WD-B

POW

CREATED AN
BRIAN MICHAEL BEND

COLOR ART
PETER PANTAZIS

TYPOGRAPHY
KEN BRUZENAK

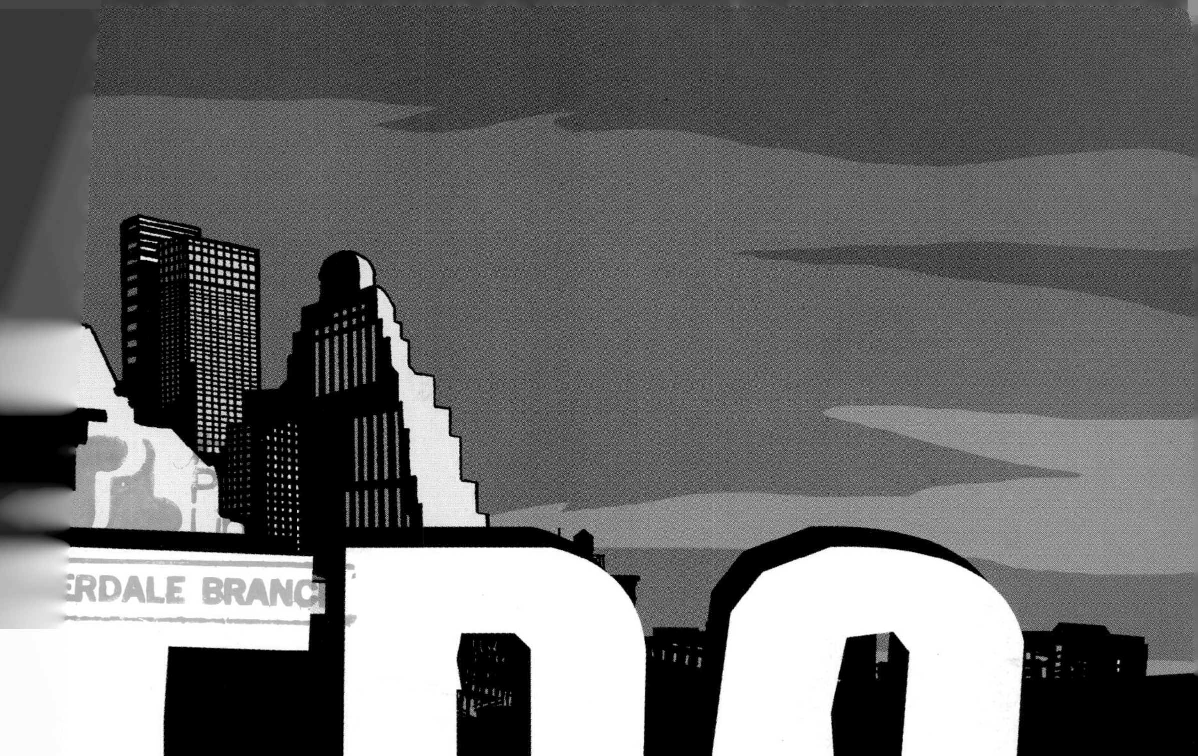
ERDALE BRANC

ERS™

ODUCED BY
ND MIKE AVON OEMING

EDITOR
KC MCCRORY

BUSINESS AFFAIRS
ALISA BENDIS

Previously in Powers

Detectives Christian Walker and Deena Pilgrim work out of the special homicide unit in charge of cases that involve Powers.

Walker has been off the force for almost a year due to his scandalous interview in the press about the federal corruption in law enforcement.

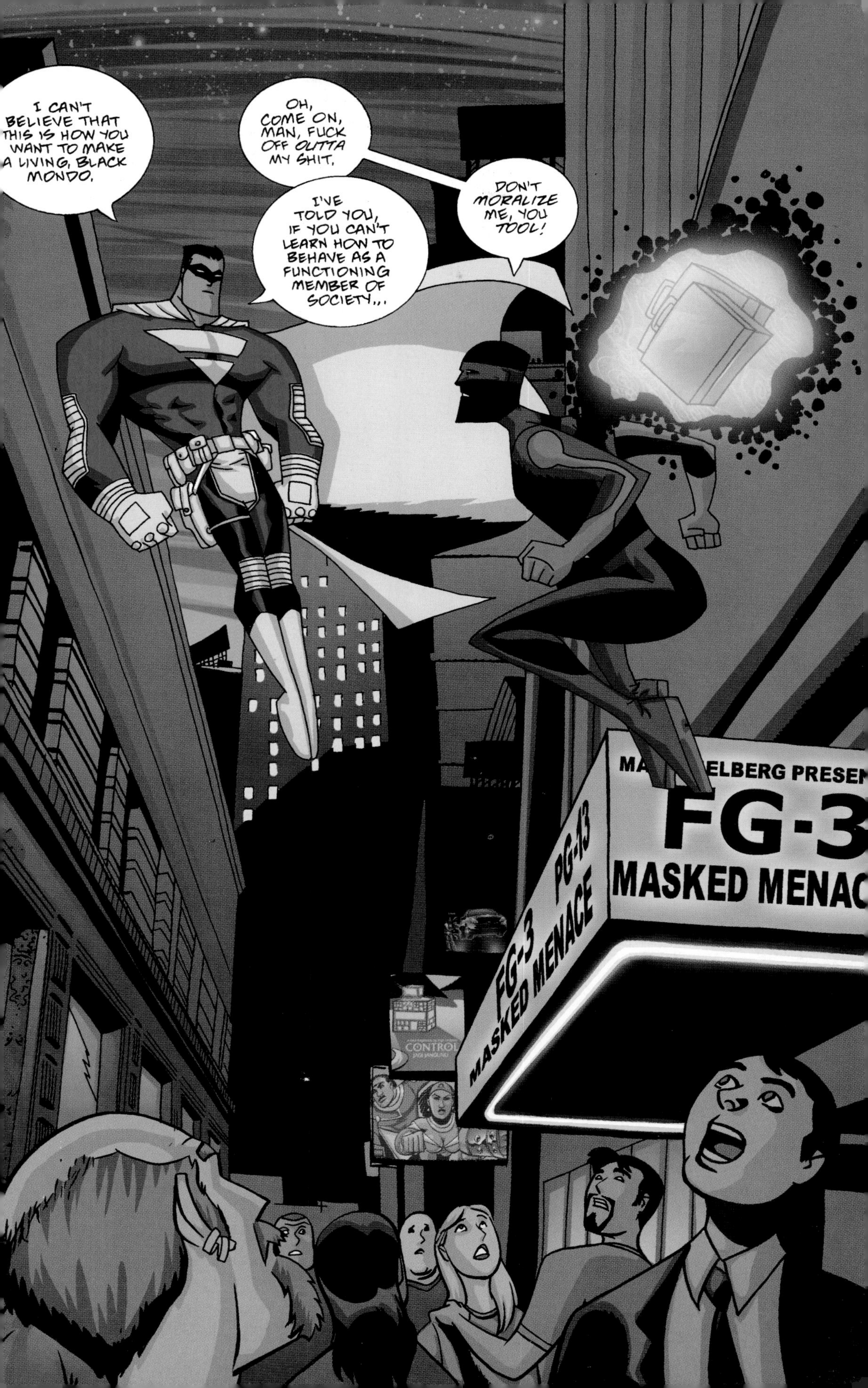

I CAN'T BELIEVE THAT THIS IS HOW YOU WANT TO MAKE A LIVING, BLACK MONDO.
OH, COME ON, MAN, FUCK OFF OUTTA MY SHIT.
I'VE TOLD YOU, IF YOU CAN'T LEARN HOW TO BEHAVE AS A FUNCTIONING MEMBER OF SOCIETY...
DON'T MORALIZE ME, YOU TOOL!
ELBERG PRESEN
FG-3
MASKED MENAC
PG-13
FG-3
MASKED MENACE
CONTROL

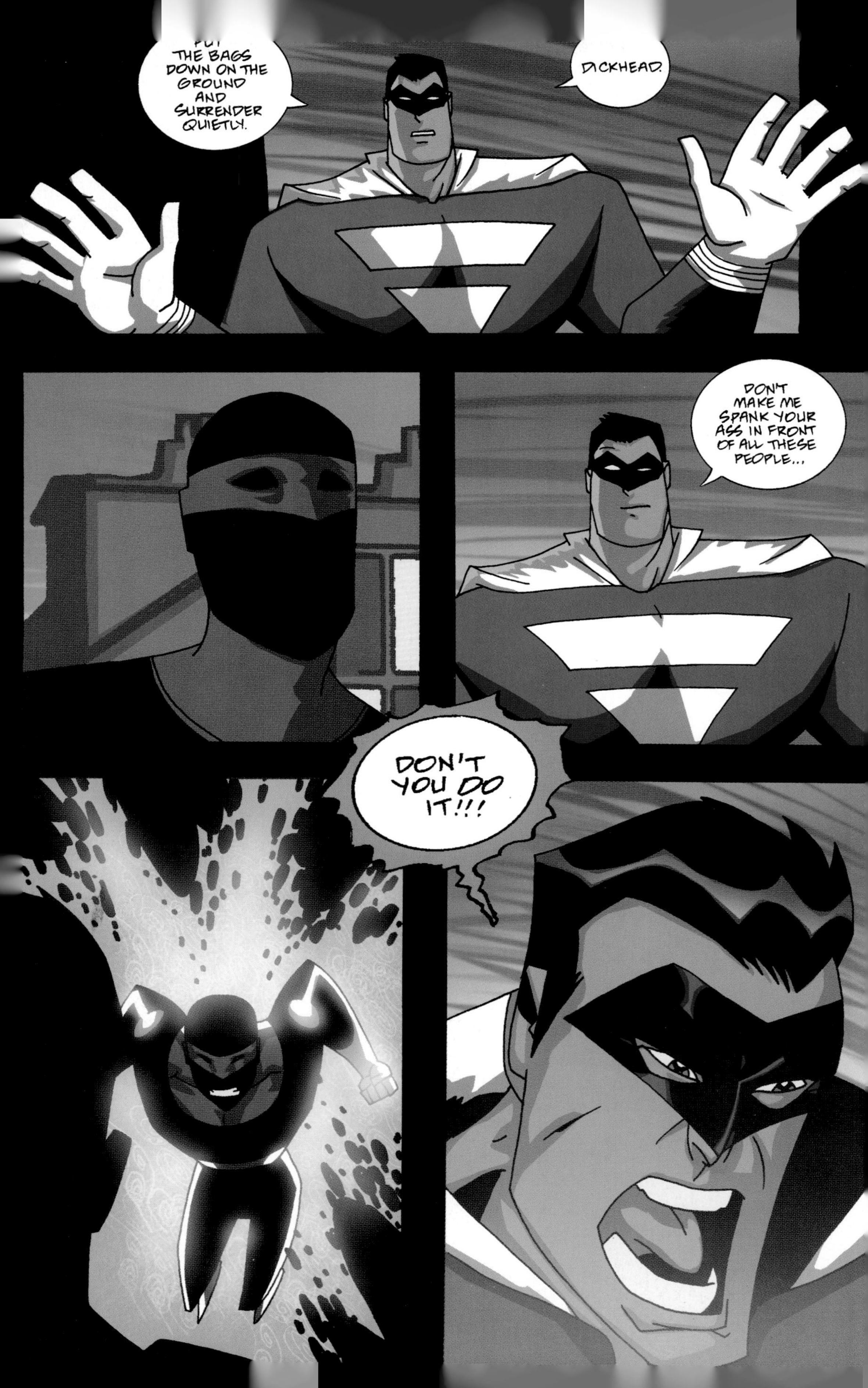
PUT THE BAGS DOWN ON THE GROUND AND SURRENDER QUIETLY.
DICKHEAD.
DON'T MAKE ME SPANK YOUR ASS IN FRONT OF ALL THESE PEOPLE...
DON'T YOU DO IT!!!

HERRAYAH!

TAAAAA...

FUCK! FUCK! FUCK!!

AACH!

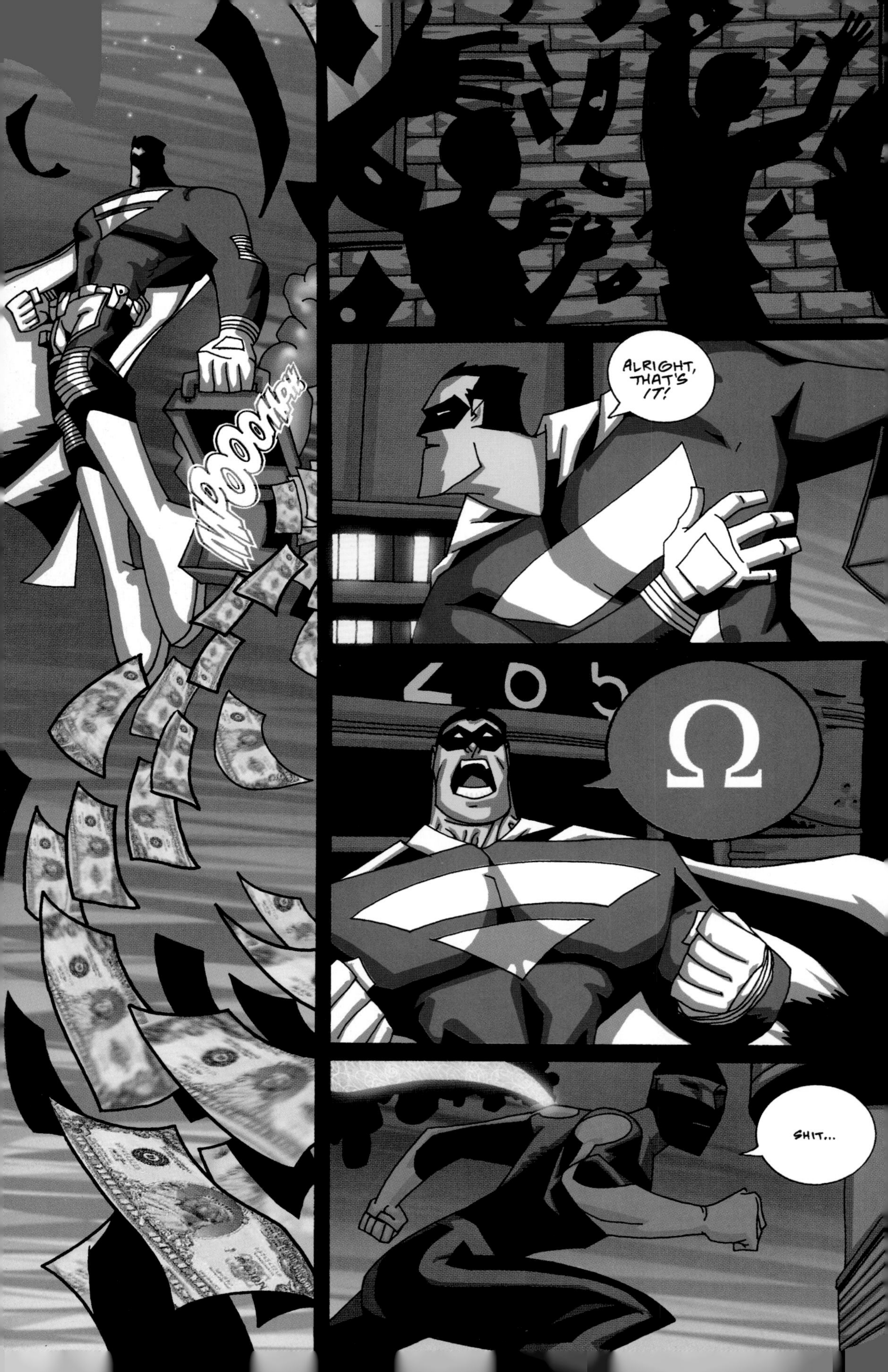
WHOOOMP!
ALRIGHT, THAT'S IT!
Ω
SHIT...

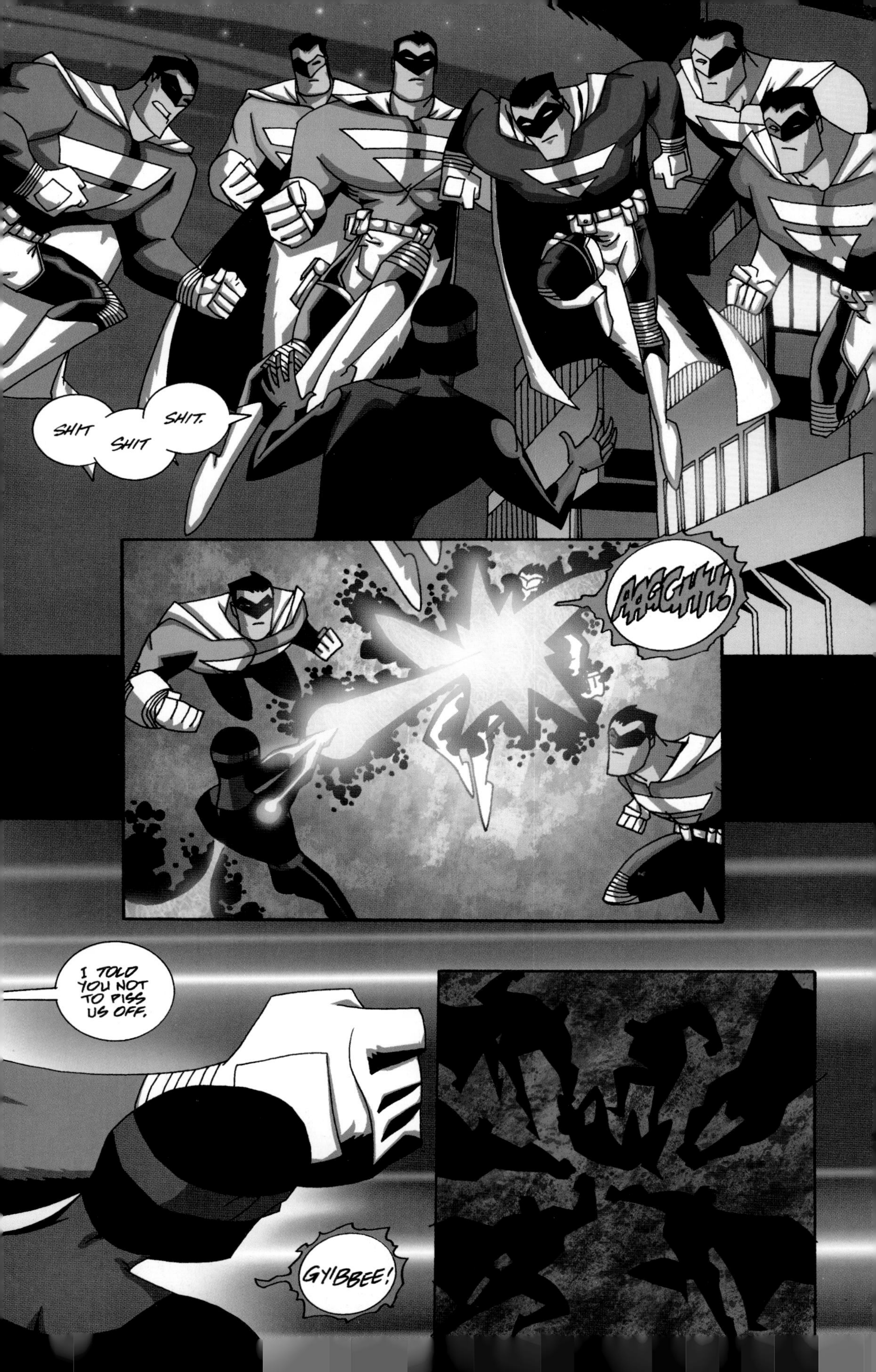
SHIT SHIT SHIT.
AAGHHH!
I TOLD YOU NOT TO PISS US OFF.
GYIBBEE!

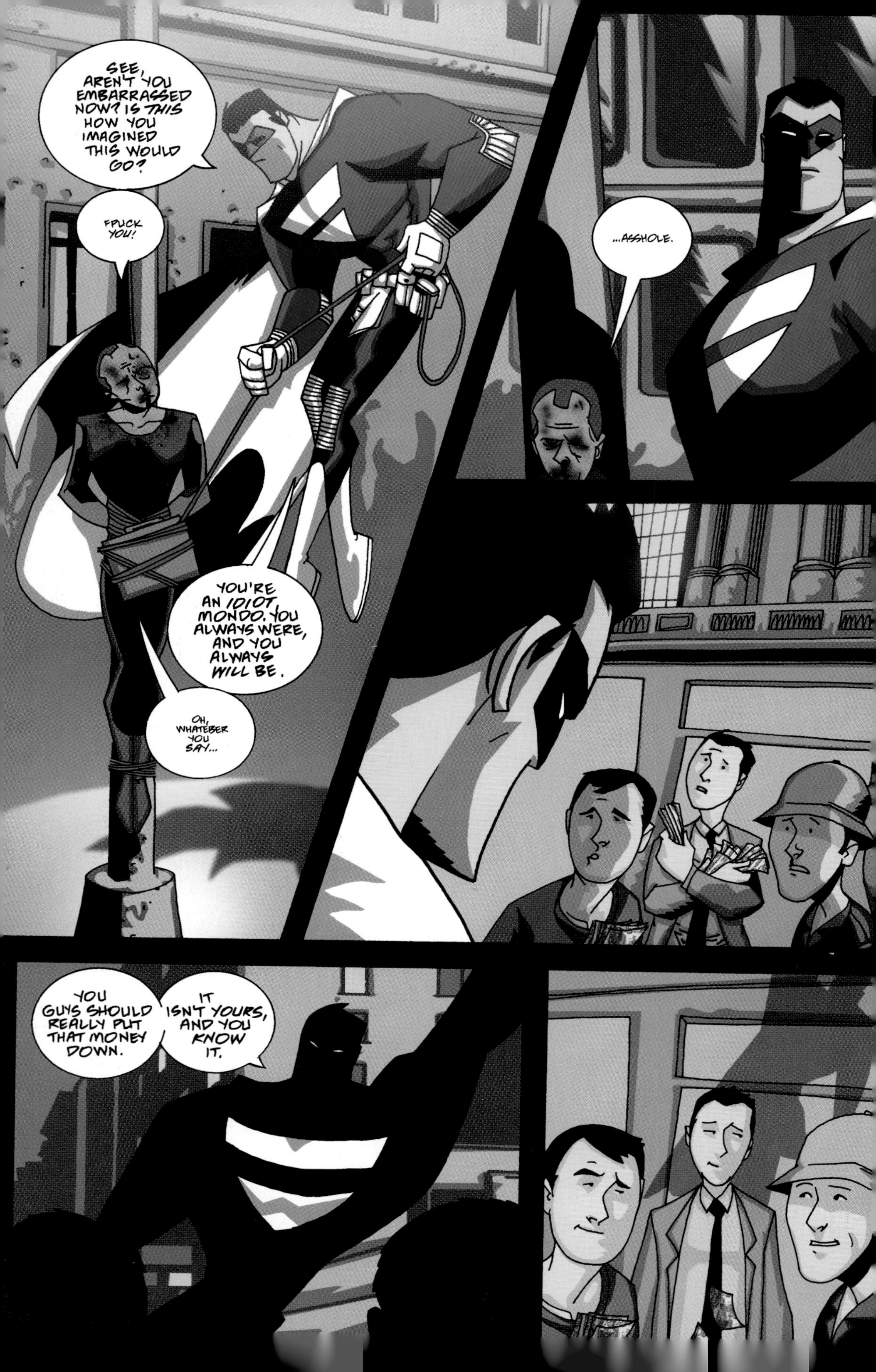
SEE, AREN'T YOU EMBARRASSED NOW? IS THIS HOW YOU IMAGINED THIS WOULD GO?
FPUCK YOU!
...ASSHOLE.
YOU'RE AN IDIOT, MONDO. YOU ALWAYS WERE, AND YOU ALWAYS WILL BE.
OH, WHATEBER YOU SAY...
YOU GUYS SHOULD REALLY PUT THAT MONEY DOWN.
IT ISN'T YOURS, AND YOU KNOW IT.

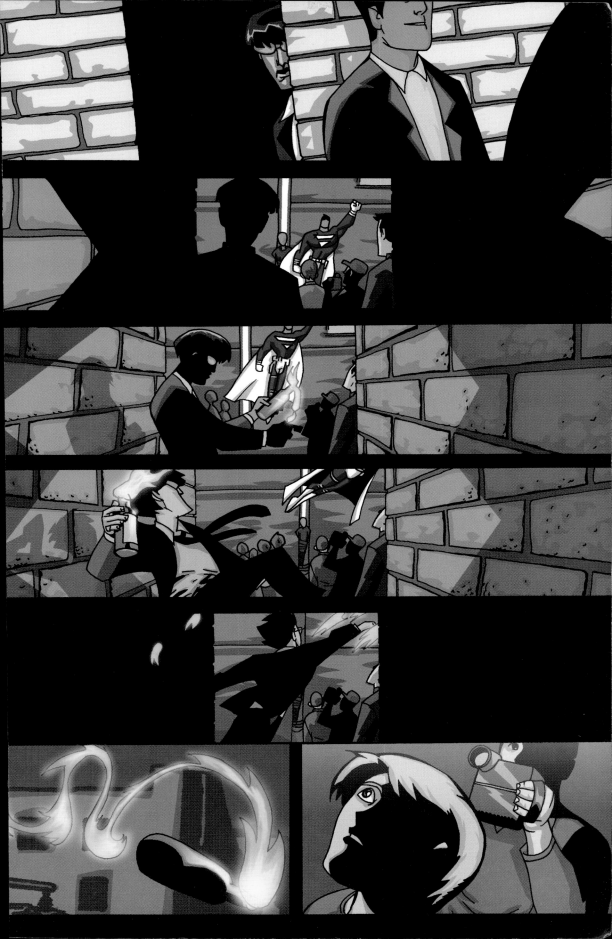

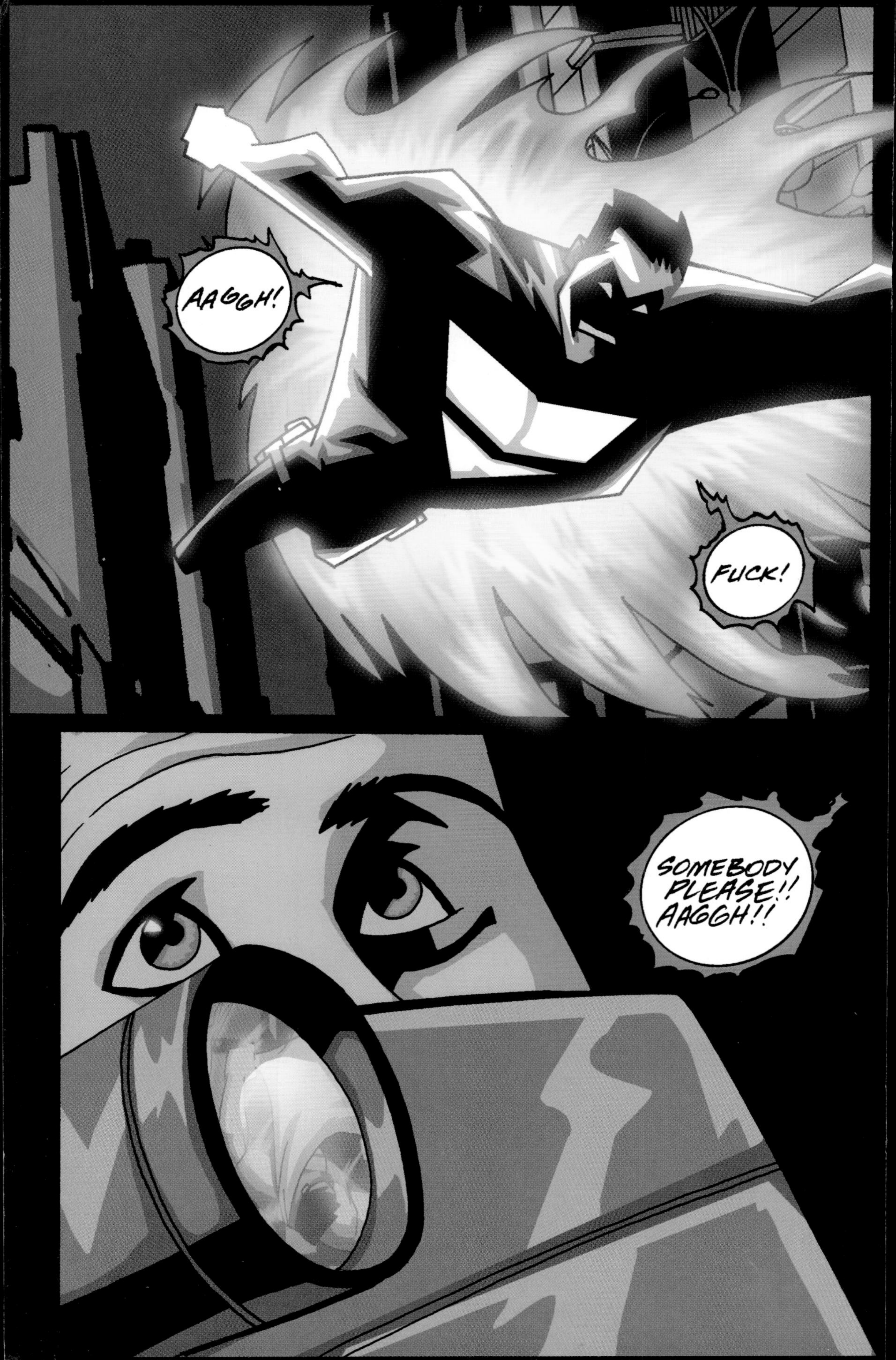
AAGGH!
FUCK!
SOMEBODY PLEASE!! AAGGH!!

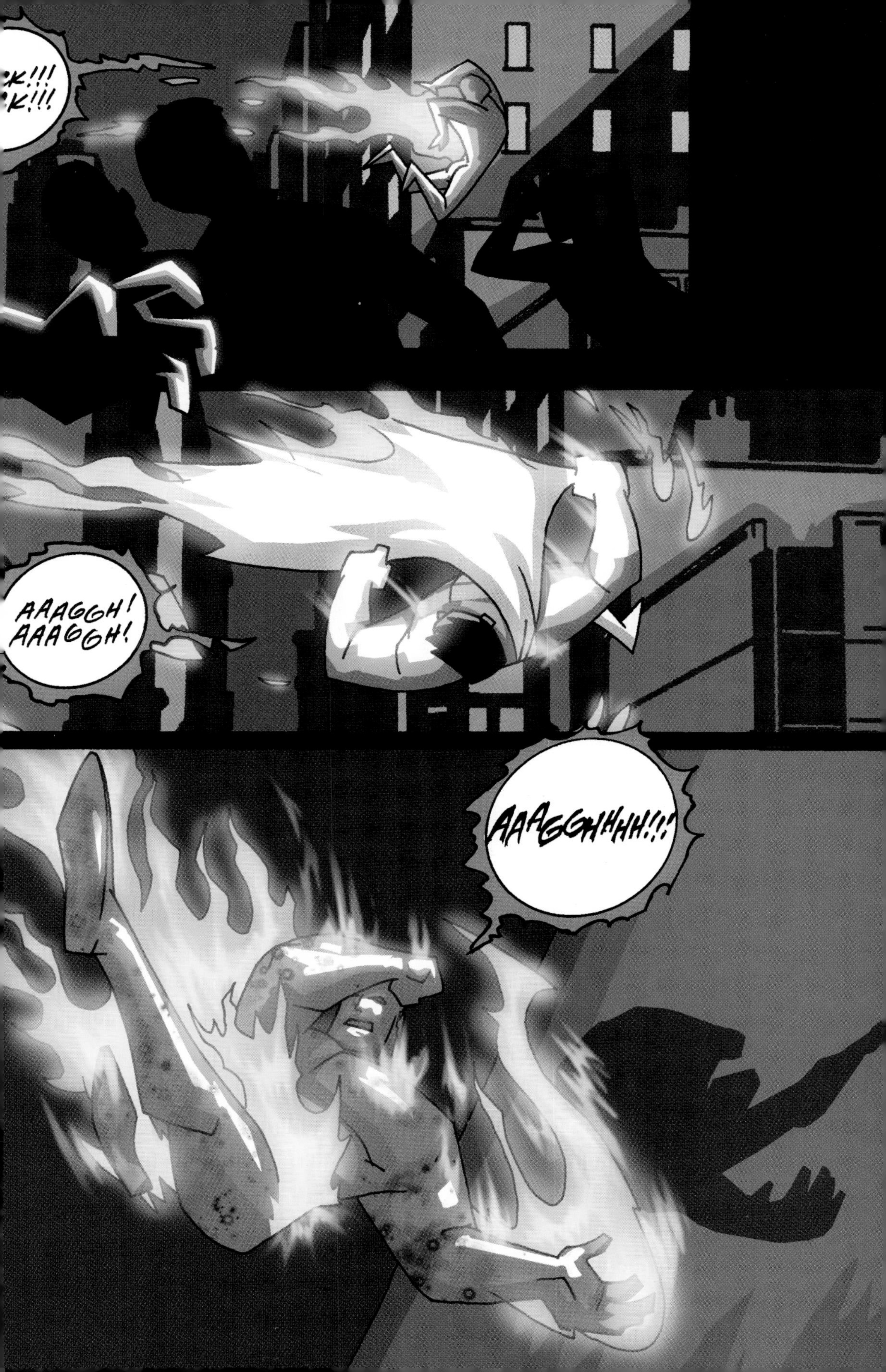
AAAGGH!
AAAGGH!
AAAGGHHHH!!!

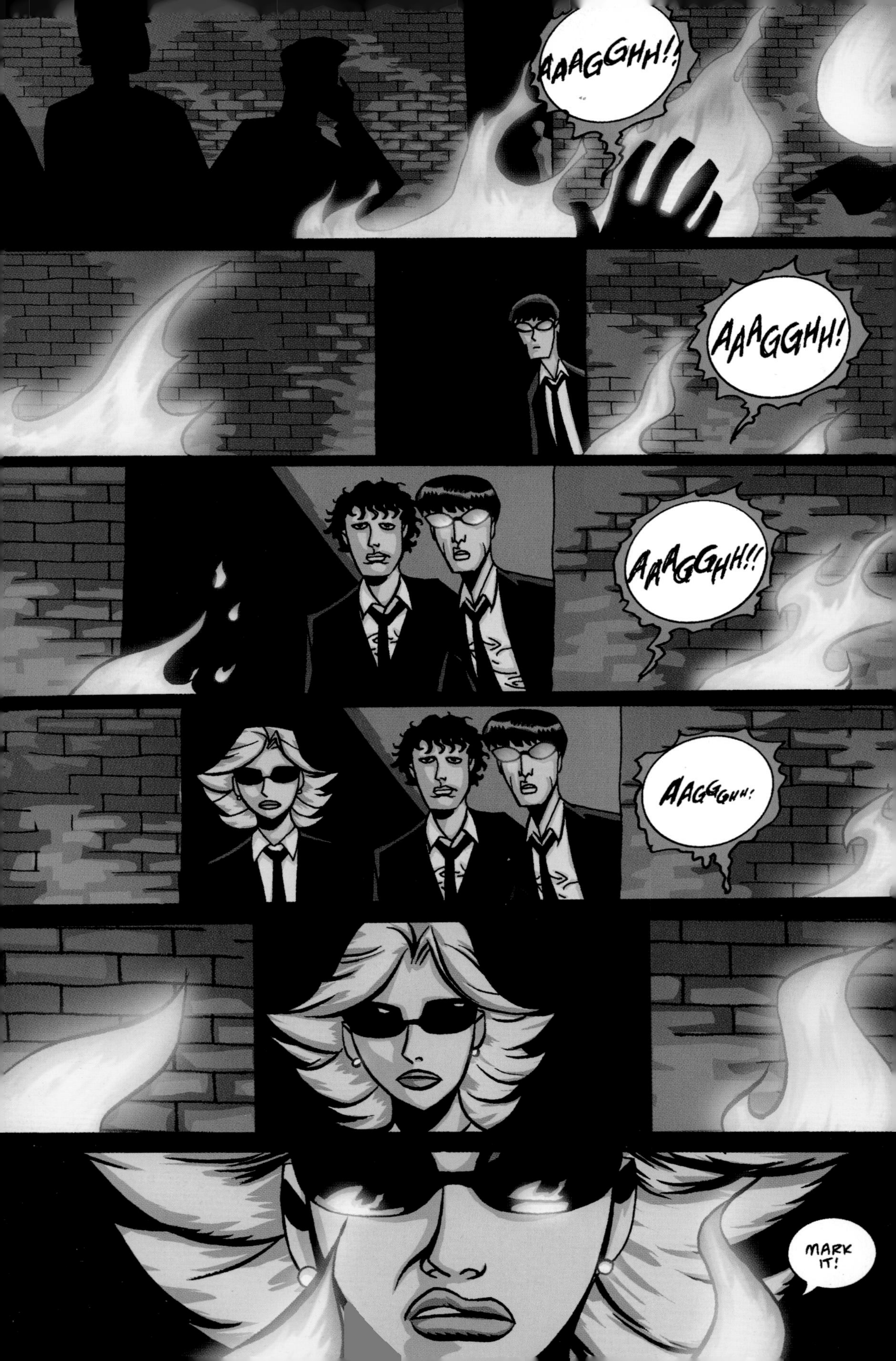
AAAGGHH!!
AAAGGHH!
AAAGGHH!!
AAGGGHH!
MARK IT!

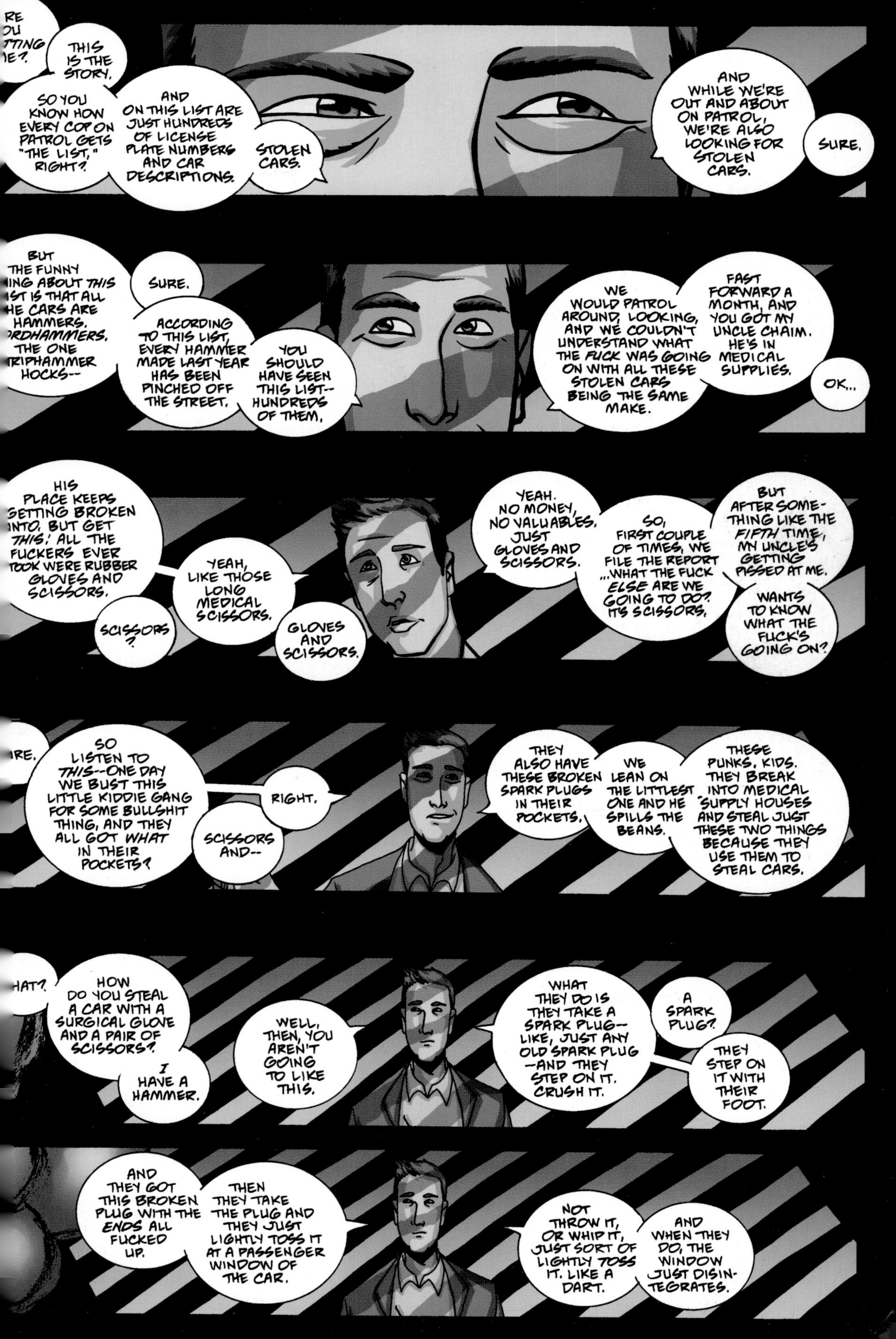

RE OU TTING IE?
THIS IS THE STORY.
SO YOU KNOW HOW EVERY COP ON PATROL GETS "THE LIST," RIGHT?
AND ON THIS LIST ARE JUST HUNDREDS OF LICENSE PLATE NUMBERS AND CAR DESCRIPTIONS.
STOLEN CARS.
AND WHILE WE'RE OUT AND ABOUT ON PATROL, WE'RE ALSO LOOKING FOR STOLEN CARS.
SURE.
BUT THE FUNNY HING ABOUT THIS IST IS THAT ALL HE CARS ARE HAMMERS. ORDHAMMERS. THE ONE TRIPHAMMER HOCKS--
SURE.
ACCORDING TO THIS LIST, EVERY HAMMER MADE LAST YEAR HAS BEEN PINCHED OFF THE STREET.
YOU SHOULD HAVE SEEN THIS LIST-- HUNDREDS OF THEM.
WE WOULD PATROL AROUND, LOOKING, AND WE COULDN'T UNDERSTAND WHAT THE FUCK WAS GOING ON WITH ALL THESE STOLEN CARS BEING THE SAME MAKE.
FAST FORWARD A MONTH, AND YOU GOT MY UNCLE CHAIM. HE'S IN MEDICAL SUPPLIES.
OK...
HIS PLACE KEEPS GETTING BROKEN INTO, BUT GET THIS! ALL THE FUCKERS EVER TOOK WERE RUBBER GLOVES AND SCISSORS.
SCISSORS?
YEAH, LIKE THOSE LONG MEDICAL SCISSORS.
GLOVES AND SCISSORS.
YEAH. NO MONEY, NO VALUABLES. JUST GLOVES AND SCISSORS.
SO, FIRST COUPLE OF TIMES, WE FILE THE REPORT ...WHAT THE FUCK ELSE ARE WE GOING TO DO? IT'S SCISSORS.
BUT AFTER SOMETHING LIKE THE FIFTH TIME, MY UNCLE'S GETTING PISSED AT ME.
WANTS TO KNOW WHAT THE FUCK'S GOING ON?
IRE.
SO LISTEN TO THIS--ONE DAY WE BUST THIS LITTLE KIDDIE GANG FOR SOME BULLSHIT THING, AND THEY ALL GOT WHAT IN THEIR POCKETS?
RIGHT.
SCISSORS AND--
THEY ALSO HAVE THESE BROKEN SPARK PLUGS IN THEIR POCKETS.
WE LEAN ON THE LITTLEST ONE AND HE SPILLS THE BEANS.
THESE PUNKS, KIDS. THEY BREAK INTO MEDICAL SUPPLY HOUSES AND STEAL JUST THESE TWO THINGS BECAUSE THEY USE THEM TO STEAL CARS.
HAT?
HOW DO YOU STEAL A CAR WITH A SURGICAL GLOVE AND A PAIR OF SCISSORS?
I HAVE A HAMMER.
WELL, THEN, YOU AREN'T GOING TO LIKE THIS.
WHAT THEY DO IS THEY TAKE A SPARK PLUG-- LIKE, JUST ANY OLD SPARK PLUG --AND THEY STEP ON IT. CRUSH IT.
A SPARK PLUG?
THEY STEP ON IT WITH THEIR FOOT.
AND THEY GOT THIS BROKEN PLUG WITH THE ENDS ALL FUCKED UP.
THEN THEY TAKE THE PLUG AND THEY JUST LIGHTLY TOSS IT AT A PASSENGER WINDOW OF THE CAR.
NOT THROW IT, OR WHIP IT, JUST SORT OF LIGHTLY TOSS IT. LIKE A DART.
AND WHEN THEY DO, THE WINDOW JUST DISINTEGRATES.

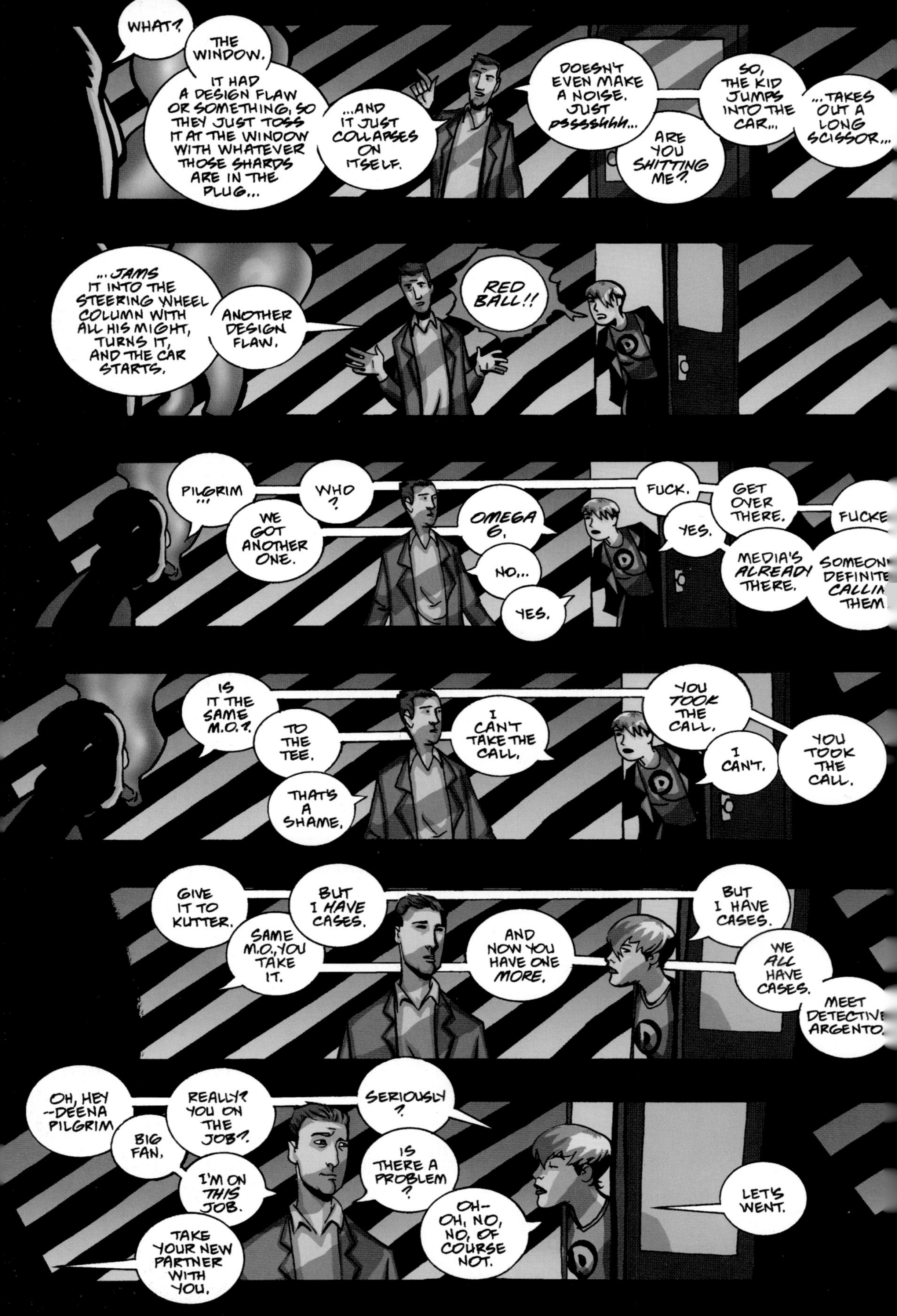
WHAT?
THE WINDOW.
IT HAD A DESIGN FLAW OR SOMETHING, SO THEY JUST TOSS IT AT THE WINDOW WITH WHATEVER THOSE SHARDS ARE IN THE PLUG...
...AND IT JUST COLLAPSES ON ITSELF.
DOESN'T EVEN MAKE A NOISE. JUST *psssshhh*...
ARE YOU SHITTING ME?
SO, THE KID JUMPS INTO THE CAR...
...TAKES OUT A LONG SCISSOR...
...*JAMS* IT INTO THE STEERING WHEEL COLUMN WITH ALL HIS MIGHT, TURNS IT, AND THE CAR STARTS.
ANOTHER DESIGN FLAW.
RED BALL!!
PILGRIM...
WHO?
WE GOT ANOTHER ONE.
OMEGA 6.
NO...
YES.
FUCK.
YES.
GET OVER THERE.
FUCKE
MEDIA'S *ALREADY* THERE.
SOMEON DEFINITE *CALLIN* THEM.
IS IT THE SAME M.O.?
TO THE TEE.
THAT'S A SHAME.
I CAN'T TAKE THE CALL.
YOU *TOOK* THE CALL.
I CAN'T.
YOU TOOK THE CALL.
GIVE IT TO KUTTER.
BUT I *HAVE* CASES.
SAME M.O., YOU TAKE IT.
AND NOW YOU HAVE ONE *MORE*.
BUT I HAVE CASES.
WE *ALL* HAVE CASES.
MEET DETECTIVE ARGENTO.
OH, HEY --DEENA PILGRIM
BIG FAN.
REALLY? YOU ON THE JOB?
I'M ON *THIS* JOB.
SERIOUSLY?
IS THERE A PROBLEM?
OH-- OH, NO, NO, OF COURSE NOT.
TAKE YOUR NEW PARTNER WITH YOU.
LET'S WENT.

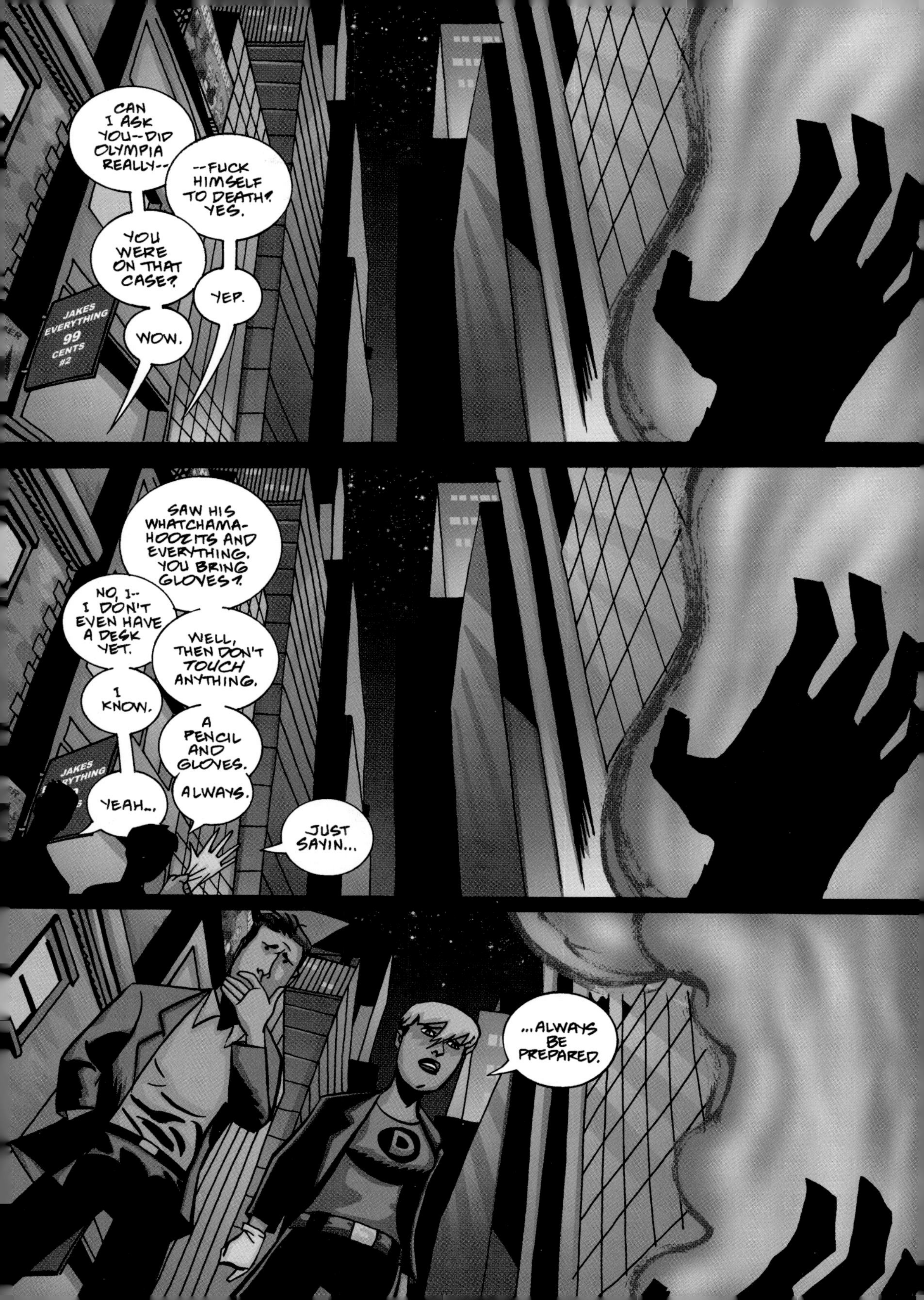
CAN I ASK YOU--DID OLYMPIA REALLY--
--FUCK HIMSELF TO DEATH? YES.
YOU WERE ON THAT CASE?
YEP.
WOW.
JAKES EVERYTHING 99 CENTS #2
SAW HIS WHATCHAMA-HOOZITS AND EVERYTHING. YOU BRING GLOVES?
NO, I-- I DON'T EVEN HAVE A DESK YET.
WELL, THEN DON'T TOUCH ANYTHING.
I KNOW.
A PENCIL AND GLOVES.
ALWAYS.
YEAH...
JUST SAYIN...
...ALWAYS BE PREPARED.

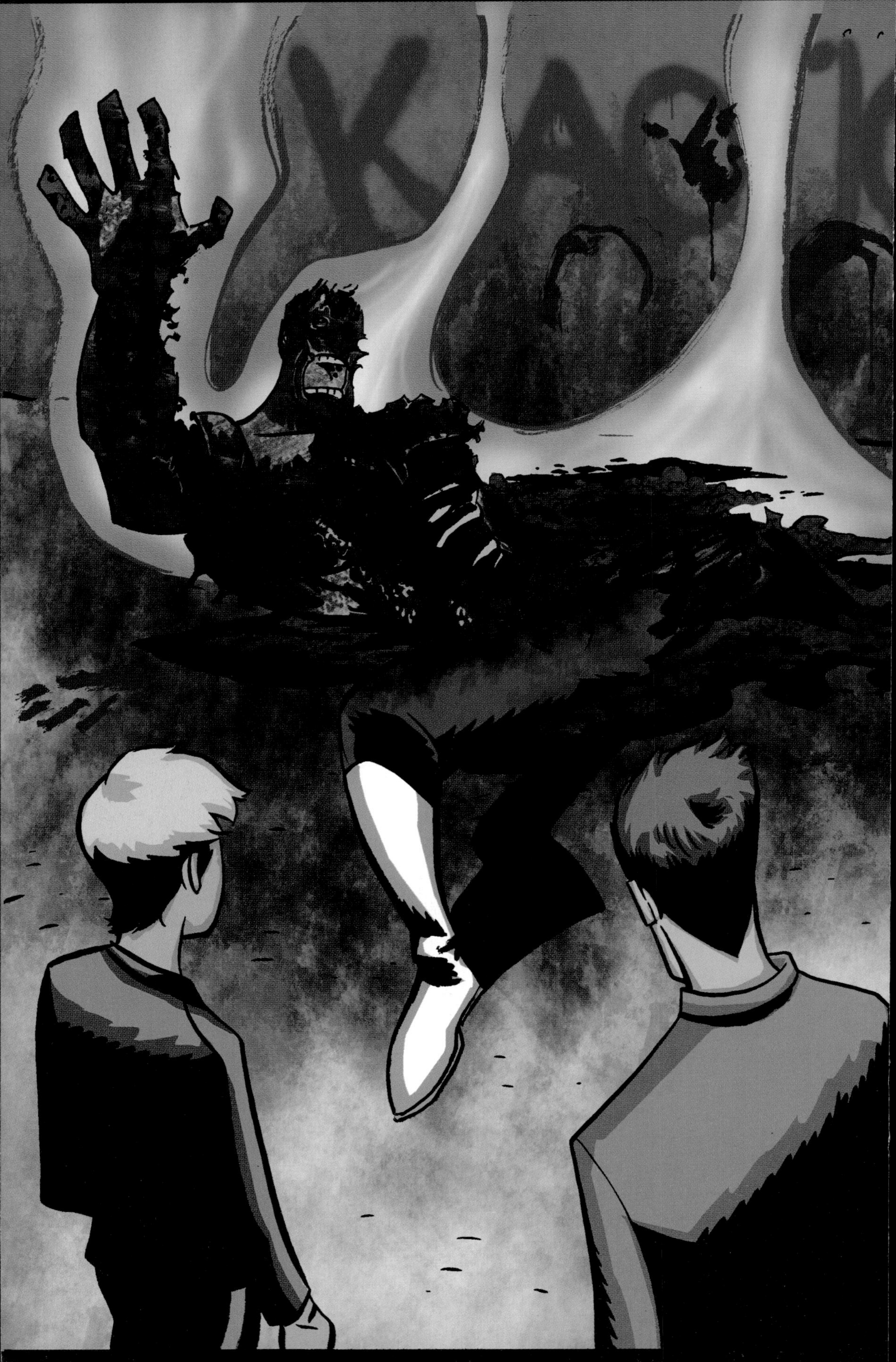

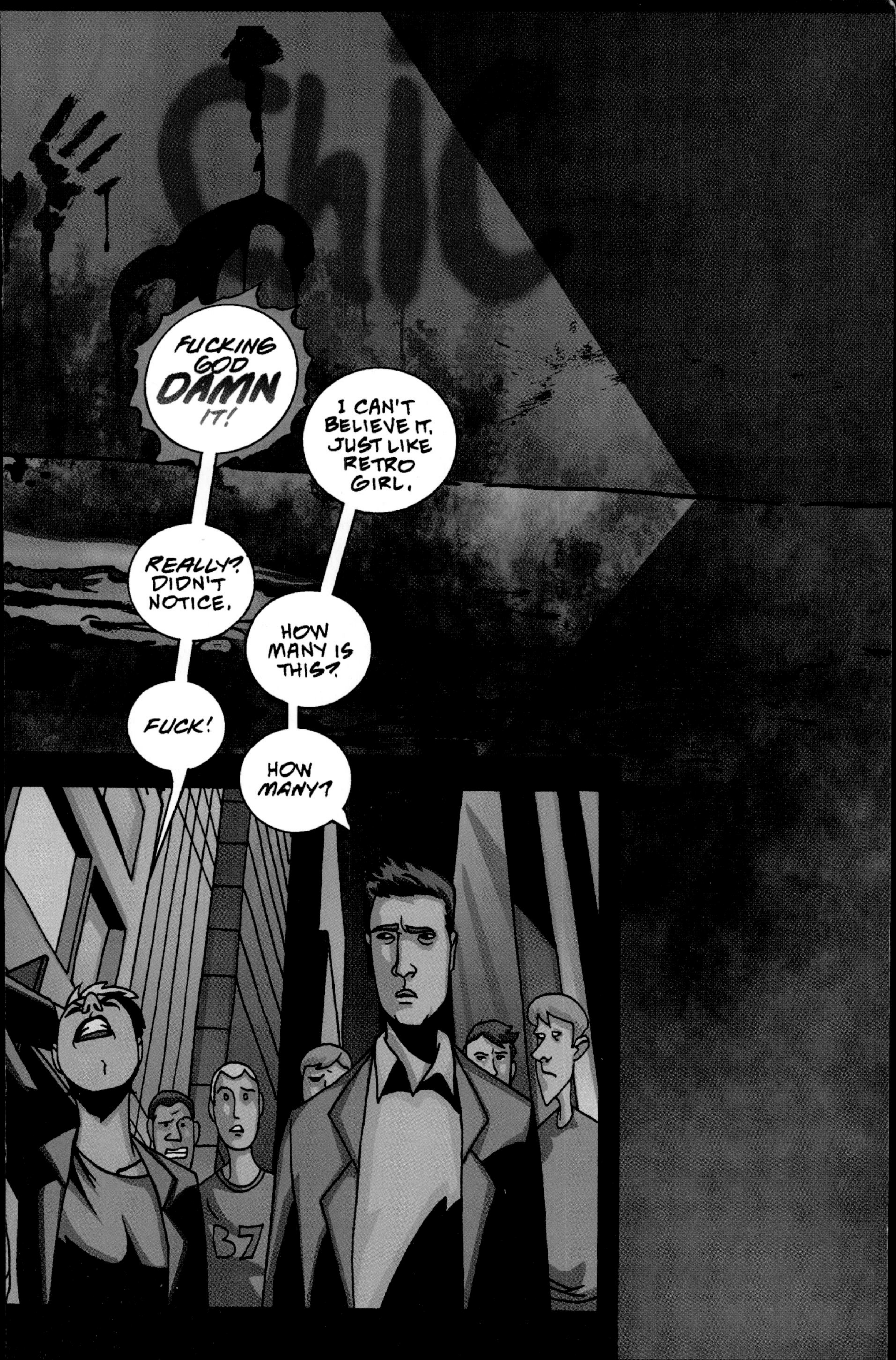
FUCKING GOD DAMN IT!
I CAN'T BELIEVE IT. JUST LIKE RETRO GIRL.
REALLY? DIDN'T NOTICE.
HOW MANY IS THIS?
FUCK!
HOW MANY?

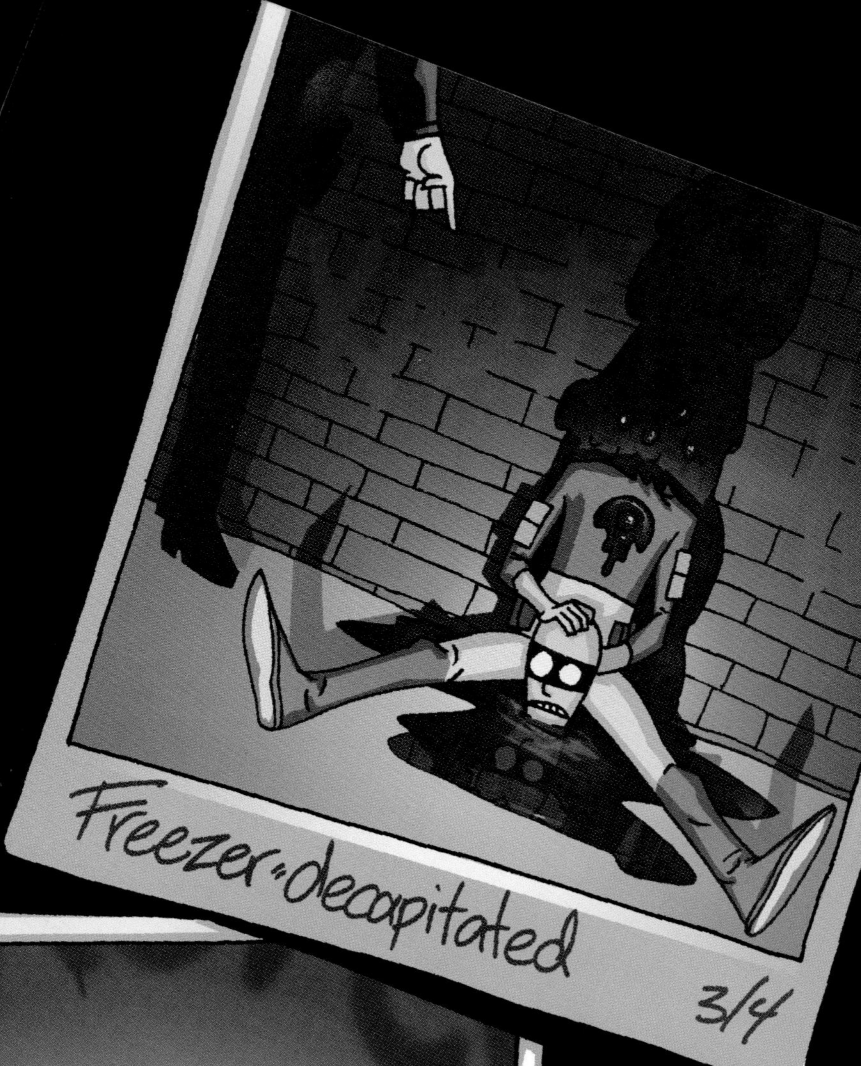
Freezer-decapitated
3/4

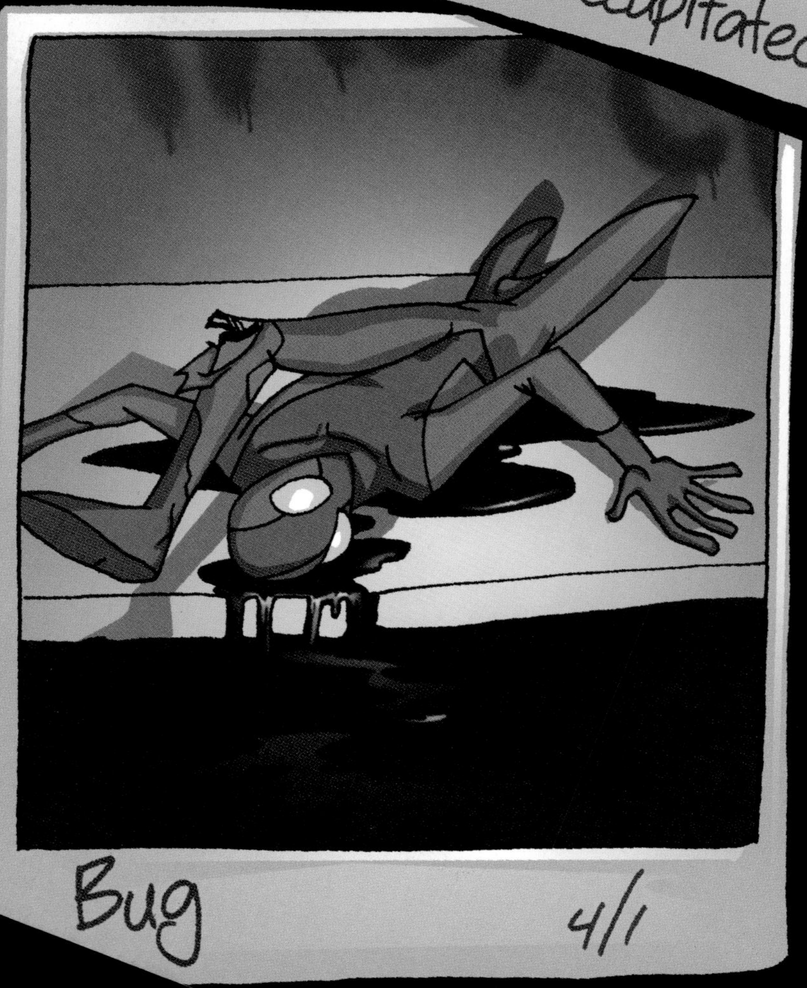
Bug
4/1

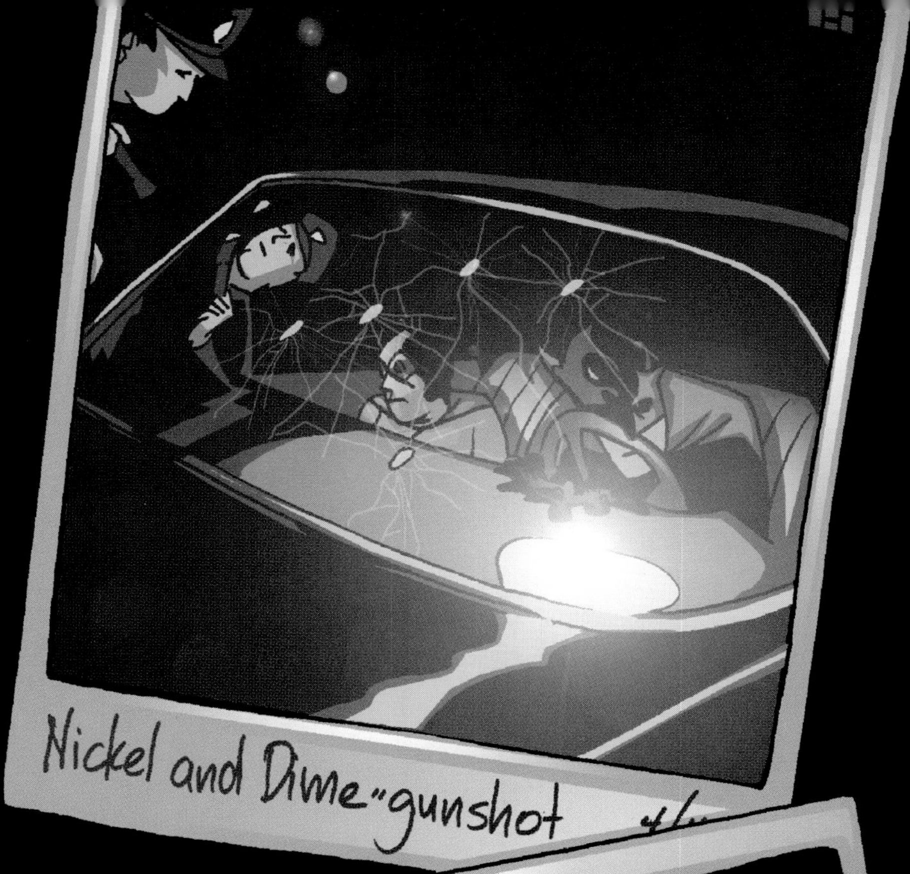
Nickel and Dime" gunshot

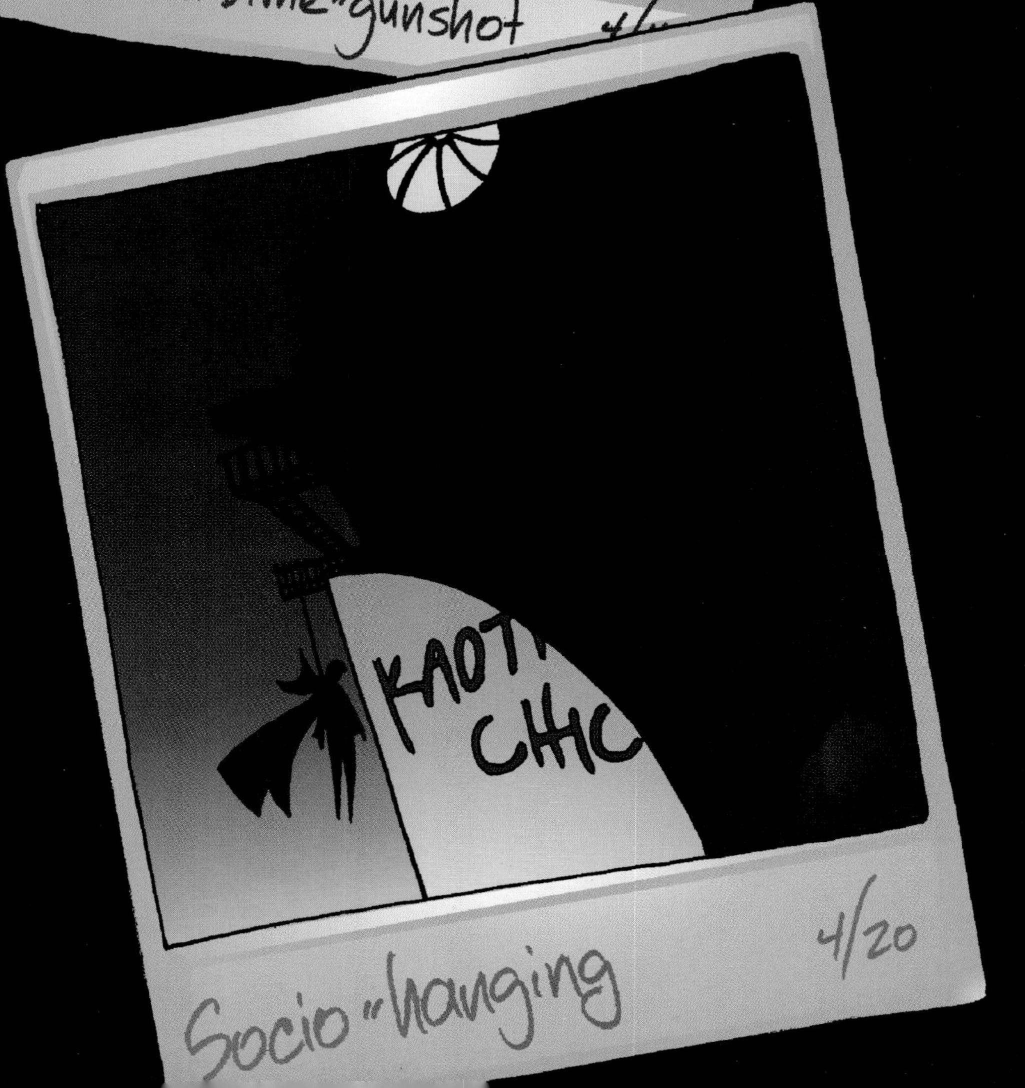
KAOT
CHIC
4/20
Socio" hanging

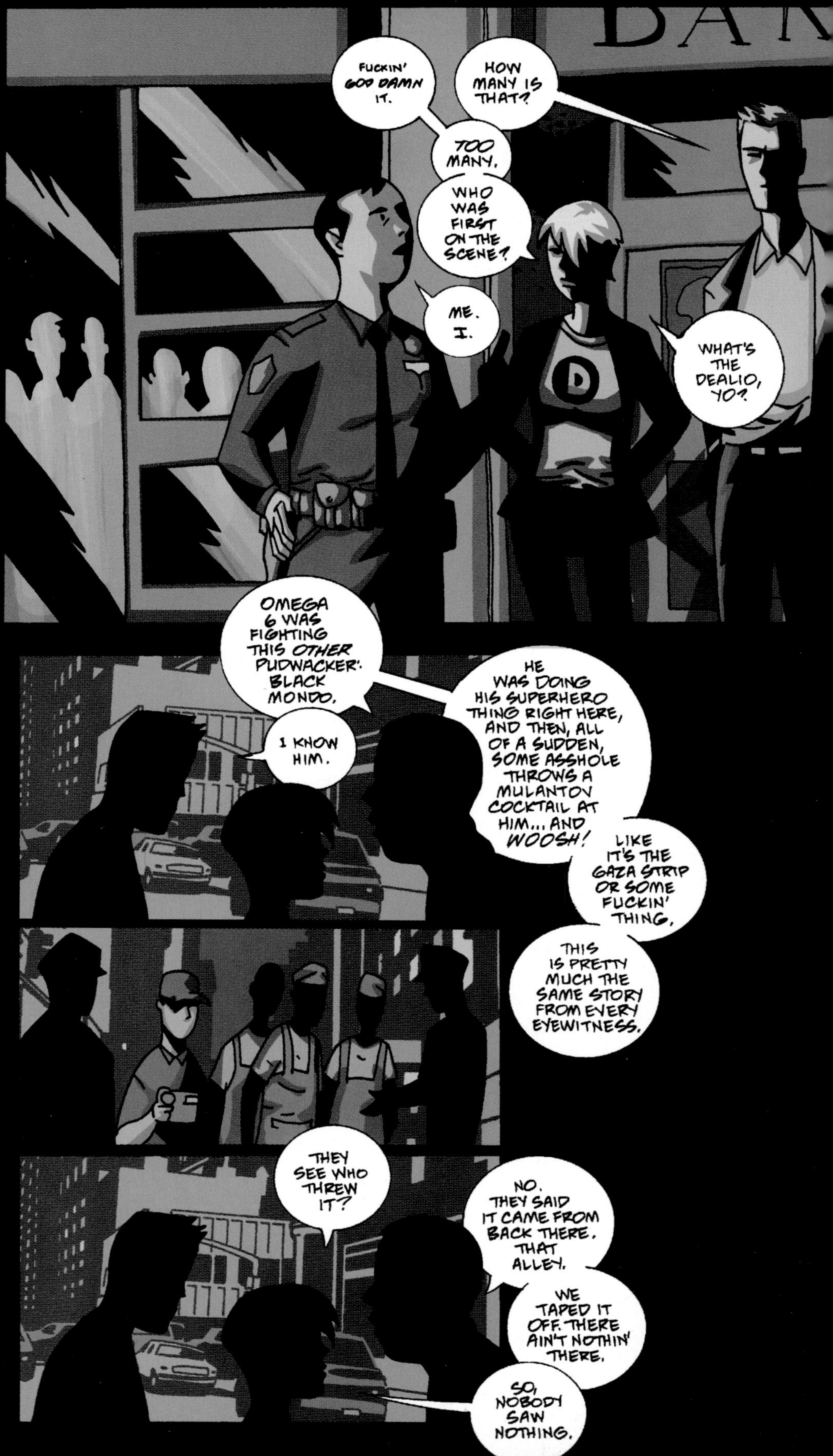
FUCKIN' GOD DAMN IT.
HOW MANY IS THAT?
TOO MANY.
WHO WAS FIRST ON THE SCENE?
ME. I.
WHAT'S THE DEALIO, YO?
OMEGA 6 WAS FIGHTING THIS OTHER PUDWACKER: BLACK MONDO.
I KNOW HIM.
HE WAS DOING HIS SUPERHERO THING RIGHT HERE, AND THEN, ALL OF A SUDDEN, SOME ASSHOLE THROWS A MULANTOV COCKTAIL AT HIM... AND WOOSH!
LIKE IT'S THE GAZA STRIP OR SOME FUCKIN' THING.
THIS IS PRETTY MUCH THE SAME STORY FROM EVERY EYEWITNESS.
THEY SEE WHO THREW IT?
NO. THEY SAID IT CAME FROM BACK THERE. THAT ALLEY.
WE TAPED IT OFF. THERE AIN'T NOTHIN' THERE.
SO, NOBODY SAW NOTHING.

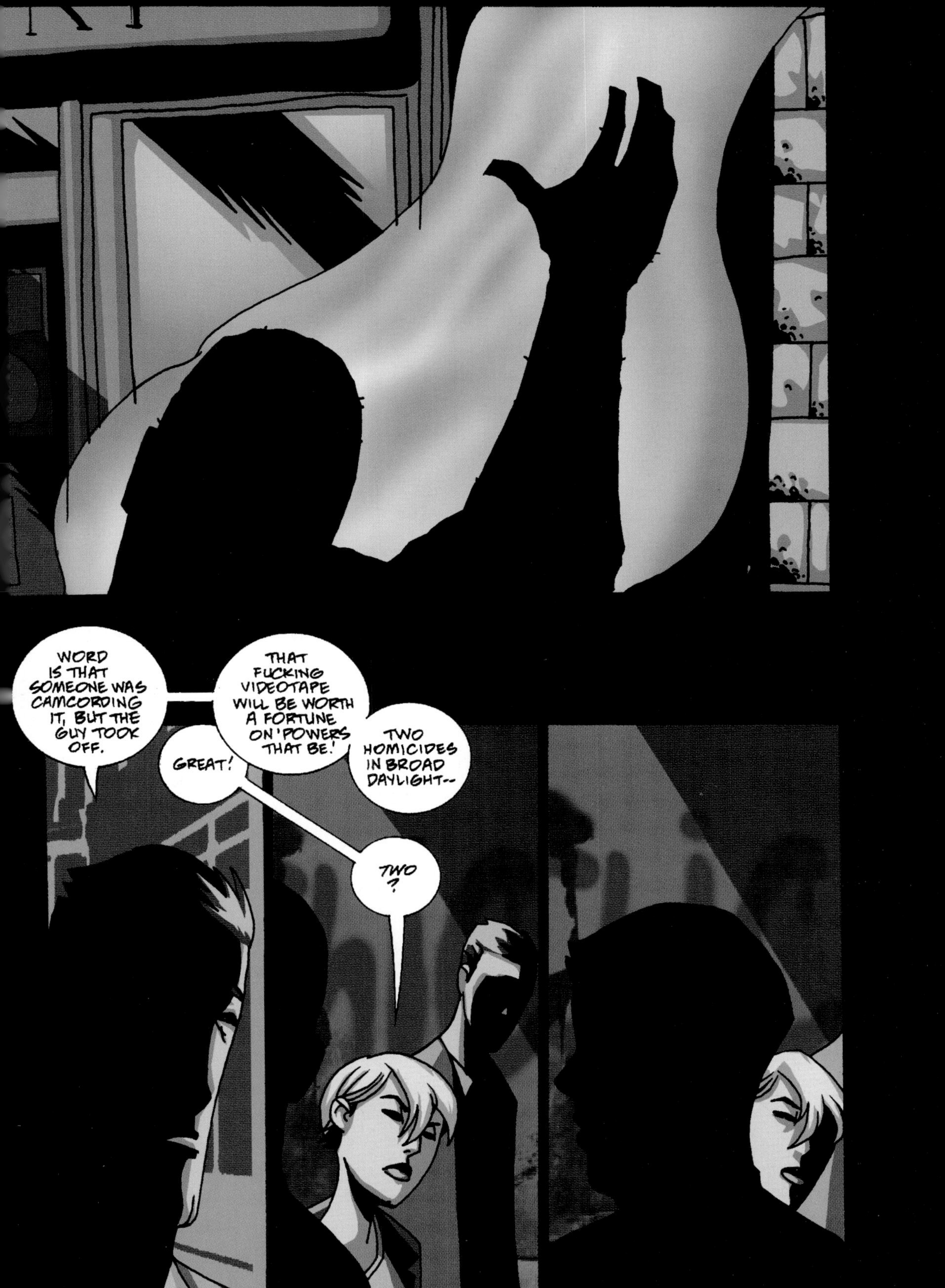
WORD IS THAT SOMEONE WAS CAMCORDING IT, BUT THE GUY TOOK OFF.
THAT FUCKING VIDEOTAPE WILL BE WORTH A FORTUNE ON 'POWERS THAT BE.'
GREAT!
TWO HOMICIDES IN BROAD DAYLIGHT--
TWO?

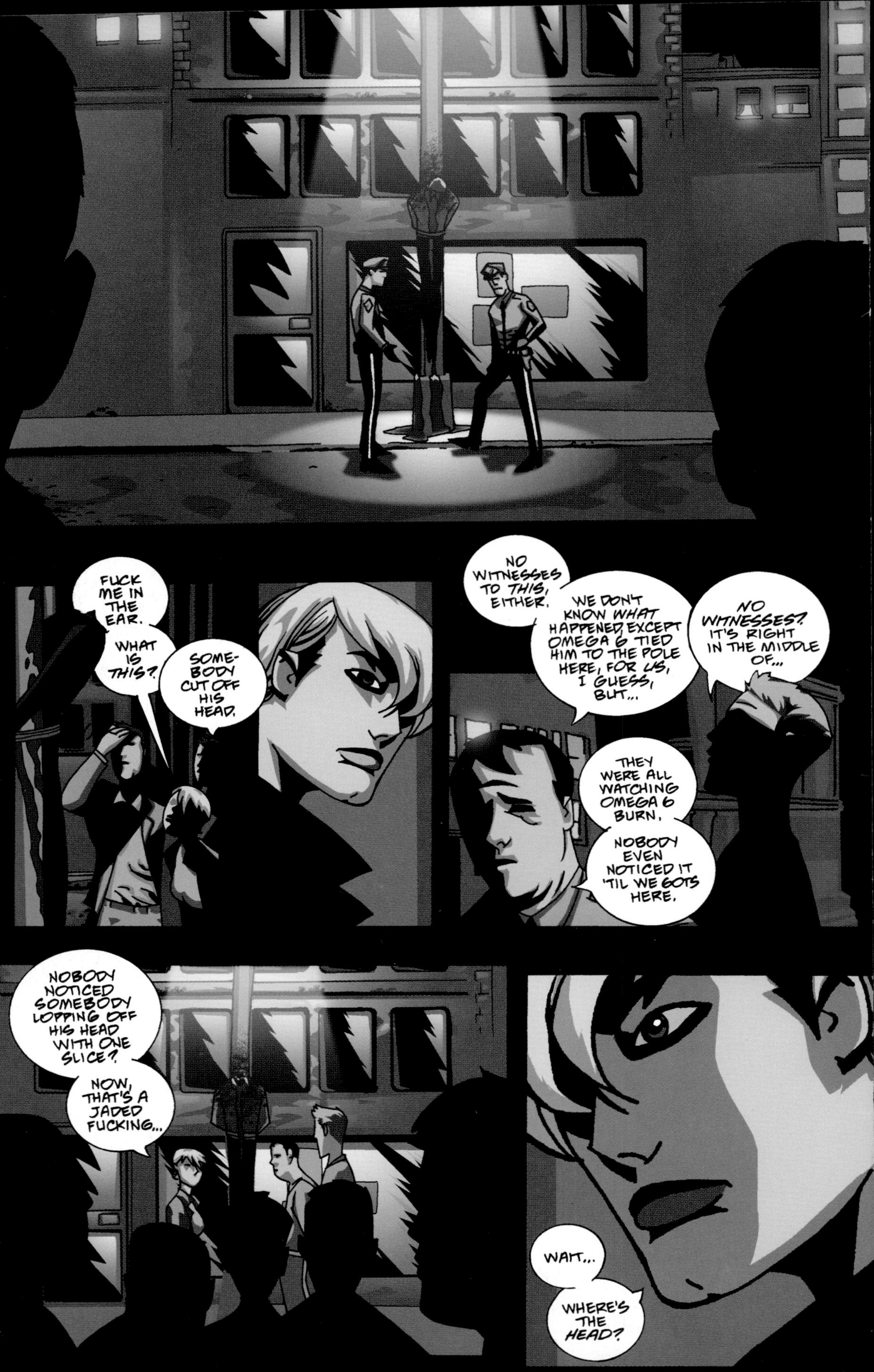
FUCK ME IN THE EAR.
WHAT IS THIS?
SOME-BODY CUT OFF HIS HEAD.
NO WITNESSES TO THIS, EITHER.
WE DON'T KNOW WHAT HAPPENED, EXCEPT OMEGA 6 TIED HIM TO THE POLE HERE, FOR US, I GUESS, BUT...
NO WITNESSES? IT'S RIGHT IN THE MIDDLE OF...
THEY WERE ALL WATCHING OMEGA 6 BURN.
NOBODY EVEN NOTICED IT 'TIL WE GOTS HERE.
NOBODY NOTICED SOMEBODY LOPPING OFF HIS HEAD WITH ONE SLICE?
NOW, THAT'S A JADED FUCKING...
WAIT...
WHERE'S THE HEAD?

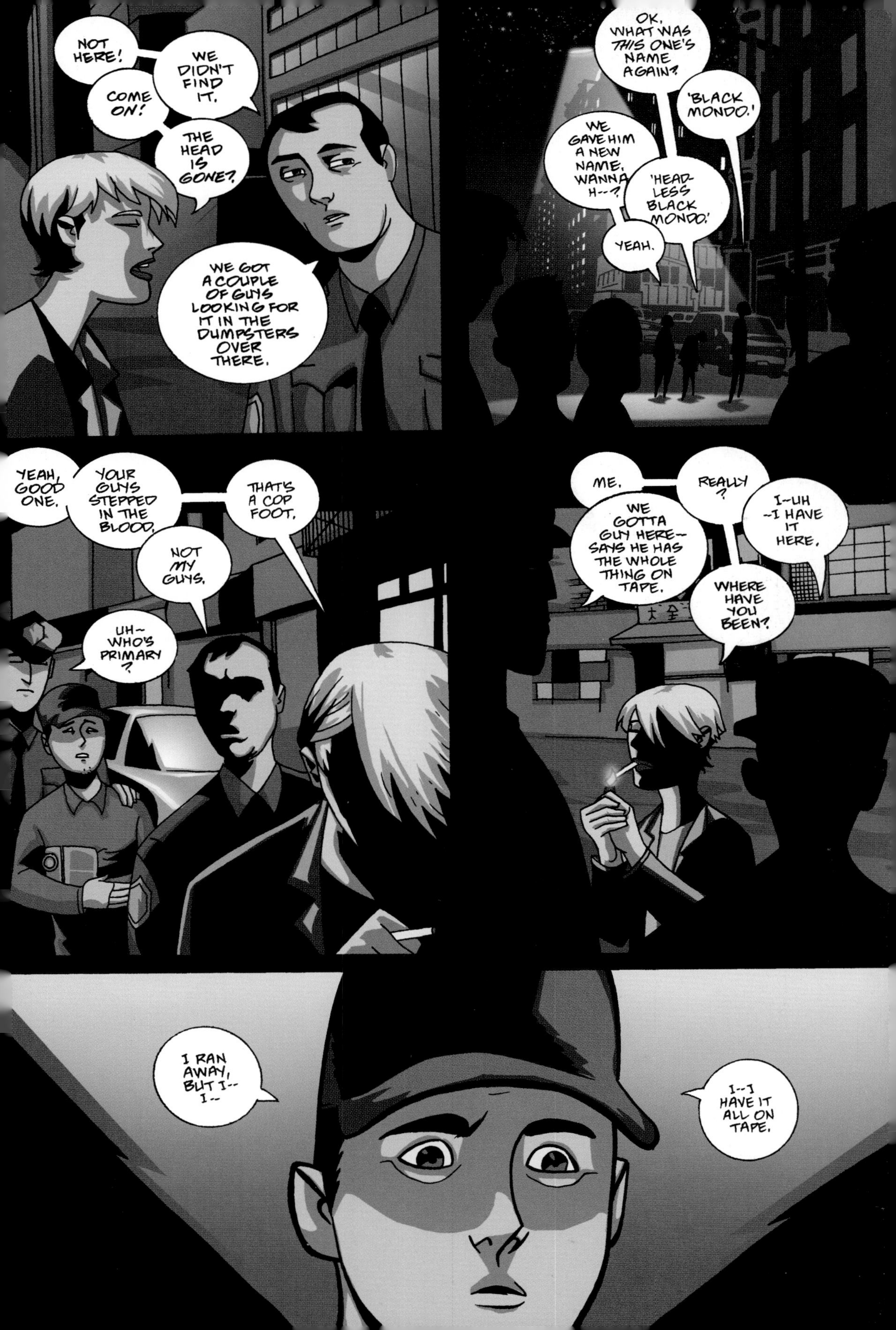
NOT HERE!
WE DIDN'T FIND IT.
COME ON!
THE HEAD IS GONE?
WE GOT A COUPLE OF GUYS LOOKING FOR IT IN THE DUMPSTERS OVER THERE.
OK, WHAT WAS THIS ONE'S NAME AGAIN?
'BLACK MONDO.'
WE GAVE HIM A NEW NAME. WANNA H--?
'HEAD-LESS BLACK MONDO.'
YEAH.
YEAH, GOOD ONE.
YOUR GUYS STEPPED IN THE BLOOD.
THAT'S A COP FOOT.
NOT MY GUYS.
UH-- WHO'S PRIMARY ?
ME.
REALLY ?
WE GOTTA GUY HERE-- SAYS HE HAS THE WHOLE THING ON TAPE.
I--UH --I HAVE IT HERE.
WHERE HAVE YOU BEEN?
I RAN AWAY, BUT I-- I--
I--I HAVE IT ALL ON TAPE.

AAAGGHHH!!

MAN, THAT'S FUCKING INSANE!

OOF!

YEAH, DON'T STOP AND HELP HIM, YOU RETARDS!

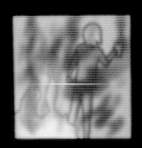
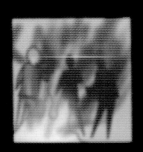
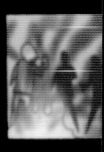

SHE LOOK FAMILIAR TO ANY OF YOU?

NOPE

FUCK!

NOPE.

NO.

CAN WE RUN IT THROUGH THE COMPUTER?

THIS ISN'T STAR TREK.

I WAS JUST ASKING.

IT DOESN'T WORK THAT WAY- FUCK!

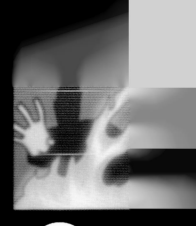

THE
MERA
WN--
JO!

THIS
IS
AWFUL!

MAN...

PEOPLE
SUCK.

EY!

THERE!
STOP!

ZOOM
IN.

W
'S WORK
'LL RUN
E OTHER
MENTS--
EDS...

AND
END UP
GOING
TO THE
MEDIA.

NOT
NECESSARILY.

PLEASE.

NOT
NECESSARILY

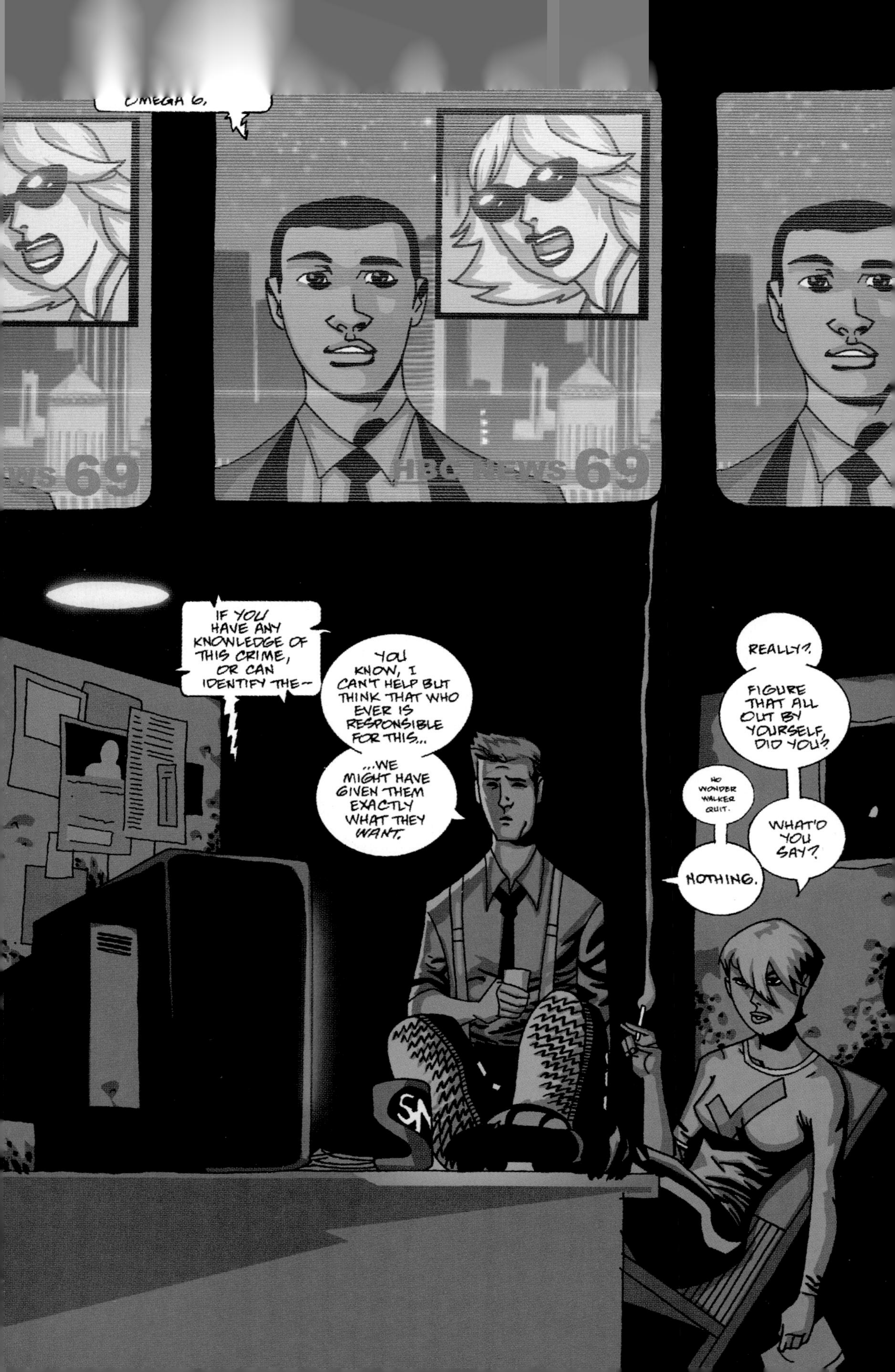
OMEGA 6.
IF YOU HAVE ANY KNOWLEDGE OF THIS CRIME, OR CAN IDENTIFY THE--
HBC NEWS 69
YOU KNOW, I CAN'T HELP BUT THINK THAT WHO EVER IS RESPONSIBLE FOR THIS...
...WE MIGHT HAVE GIVEN THEM EXACTLY WHAT THEY WANT.
REALLY?
FIGURE THAT ALL OUT BY YOURSELF, DID YOU?
NO WONDER WALKER QUIT.
WHAT'D YOU SAY?
NOTHING.

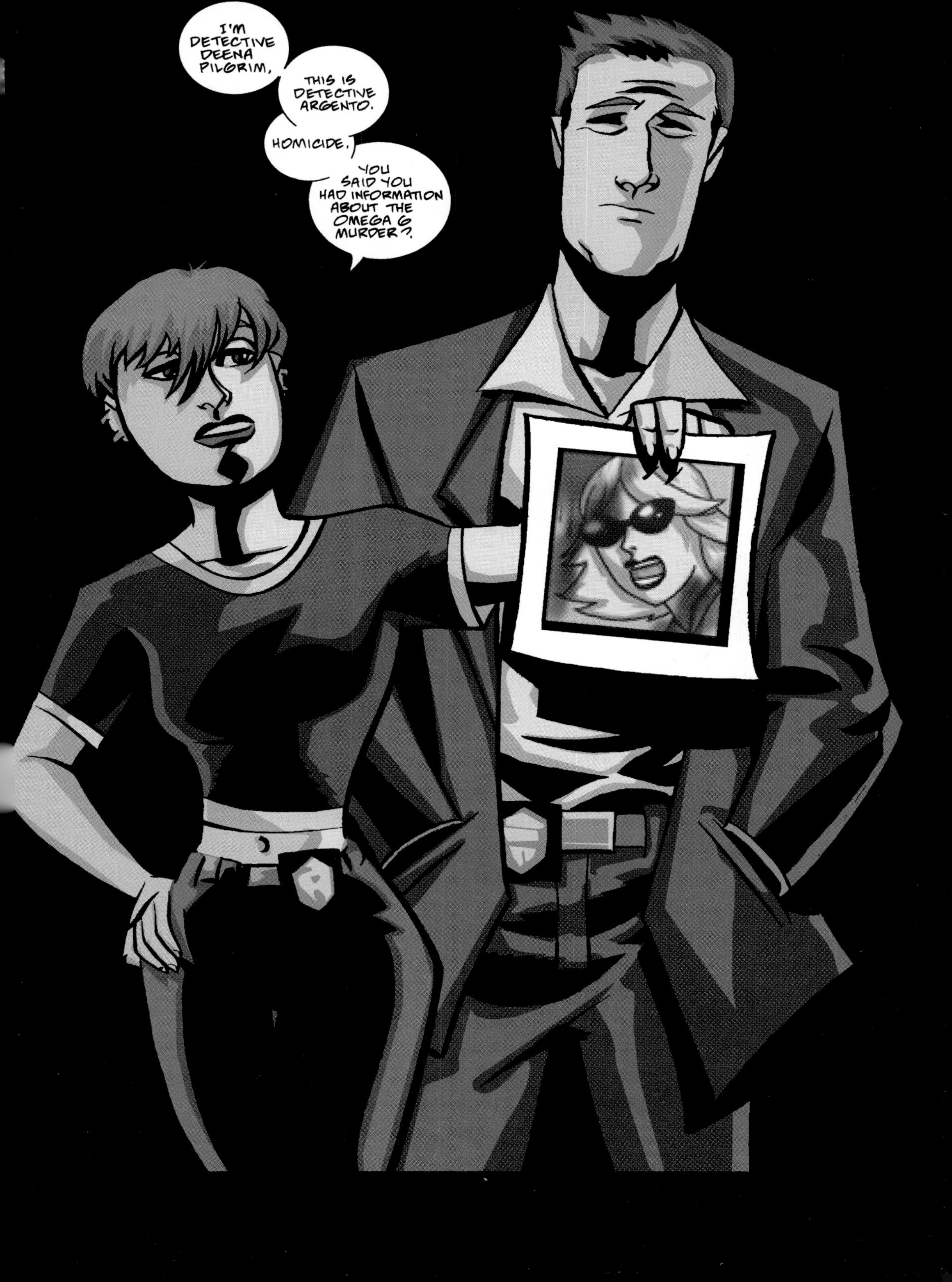
I'M DETECTIVE DEENA PILGRIM,
THIS IS DETECTIVE ARGENTO.
HOMICIDE.
YOU SAID YOU HAD INFORMATION ABOUT THE OMEGA 6 MURDER?.

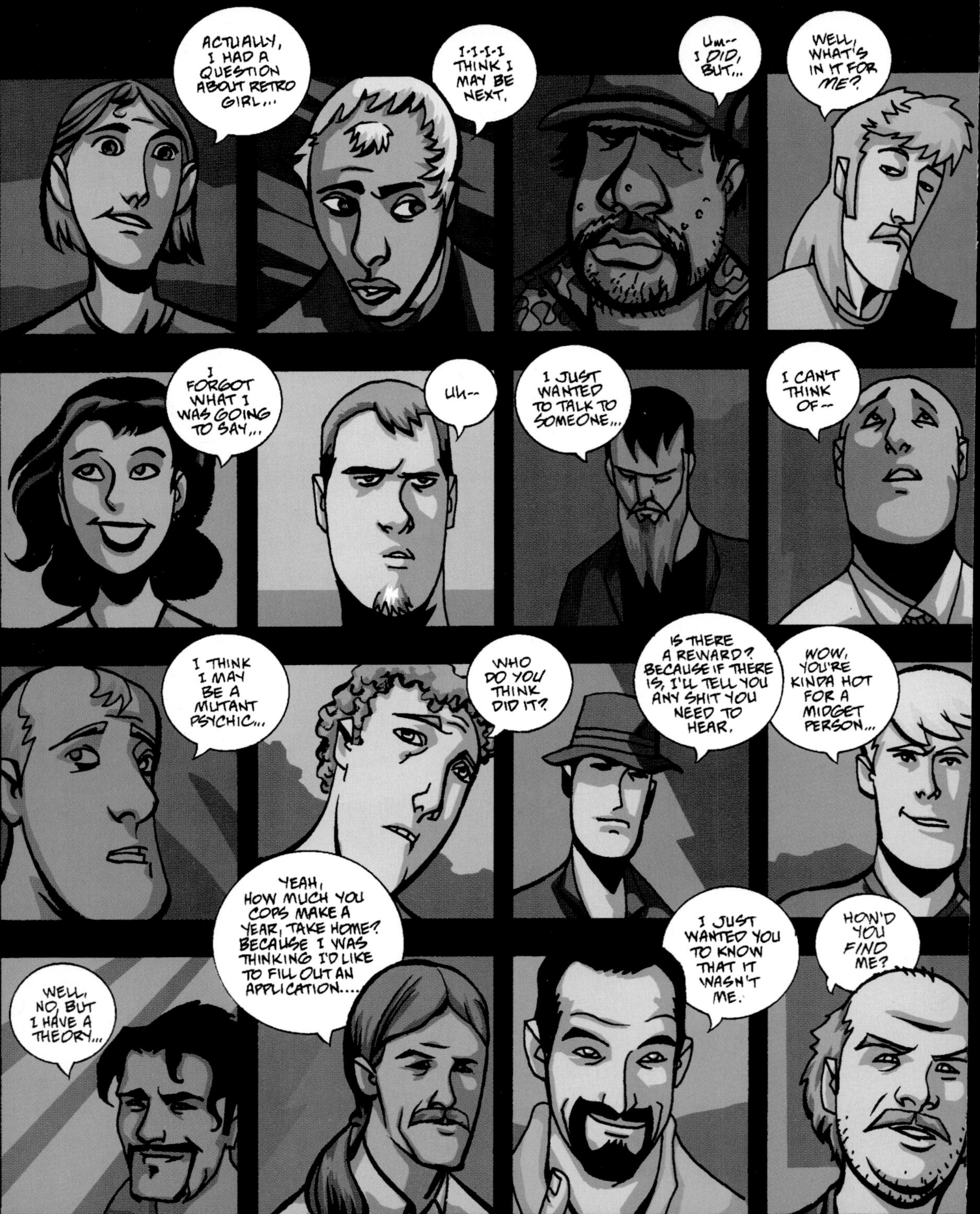
ACTUALLY, I HAD A QUESTION ABOUT RETRO GIRL...
I-I-I-I THINK I MAY BE NEXT.
UM-- I DID, BUT...
WELL, WHAT'S IN IT FOR ME?
I FORGOT WHAT I WAS GOING TO SAY...
UH--
I JUST WANTED TO TALK TO SOMEONE...
I CAN'T THINK OF--
I THINK I MAY BE A MUTANT PSYCHIC...
WHO DO YOU THINK DID IT?
IS THERE A REWARD? BECAUSE IF THERE IS, I'LL TELL YOU ANY SHIT YOU NEED TO HEAR.
WOW, YOU'RE KINDA HOT FOR A MIDGET PERSON...
WELL, NO, BUT I HAVE A THEORY...
YEAH, HOW MUCH YOU COPS MAKE A YEAR, TAKE HOME? BECAUSE I WAS THINKING I'D LIKE TO FILL OUT AN APPLICATION....
I JUST WANTED YOU TO KNOW THAT IT WASN'T ME.
HOW'D YOU FIND ME?

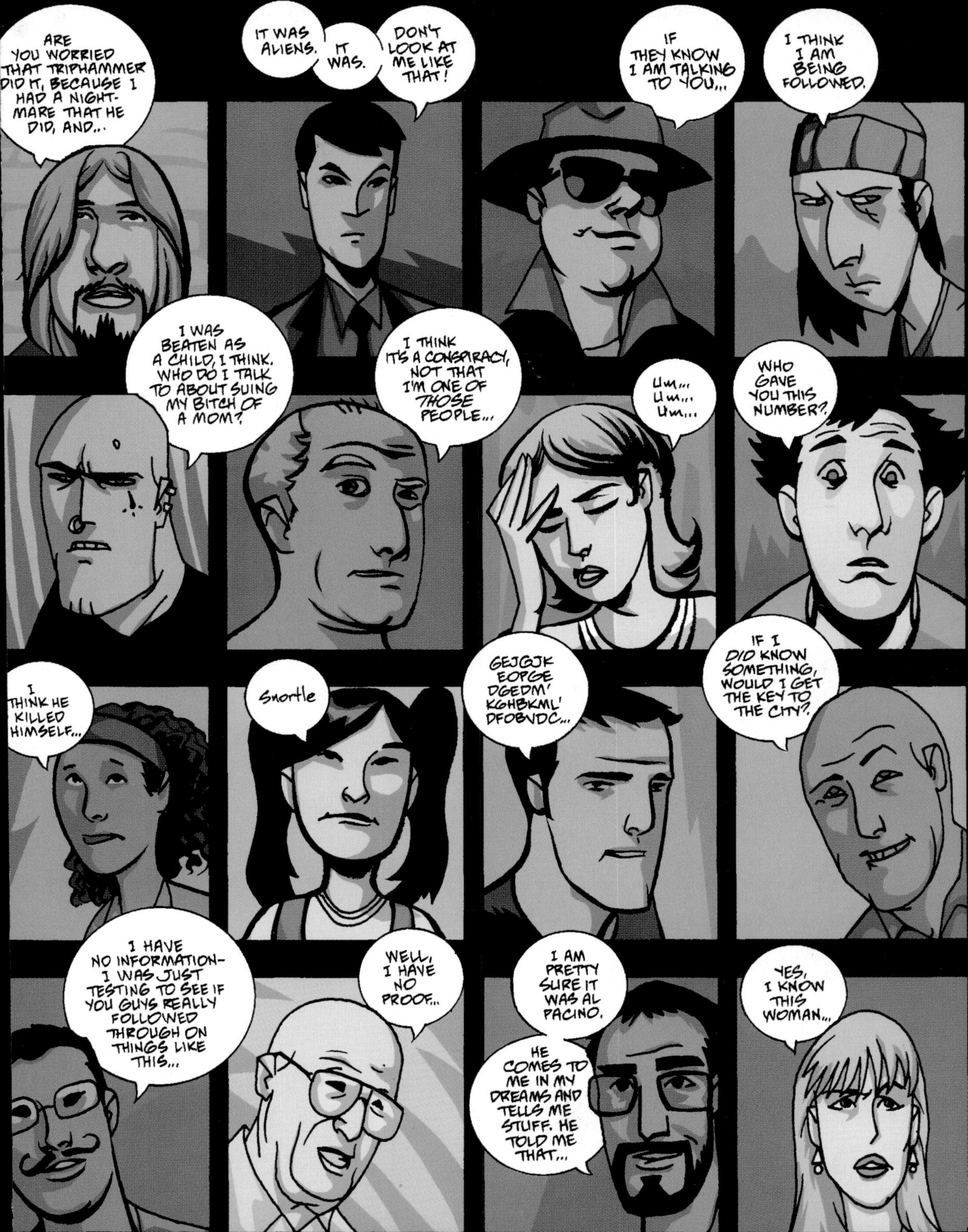
ARE YOU WORRIED THAT TRIPHAMMER DID IT, BECAUSE I HAD A NIGHT-MARE THAT HE DID, AND...
IT WAS ALIENS.
IT WAS.
DON'T LOOK AT ME LIKE THAT!
IF THEY KNOW I AM TALKING TO YOU...
I THINK I AM BEING FOLLOWED.
I WAS BEATEN AS A CHILD, I THINK. WHO DO I TALK TO ABOUT SUING MY BITCH OF A MOM?
I THINK IT'S A CONSPIRACY, NOT THAT I'M ONE OF THOSE PEOPLE...
Um... Um... Um...
WHO GAVE YOU THIS NUMBER?
I THINK HE KILLED HIMSELF...
Snortle
GEJGJK EOPGE DGEDM' KGHBKML' DFOBVDC...
IF I DID KNOW SOMETHING, WOULD I GET THE KEY TO THE CITY?
I HAVE NO INFORMATION- I WAS JUST TESTING TO SEE IF YOU GUYS REALLY FOLLOWED THROUGH ON THINGS LIKE THIS...
WELL, I HAVE NO PROOF...
I AM PRETTY SURE IT WAS AL PACINO.
HE COMES TO ME IN MY DREAMS AND TELLS ME STUFF. HE TOLD ME THAT...
YES, I KNOW THIS WOMAN...

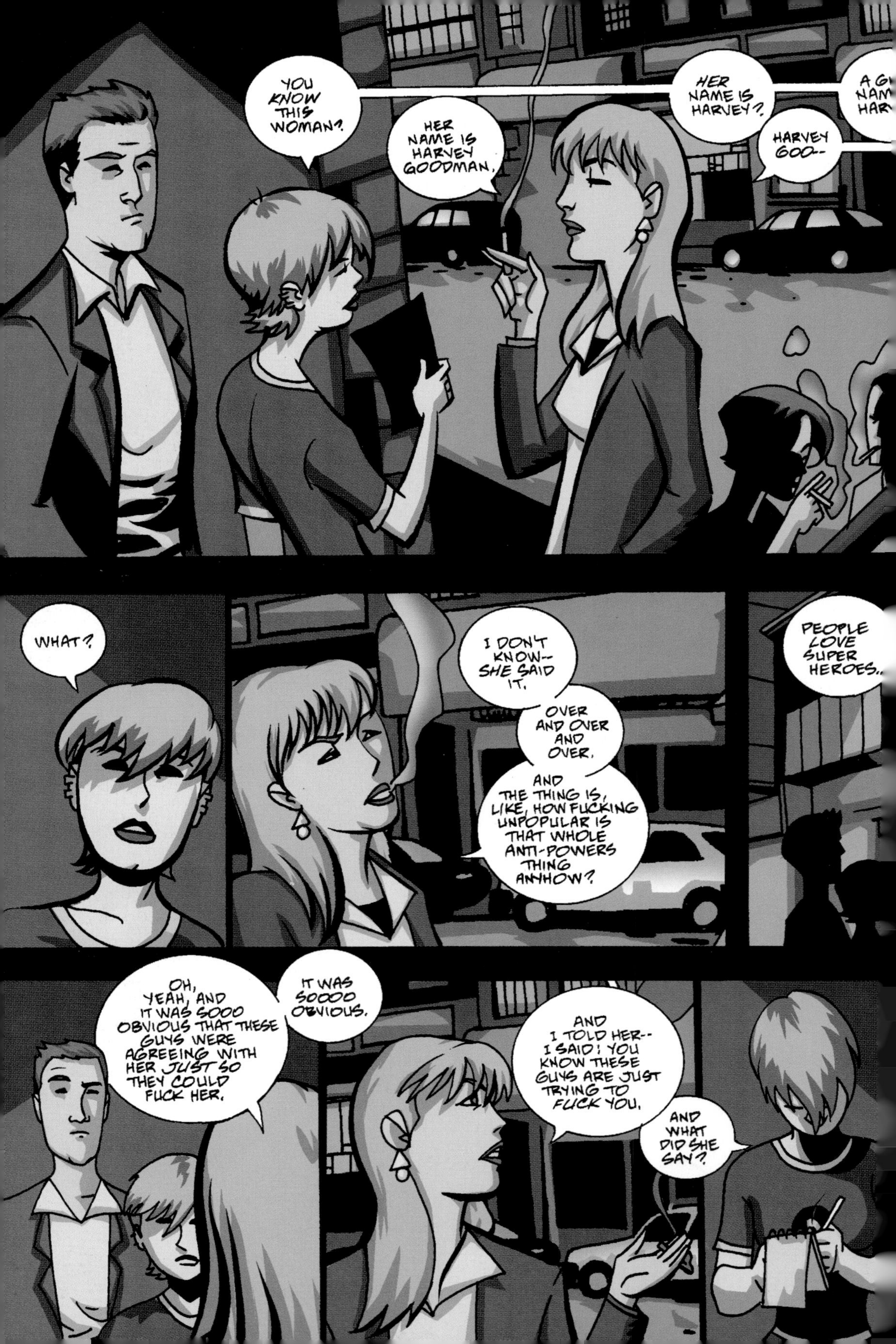
YOU KNOW THIS WOMAN?
HER NAME IS HARVEY GOODMAN.
HER NAME IS HARVEY?
HARVEY GOO--
WHAT?
I DON'T KNOW-- SHE SAID IT.
OVER AND OVER AND OVER.
AND THE THING IS, LIKE, HOW FUCKING UNPOPULAR IS THAT WHOLE ANTI-POWERS THING ANYHOW?
PEOPLE LOVE SUPER HEROES...
OH, YEAH, AND IT WAS SOOO OBVIOUS THAT THESE GUYS WERE AGREEING WITH HER *JUST* SO THEY COULD FUCK HER.
IT WAS SOOOO OBVIOUS.
AND I TOLD HER-- I SAID: YOU KNOW THESE GUYS ARE JUST TRYING TO *FUCK* YOU.
AND WHAT DID SHE SAY?

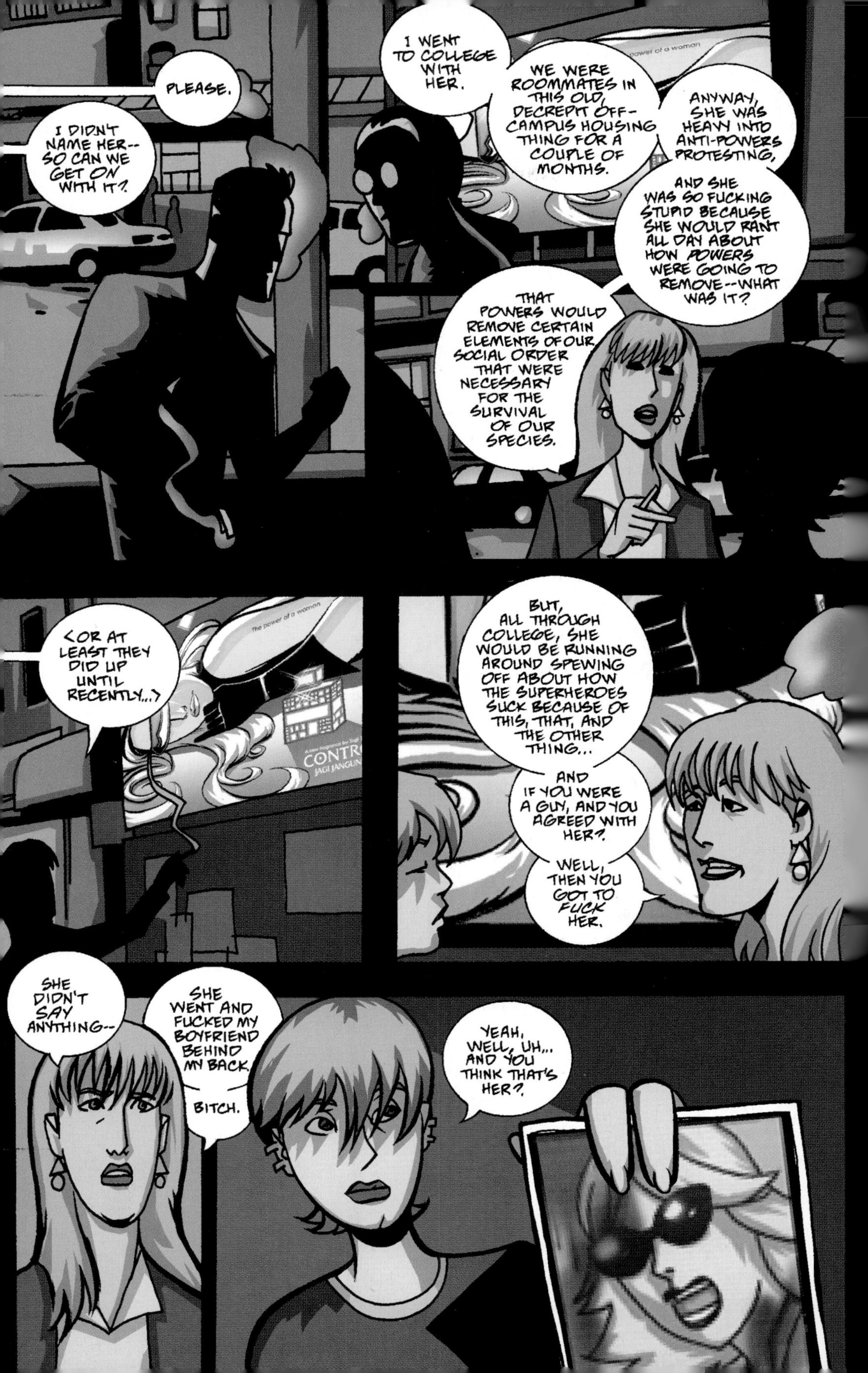
PLEASE.
I DIDN'T NAME HER-- SO CAN WE GET ON WITH IT?
I WENT TO COLLEGE WITH HER.
WE WERE ROOMMATES IN THIS OLD, DECREPIT OFF-CAMPUS HOUSING THING FOR A COUPLE OF MONTHS.
ANYWAY, SHE WAS HEAVY INTO ANTI-POWERS PROTESTING,
AND SHE WAS SO FUCKING STUPID BECAUSE SHE WOULD RANT ALL DAY ABOUT HOW POWERS WERE GOING TO REMOVE--WHAT WAS IT?
THAT POWERS WOULD REMOVE CERTAIN ELEMENTS OF OUR SOCIAL ORDER THAT WERE NECESSARY FOR THE SURVIVAL OF OUR SPECIES.
the power of a woman
<OR AT LEAST THEY DID UP UNTIL RECENTLY...>
CONTR
JAGI JANGUN
BUT, ALL THROUGH COLLEGE, SHE WOULD BE RUNNING AROUND SPEWING OFF ABOUT HOW THE SUPERHEROES SUCK BECAUSE OF THIS, THAT, AND THE OTHER THING...
AND IF YOU WERE A GUY, AND YOU AGREED WITH HER?
WELL, THEN YOU GOT TO FUCK HER.
SHE DIDN'T SAY ANYTHING--
SHE WENT AND FUCKED MY BOYFRIEND BEHIND MY BACK.
BITCH.
YEAH, WELL, UH... AND YOU THINK THAT'S HER?

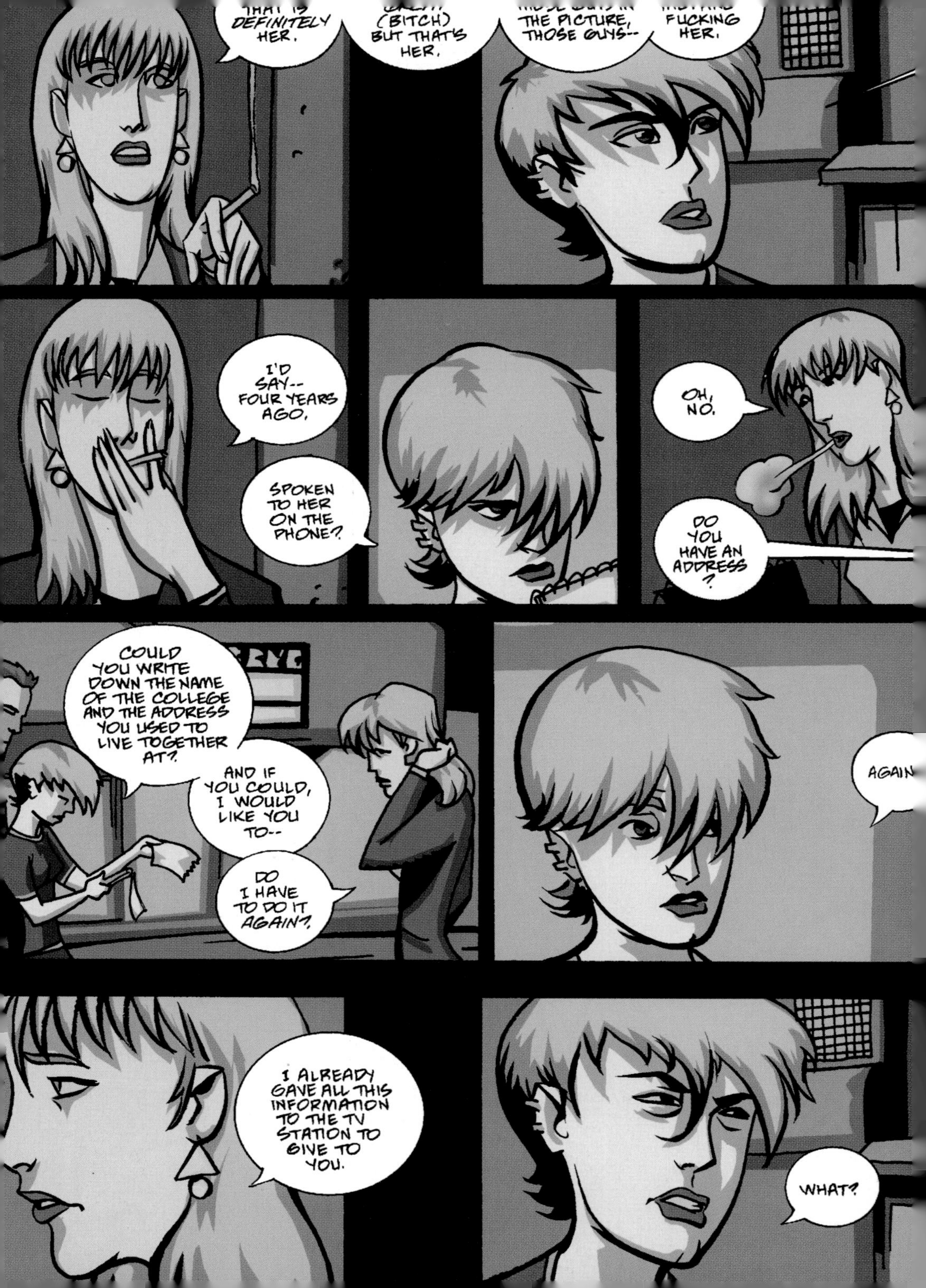
DEFINITELY HER.
(BITCH) BUT THAT'S HER.
THE PICTURE, THOSE GUYS--
FUCKING HER.
I'D SAY-- FOUR YEARS AGO.
SPOKEN TO HER ON THE PHONE?
OH, NO.
DO YOU HAVE AN ADDRESS?
COULD YOU WRITE DOWN THE NAME OF THE COLLEGE AND THE ADDRESS YOU USED TO LIVE TOGETHER AT?
AND IF YOU COULD, I WOULD LIKE YOU TO--
DO I HAVE TO DO IT AGAIN?
AGAIN
I ALREADY GAVE ALL THIS INFORMATION TO THE TV STATION TO GIVE TO YOU.
WHAT?

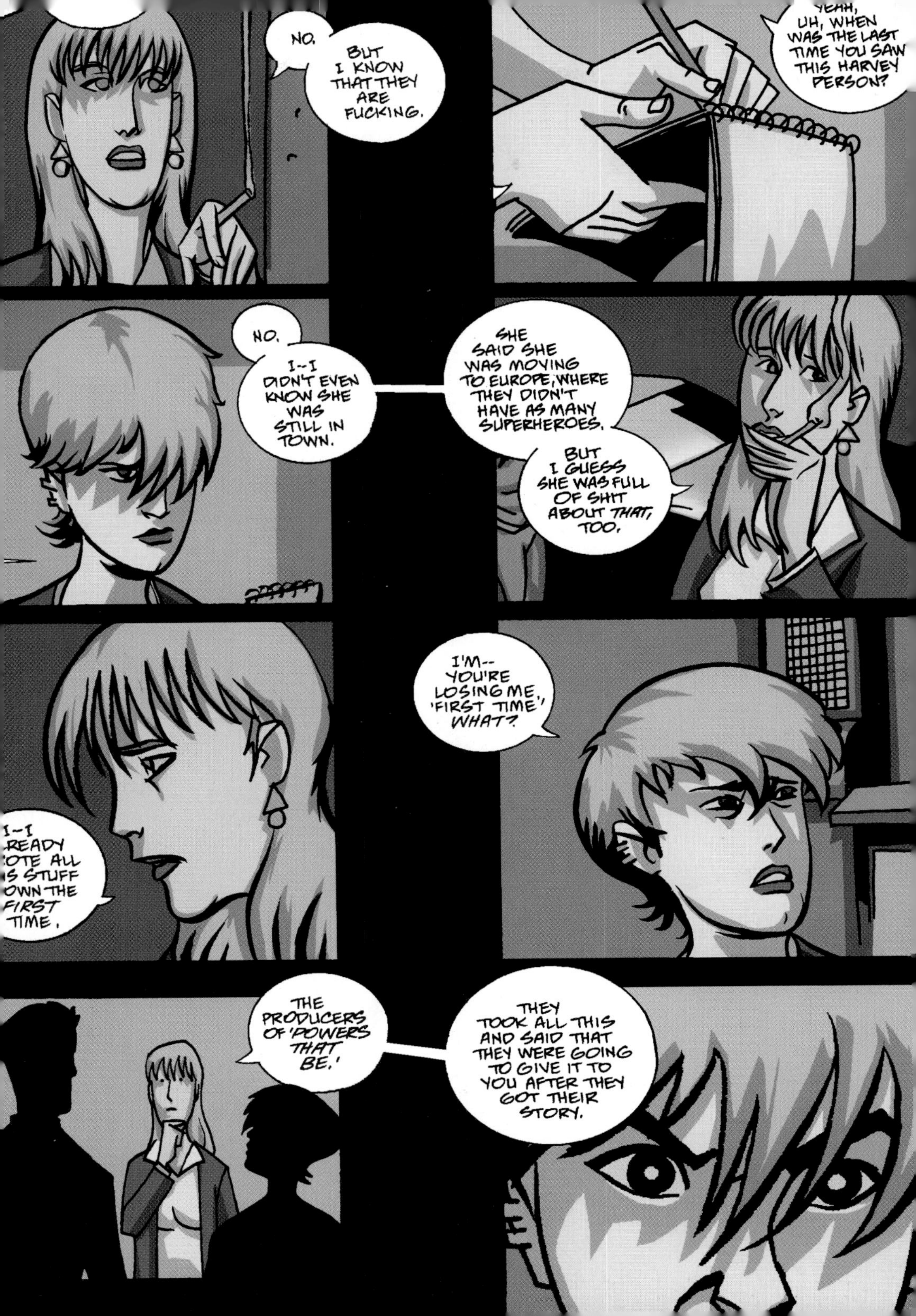
NO.
BUT I KNOW THAT THEY ARE FUCKING.
YEAH, UH, WHEN WAS THE LAST TIME YOU SAW THIS HARVEY PERSON?
NO.
I--I DIDN'T EVEN KNOW SHE WAS STILL IN TOWN.
SHE SAID SHE WAS MOVING TO EUROPE, WHERE THEY DIDN'T HAVE AS MANY SUPERHEROES.
BUT I GUESS SHE WAS FULL OF SHIT ABOUT THAT, TOO.
I--I
TIME.
I'M-- YOU'RE LOSING ME, 'FIRST TIME', WHAT?
THE PRODUCERS OF 'POWERS THAT BE.'
THEY TOOK ALL THIS AND SAID THAT THEY WERE GOING TO GIVE IT TO YOU AFTER THEY GOT THEIR STORY.

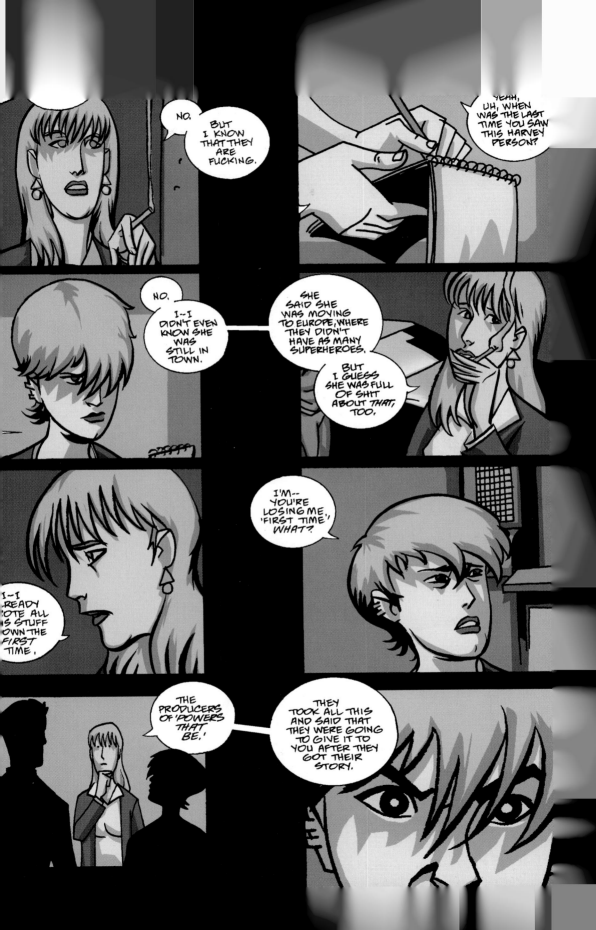

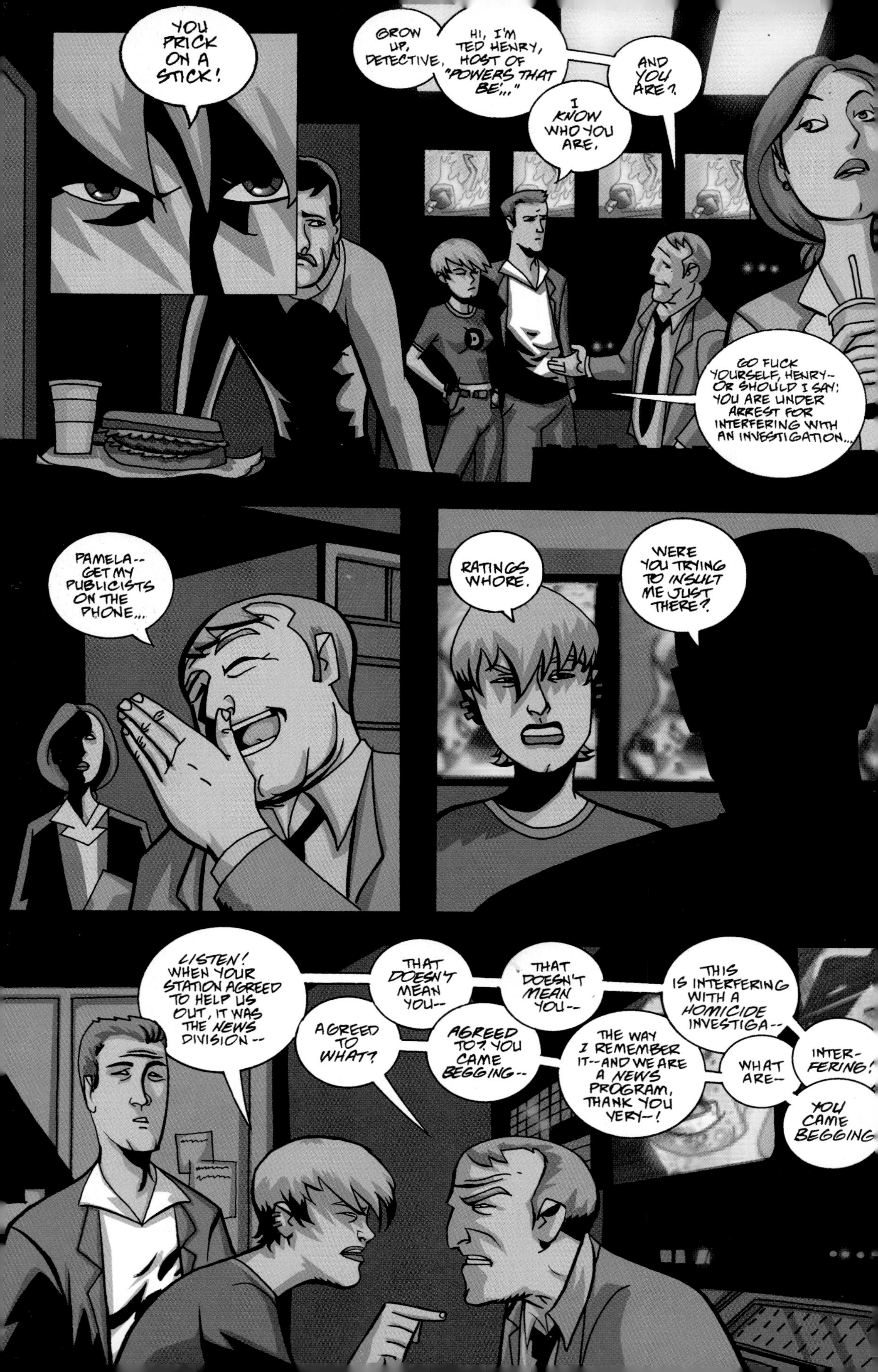

YOU PRICK ON A STICK!
GROW UP, DETECTIVE.
HI, I'M TED HENRY, HOST OF "POWERS THAT BE"...
AND YOU ARE?
I KNOW WHO YOU ARE.
GO FUCK YOURSELF, HENRY-- OR SHOULD I SAY: YOU ARE UNDER ARREST FOR INTERFERING WITH AN INVESTIGATION...
PAMELA-- GET MY PUBLICISTS ON THE PHONE...
RATINGS WHORE.
WERE YOU TRYING TO INSULT ME JUST THERE?
LISTEN! WHEN YOUR STATION AGREED TO HELP US OUT, IT WAS THE NEWS DIVISION--
AGREED TO WHAT?
THAT DOESN'T MEAN YOU--
AGREED TO? YOU CAME BEGGING--
THAT DOESN'T MEAN YOU--
THE WAY I REMEMBER IT--AND WE ARE A NEWS PROGRAM, THANK YOU VERY--!
THIS IS INTERFERING WITH A HOMICIDE INVESTIGA--
WHAT ARE--
INTER-FERING!
YOU CAME BEGGING

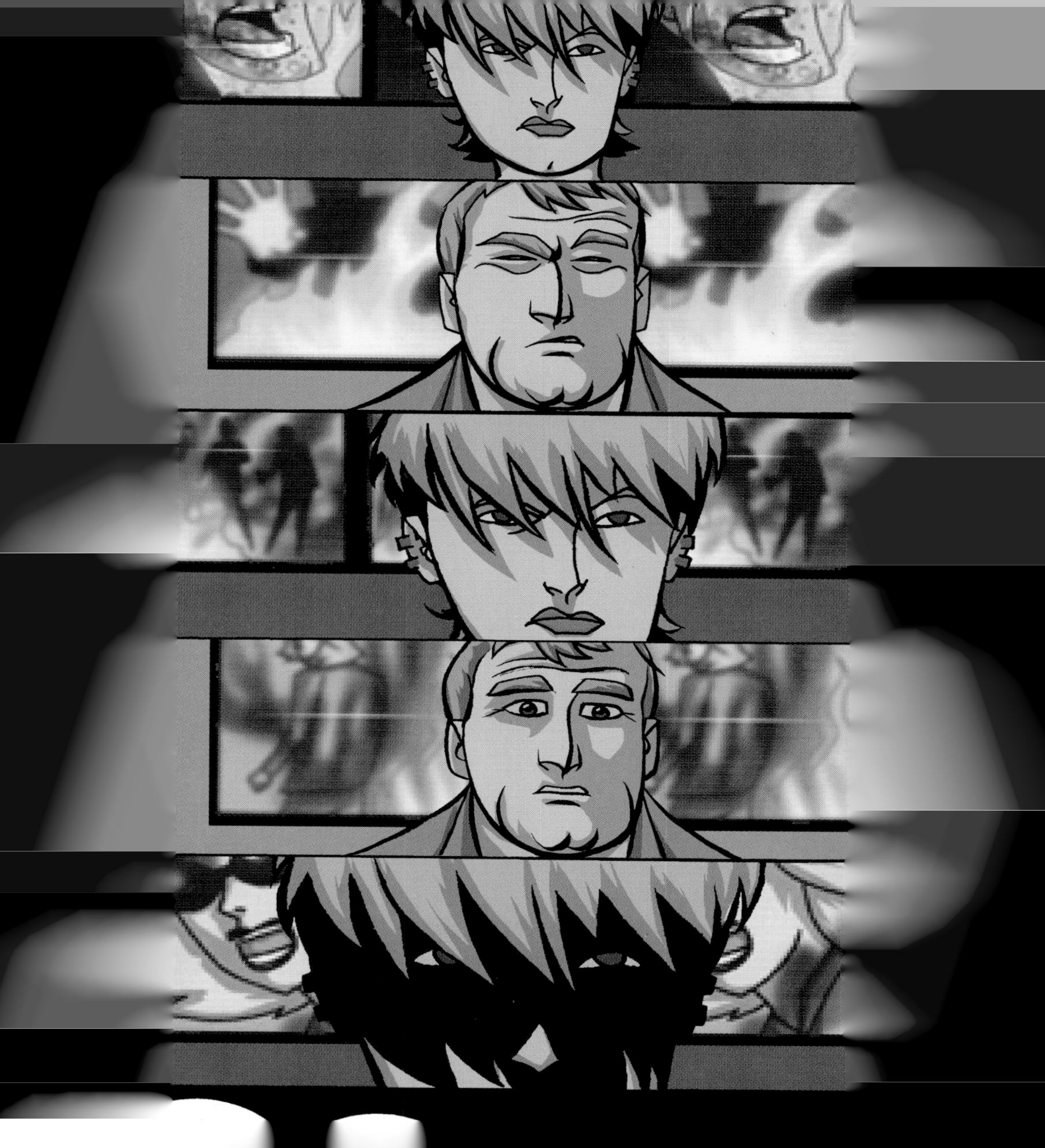

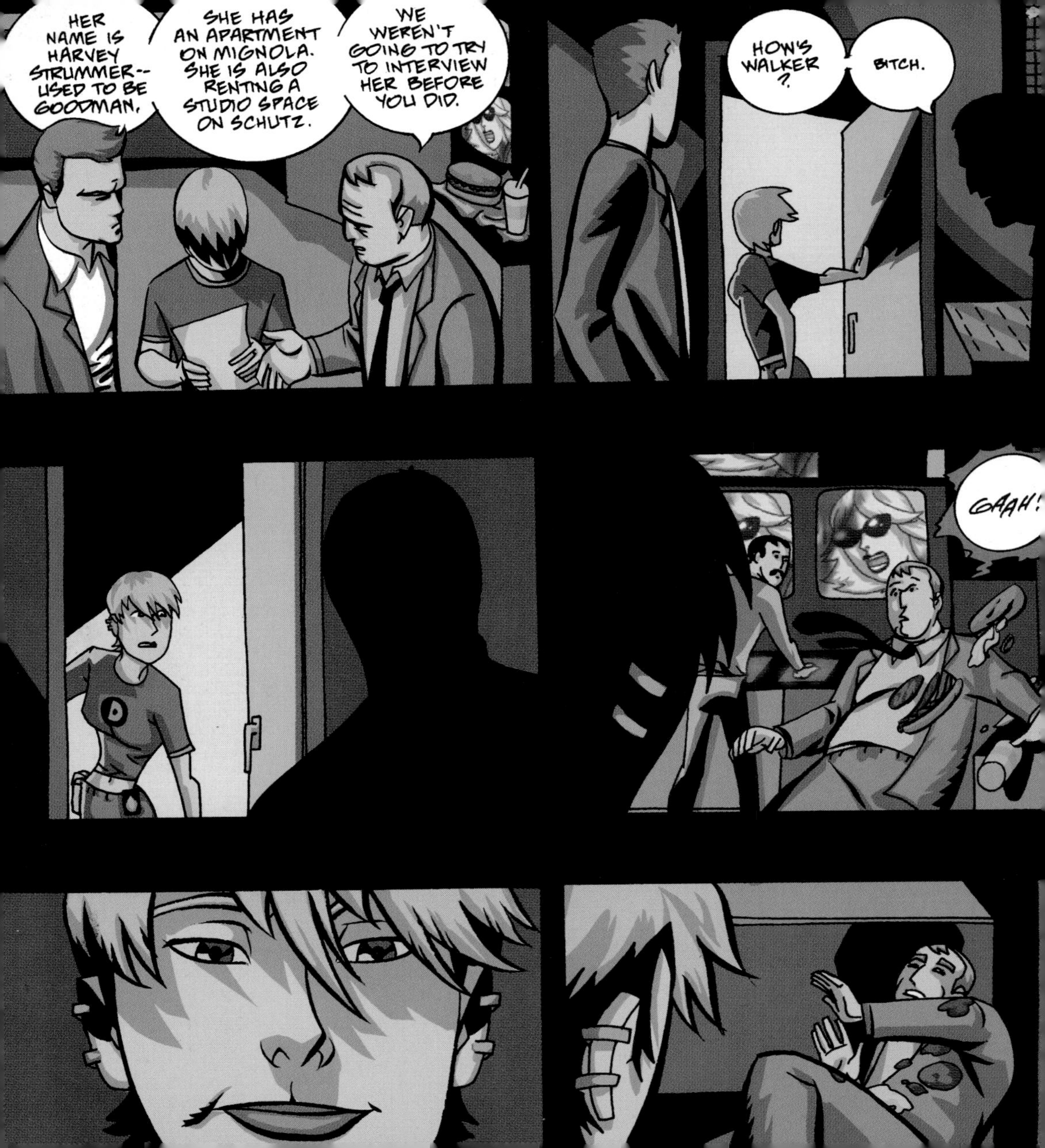
HER NAME IS HARVEY STRUMMER-- USED TO BE GOODMAN.
SHE HAS AN APARTMENT ON MIGNOLA. SHE IS ALSO RENTING A STUDIO SPACE ON SCHUTZ.
WE WEREN'T GOING TO TRY TO INTERVIEW HER BEFORE YOU DID.
HOW'S WALKER?
BITCH.
GAAH!

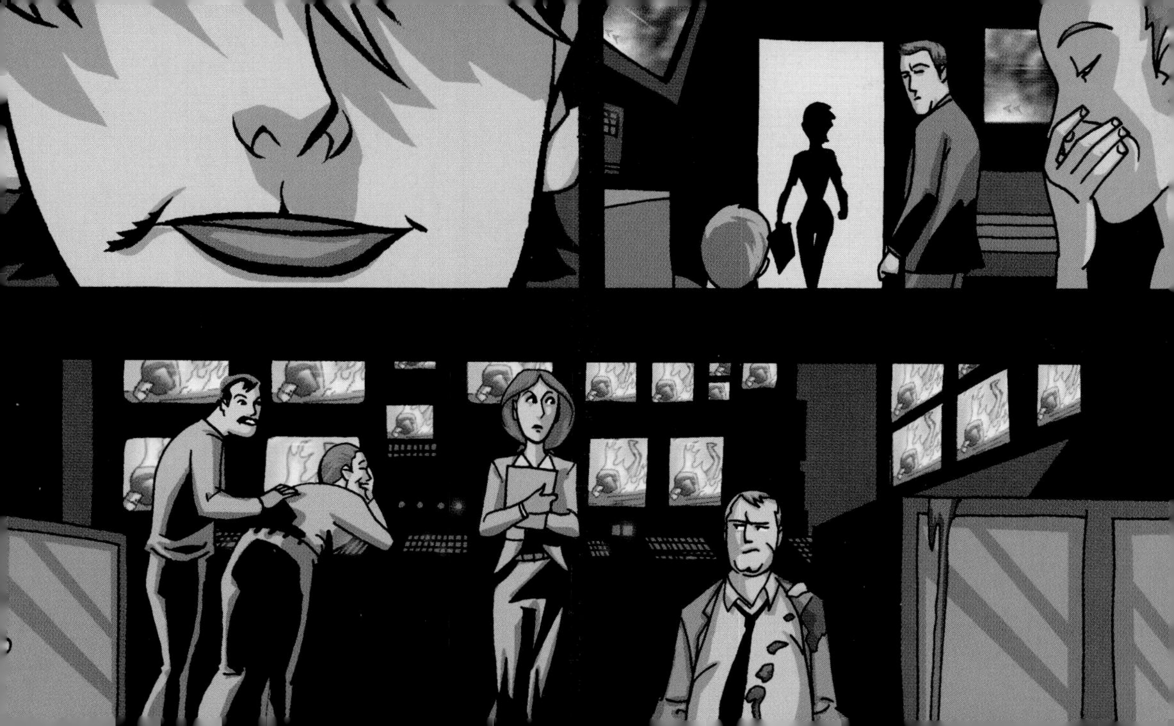

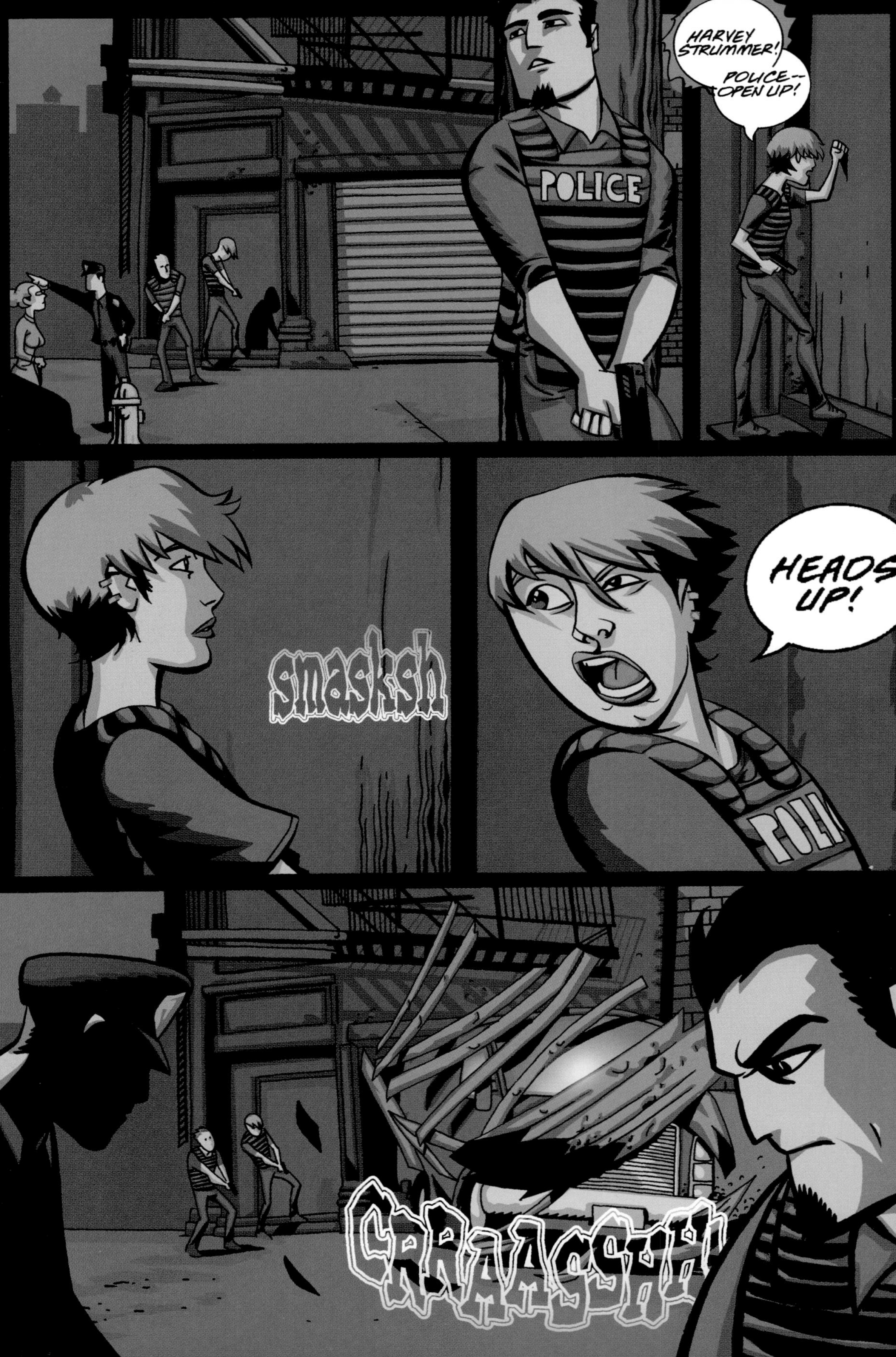

HARVEY STRUMMER!
POLICE-- OPEN UP!
POLICE
smasksh
HEADS UP!
POLI
CRRAAASHH

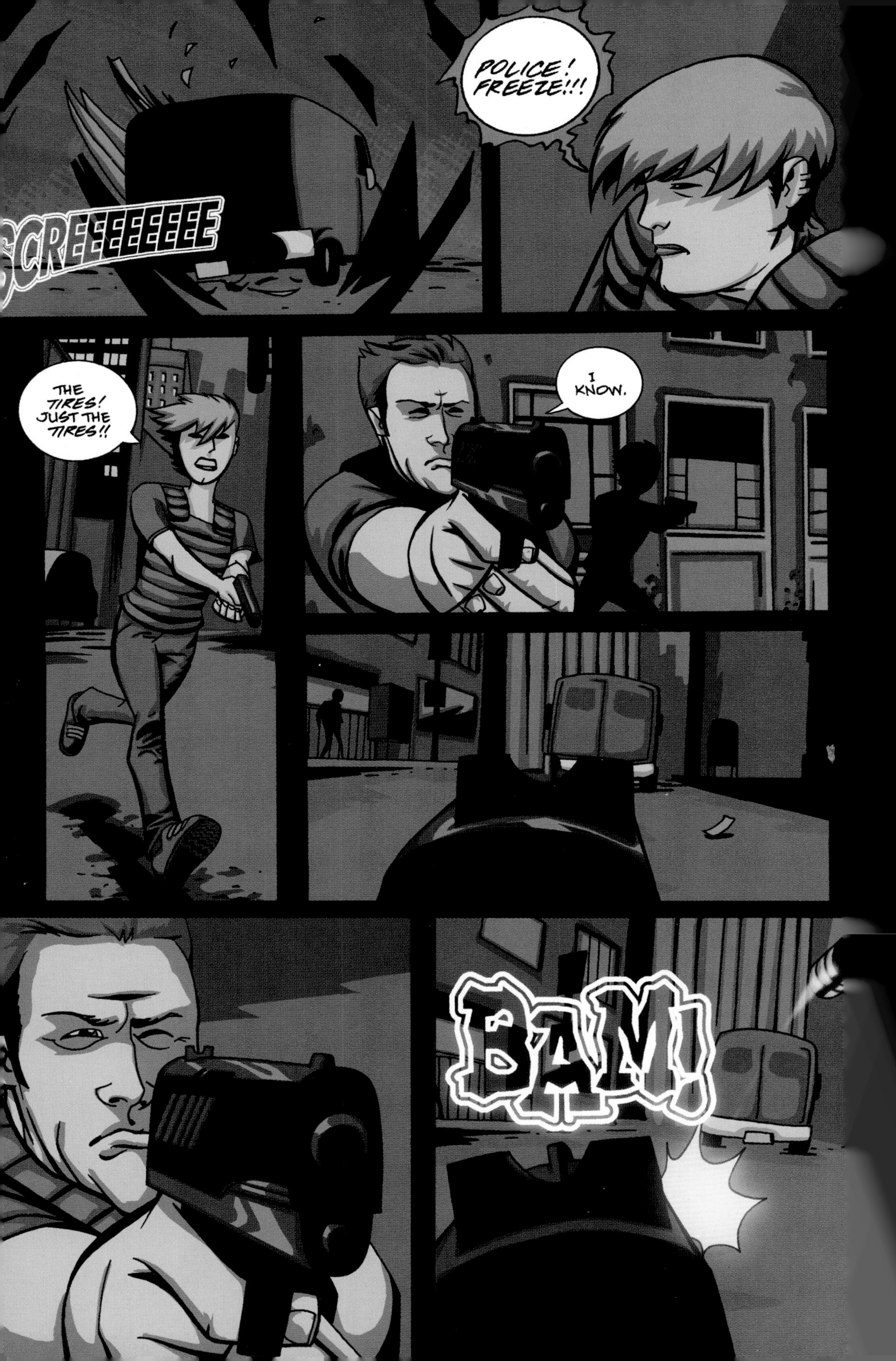
SCREEEEEEEE
POLICE! FREEZE!!!
THE TIRES! JUST THE TIRES!!
I KNOW.
BAM!

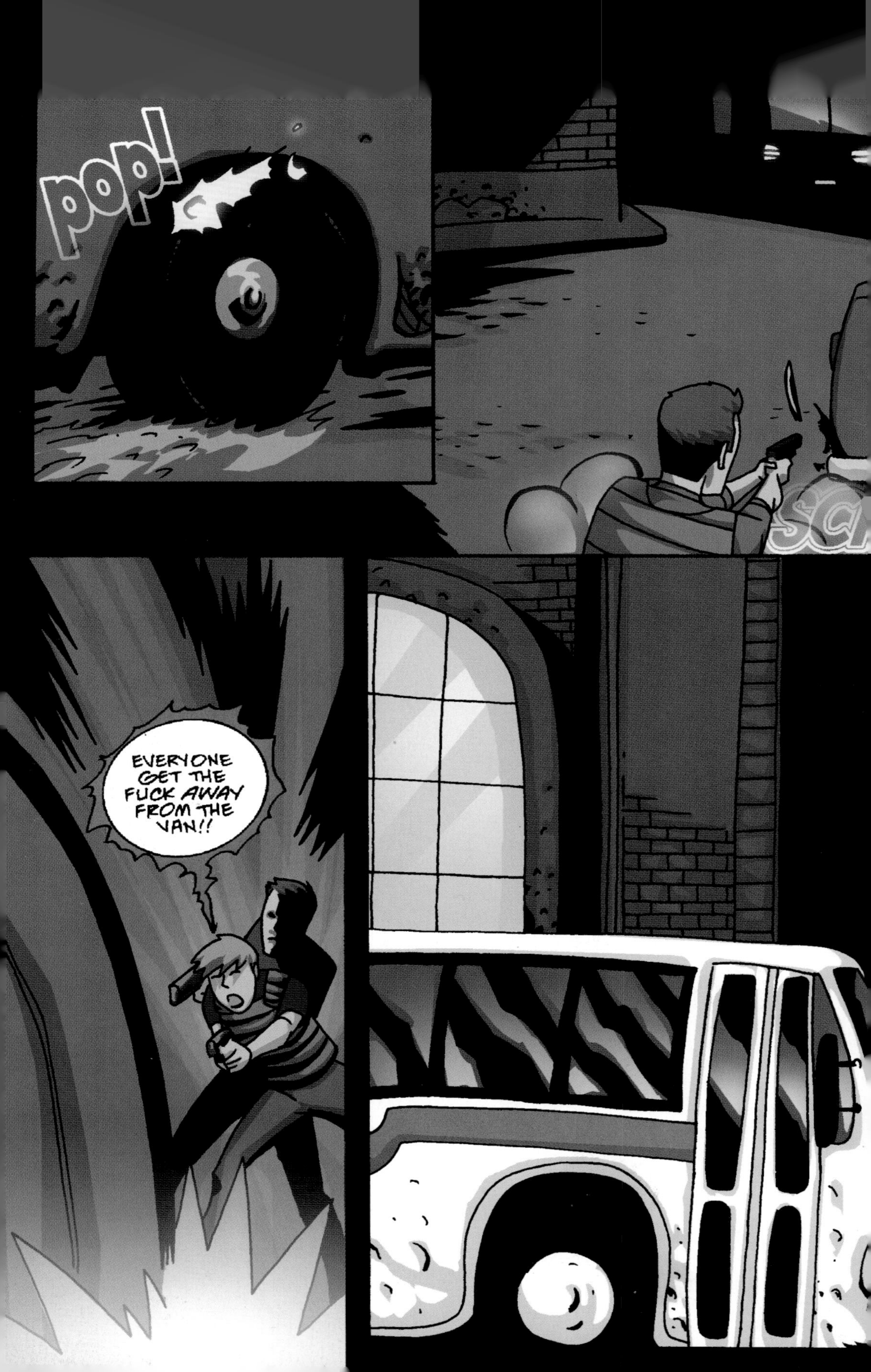
pop!
EVERYONE GET THE FUCK AWAY FROM THE VAN!!

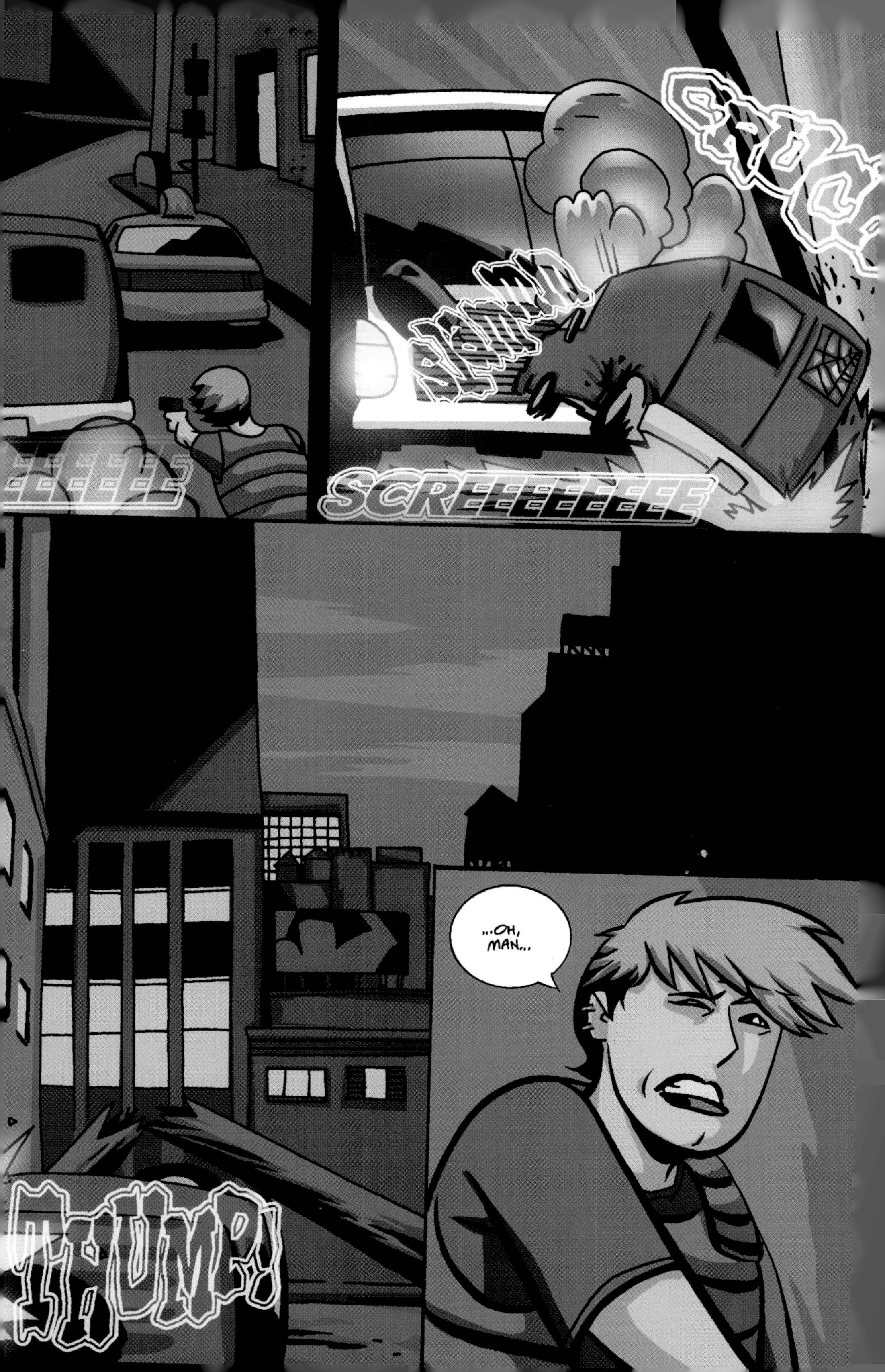
SCREEEEEEEEE
...OH, MAN...
THUMP!

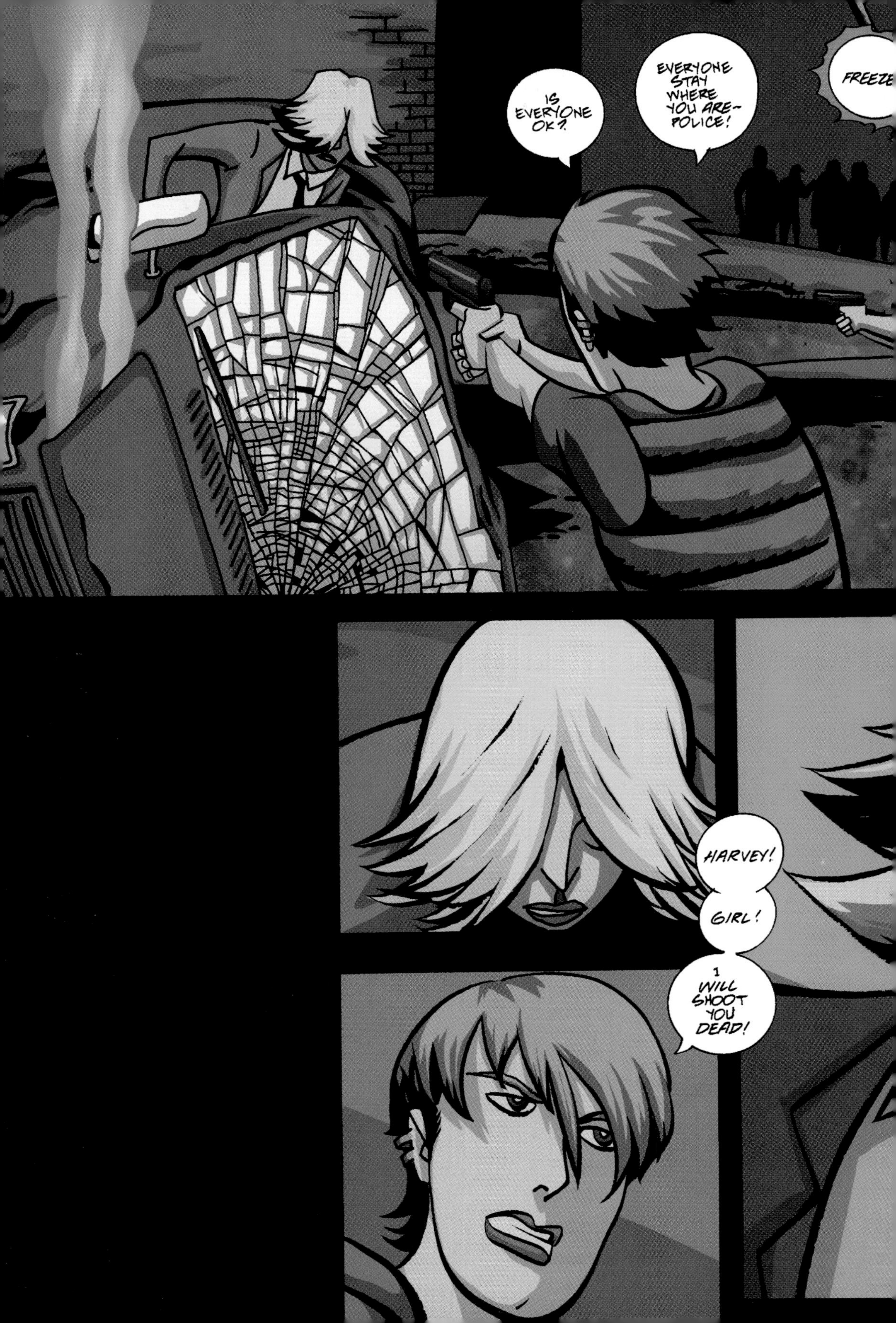
IS EVERYONE OK?
EVERYONE STAY WHERE YOU ARE-POLICE!
FREEZE
HARVEY!
GIRL!
I WILL SHOOT YOU DEAD!

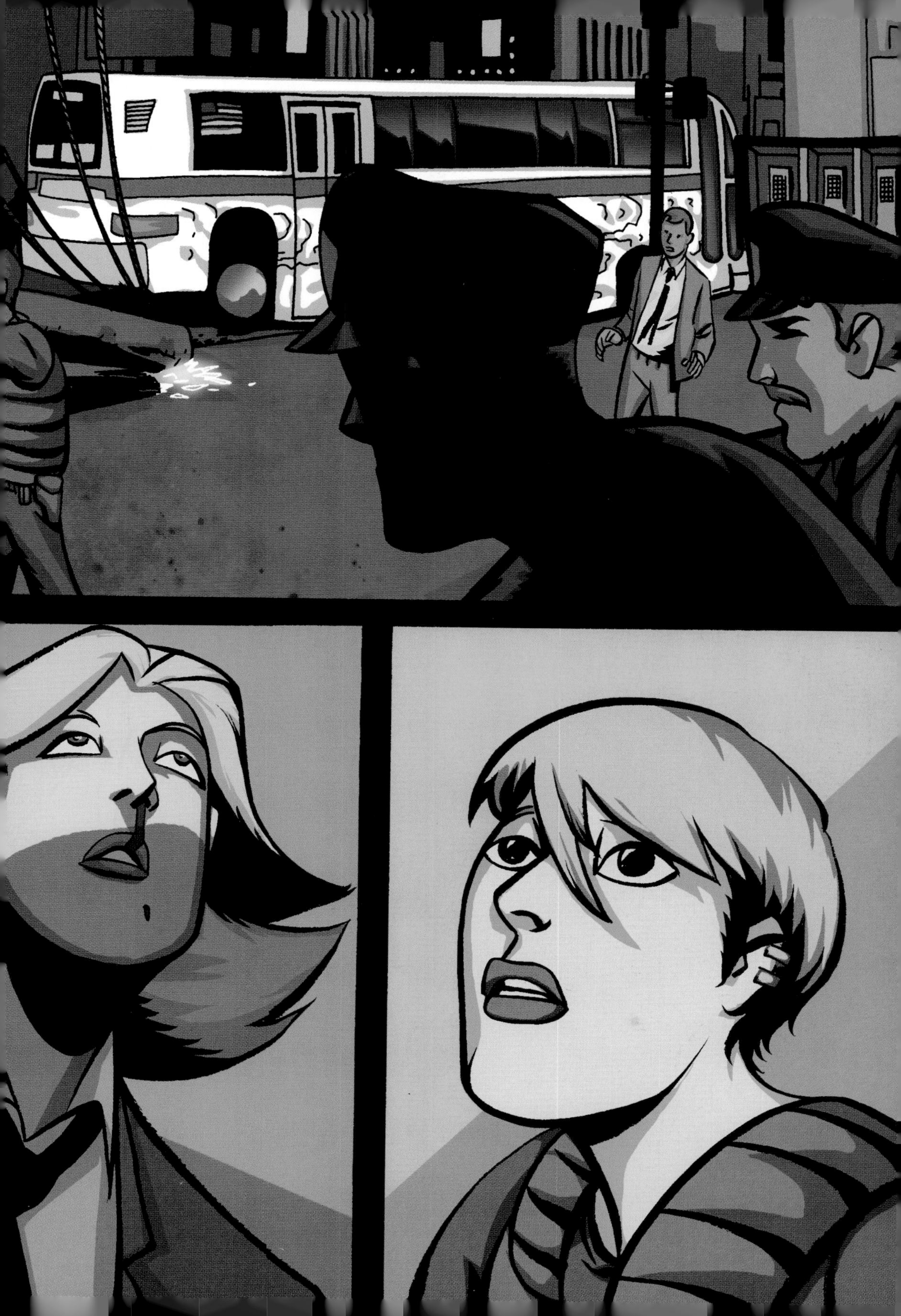

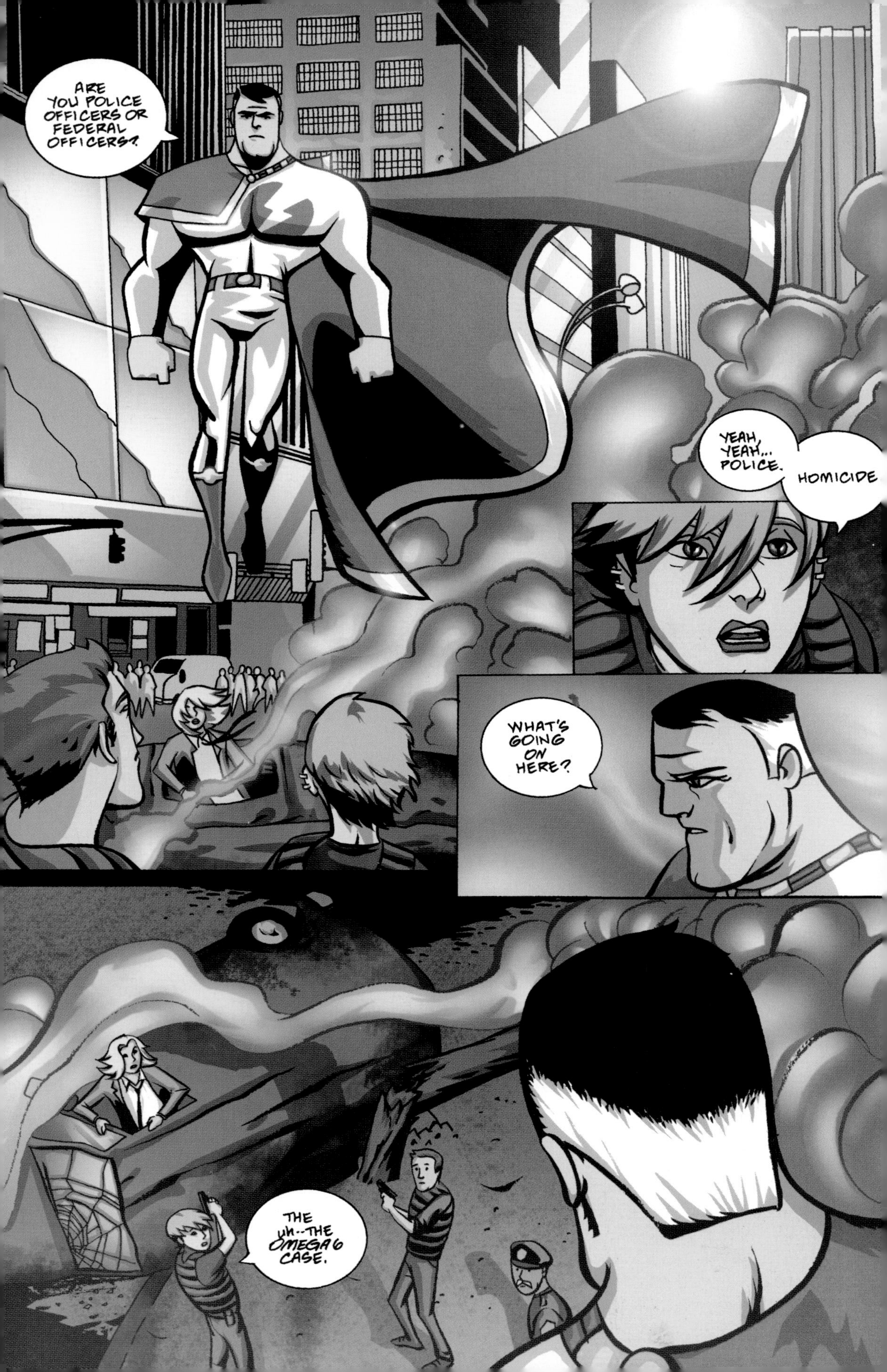
ARE YOU POLICE OFFICERS OR FEDERAL OFFICERS?
YEAH, YEAH... POLICE.
HOMICIDE
WHAT'S GOING ON HERE?
THE uh--THE OMEGA 6 CASE.

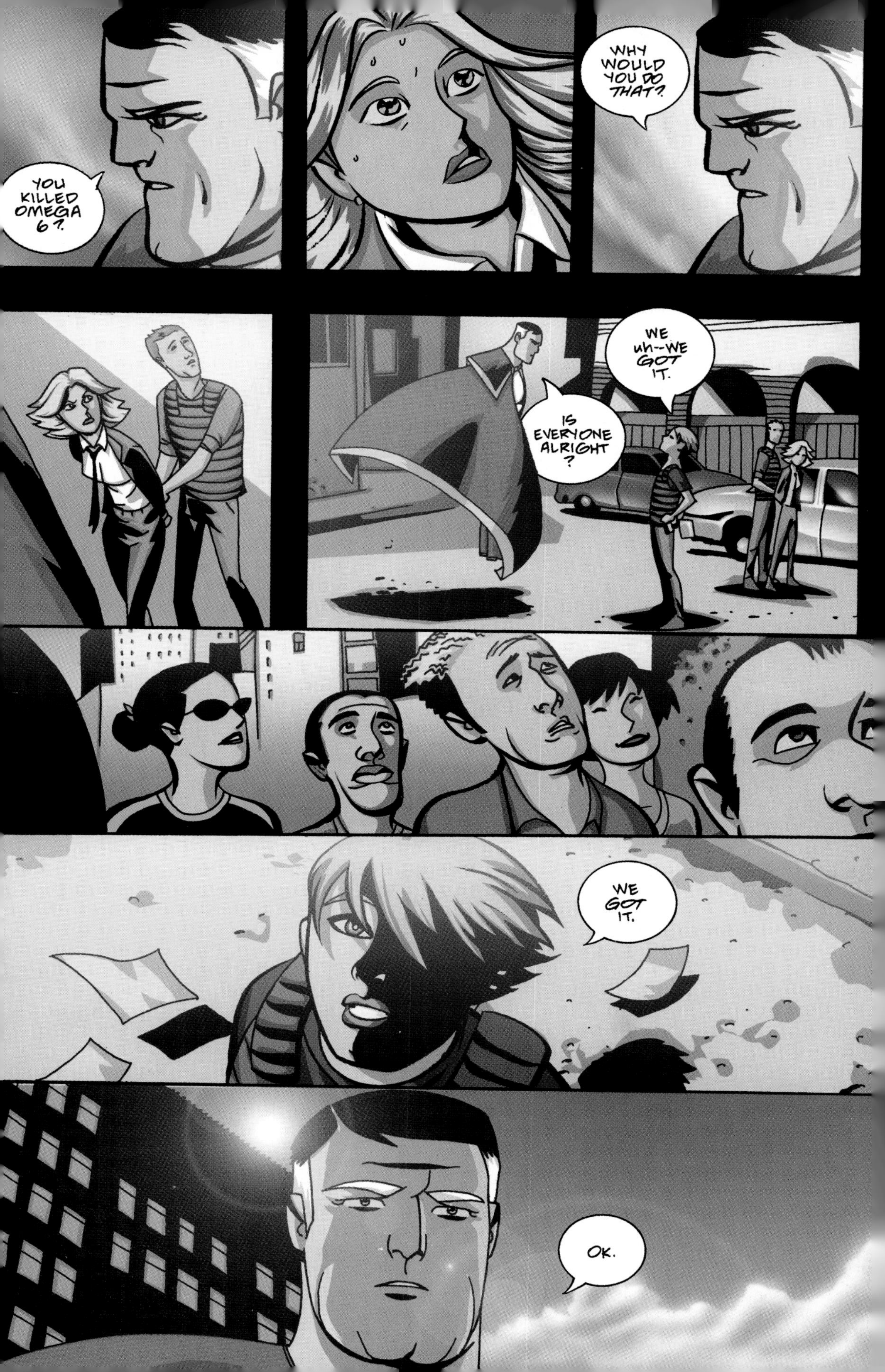
YOU KILLED OMEGA 6?
WHY WOULD YOU DO THAT?
IS EVERYONE ALRIGHT?
WE uh--WE GOT IT.
WE GOT IT.
OK.

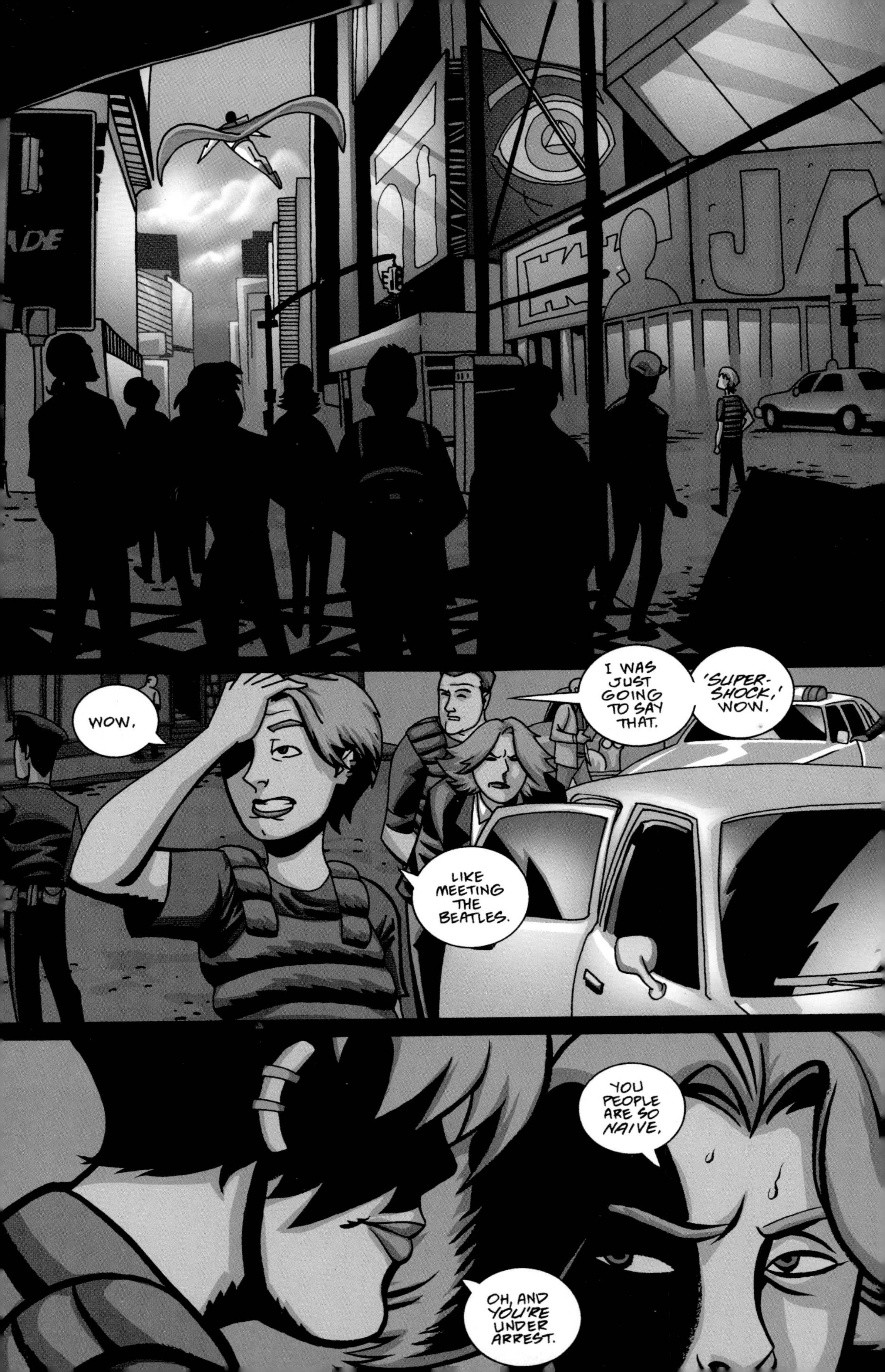
WOW.
I WAS JUST GOING TO SAY THAT.
'SUPER-SHOCK,' WOW.
LIKE MEETING THE BEATLES.
YOU PEOPLE ARE SO NAIVE.
OH, AND YOU'RE UNDER ARREST.

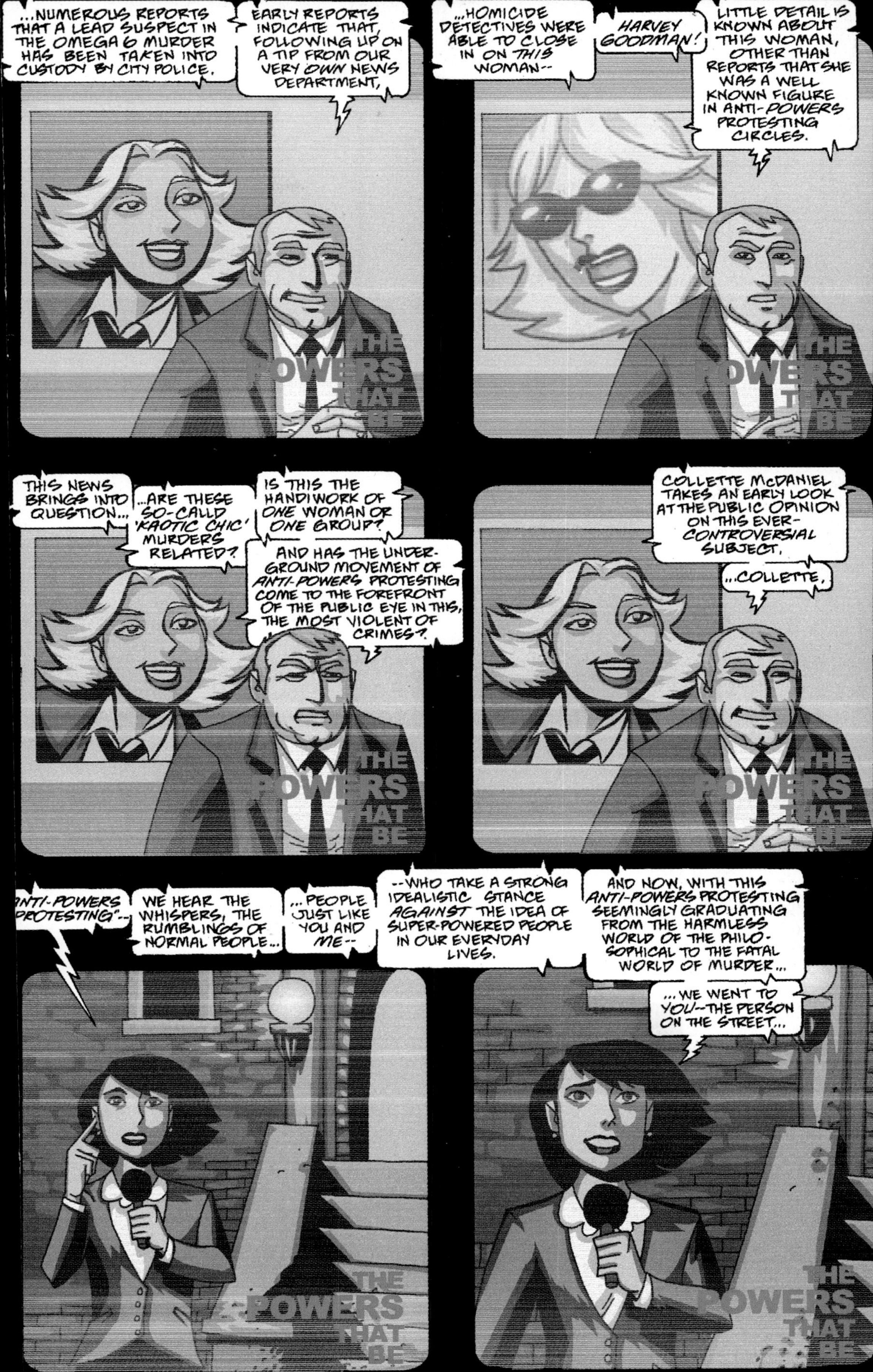
...NUMEROUS REPORTS THAT A LEAD SUSPECT IN THE OMEGA 6 MURDER HAS BEEN TAKEN INTO CUSTODY BY CITY POLICE.
EARLY REPORTS INDICATE THAT, FOLLOWING UP ON A TIP FROM OUR VERY OWN NEWS DEPARTMENT,
THE POWERS THAT BE
...HOMICIDE DETECTIVES WERE ABLE TO CLOSE IN ON THIS WOMAN--
HARVEY GOODMAN!
LITTLE DETAIL IS KNOWN ABOUT THIS WOMAN, OTHER THAN REPORTS THAT SHE WAS A WELL KNOWN FIGURE IN ANTI-POWERS PROTESTING CIRCLES.
THE POWERS THAT BE
THIS NEWS BRINGS INTO QUESTION...
...ARE THESE SO-CALLD 'KAOTIC CHIC' MURDERS RELATED?
IS THIS THE HANDIWORK OF ONE WOMAN OR ONE GROUP?
AND HAS THE UNDERGROUND MOVEMENT OF ANTI-POWERS PROTESTING COME TO THE FOREFRONT OF THE PUBLIC EYE IN THIS, THE MOST VIOLENT OF CRIMES?
THE POWERS THAT BE
COLLETTE McDANIEL TAKES AN EARLY LOOK AT THE PUBLIC OPINION ON THIS EVER-CONTROVERSIAL SUBJECT,
...COLLETTE.
THE POWERS THAT BE
NTI-POWERS PROTESTING"--
WE HEAR THE WHISPERS, THE RUMBLINGS OF NORMAL PEOPLE...
...PEOPLE JUST LIKE YOU AND ME--
--WHO TAKE A STRONG IDEALISTIC STANCE AGAINST THE IDEA OF SUPER-POWERED PEOPLE IN OUR EVERYDAY LIVES.
THE POWERS THAT BE
AND NOW, WITH THIS ANTI-POWERS PROTESTING SEEMINGLY GRADUATING FROM THE HARMLESS WORLD OF THE PHILOSOPHICAL TO THE FATAL WORLD OF MURDER...
...WE WENT TO YOU--THE PERSON ON THE STREET...
THE POWERS THAT BE

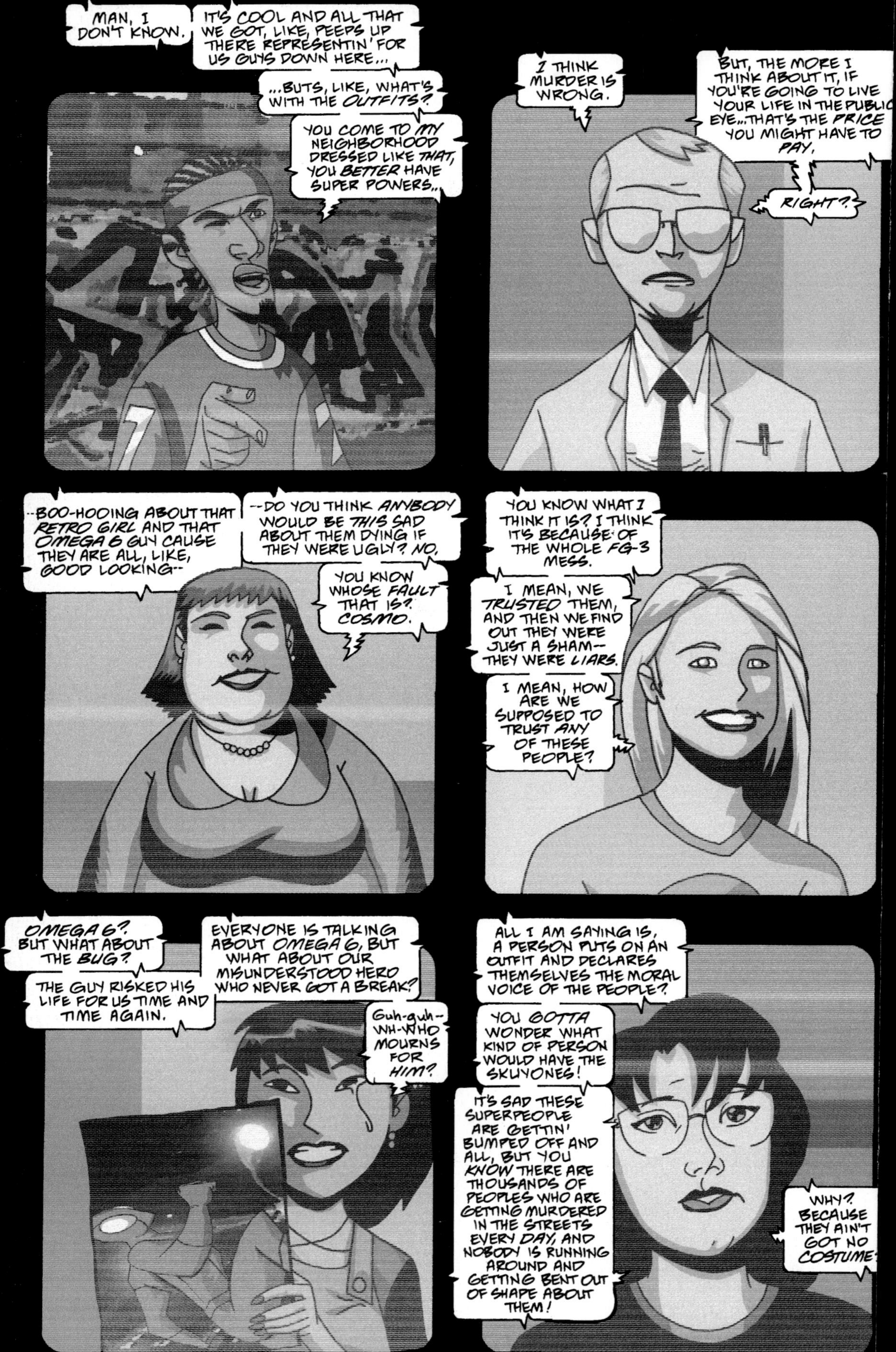
MAN, I DON'T KNOW.
IT'S COOL AND ALL THAT WE GOT, LIKE, PEEPS UP THERE REPRESENTIN' FOR US GUYS DOWN HERE...
...BUTS, LIKE, WHAT'S WITH THE OUTFITS?
YOU COME TO MY NEIGHBORHOOD DRESSED LIKE THAT, YOU BETTER HAVE SUPER POWERS...
I THINK MURDER IS WRONG.
BUT, THE MORE I THINK ABOUT IT, IF YOU'RE GOING TO LIVE YOUR LIFE IN THE PUBLIC EYE...THAT'S THE PRICE YOU MIGHT HAVE TO PAY.
RIGHT?
--BOO-HOOING ABOUT THAT RETRO GIRL AND THAT OMEGA 6 GUY CAUSE THEY ARE ALL, LIKE, GOOD LOOKING--
--DO YOU THINK ANYBODY WOULD BE THIS SAD ABOUT THEM DYING IF THEY WERE UGLY? NO.
YOU KNOW WHOSE FAULT THAT IS? COSMO.
YOU KNOW WHAT I THINK IT IS? I THINK IT'S BECAUSE OF THE WHOLE FG-3 MESS.
I MEAN, WE TRUSTED THEM, AND THEN WE FIND OUT THEY WERE JUST A SHAM--THEY WERE LIARS.
I MEAN, HOW ARE WE SUPPOSED TO TRUST ANY OF THESE PEOPLE?
OMEGA 6? BUT WHAT ABOUT THE BUG?
THE GUY RISKED HIS LIFE FOR US TIME AND TIME AGAIN.
EVERYONE IS TALKING ABOUT OMEGA 6, BUT WHAT ABOUT OUR MISUNDERSTOOD HERO WHO NEVER GOT A BREAK?
Guh-guh-WH-WHO MOURNS FOR HIM?
ALL I AM SAYING IS, A PERSON PUTS ON AN OUTFIT AND DECLARES THEMSELVES THE MORAL VOICE OF THE PEOPLE?
YOU GOTTA WONDER WHAT KIND OF PERSON WOULD HAVE THE SKUYONES!
IT'S SAD THESE SUPERPEOPLE ARE GETTIN' BUMPED OFF AND ALL, BUT YOU KNOW THERE ARE THOUSANDS OF PEOPLES WHO ARE GETTING MURDERED IN THE STREETS EVERY DAY, AND NOBODY IS RUNNING AROUND AND GETTING BENT OUT OF SHAPE ABOUT THEM!
WHY? BECAUSE THEY AIN'T GOT NO COSTUME!

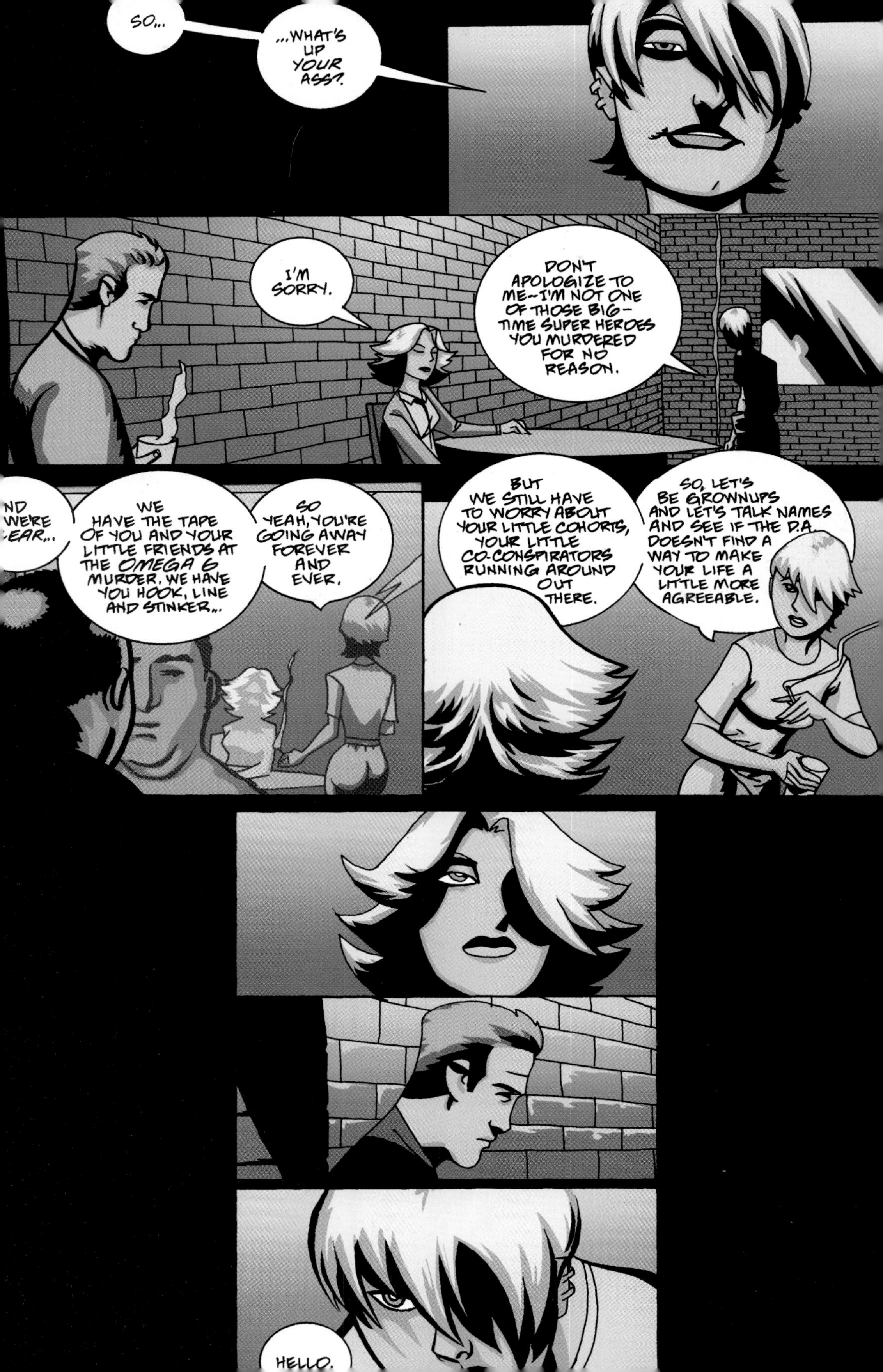
SO...
...WHAT'S UP YOUR ASS?
I'M SORRY.
DON'T APOLOGIZE TO ME--I'M NOT ONE OF THOSE BIG-TIME SUPER HEROES YOU MURDERED FOR NO REASON.
ND WE'RE EAR...
WE HAVE THE TAPE OF YOU AND YOUR LITTLE FRIENDS AT THE OMEGA 6 MURDER. WE HAVE YOU HOOK, LINE AND STINKER...
SO YEAH, YOU'RE GOING AWAY FOREVER AND EVER.
BUT WE STILL HAVE TO WORRY ABOUT YOUR LITTLE COHORTS, YOUR LITTLE CO-CONSPIRATORS RUNNING AROUND OUT THERE.
SO, LET'S BE GROWNUPS AND LET'S TALK NAMES AND SEE IF THE D.A. DOESN'T FIND A WAY TO MAKE YOUR LIFE A LITTLE MORE AGREEABLE.
HELLO.

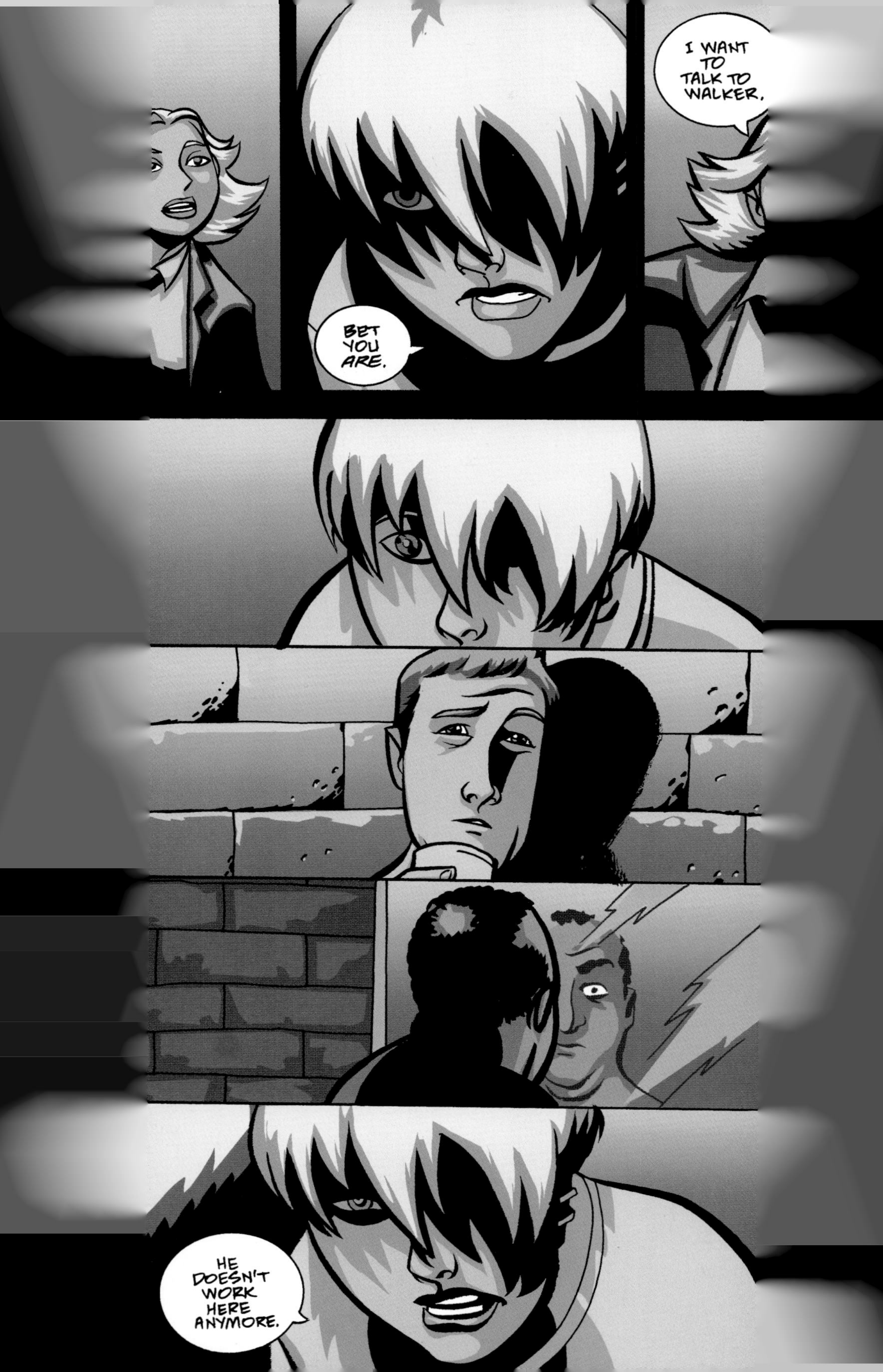
I WANT TO TALK TO WALKER.
BET YOU ARE.
HE DOESN'T WORK HERE ANYMORE.

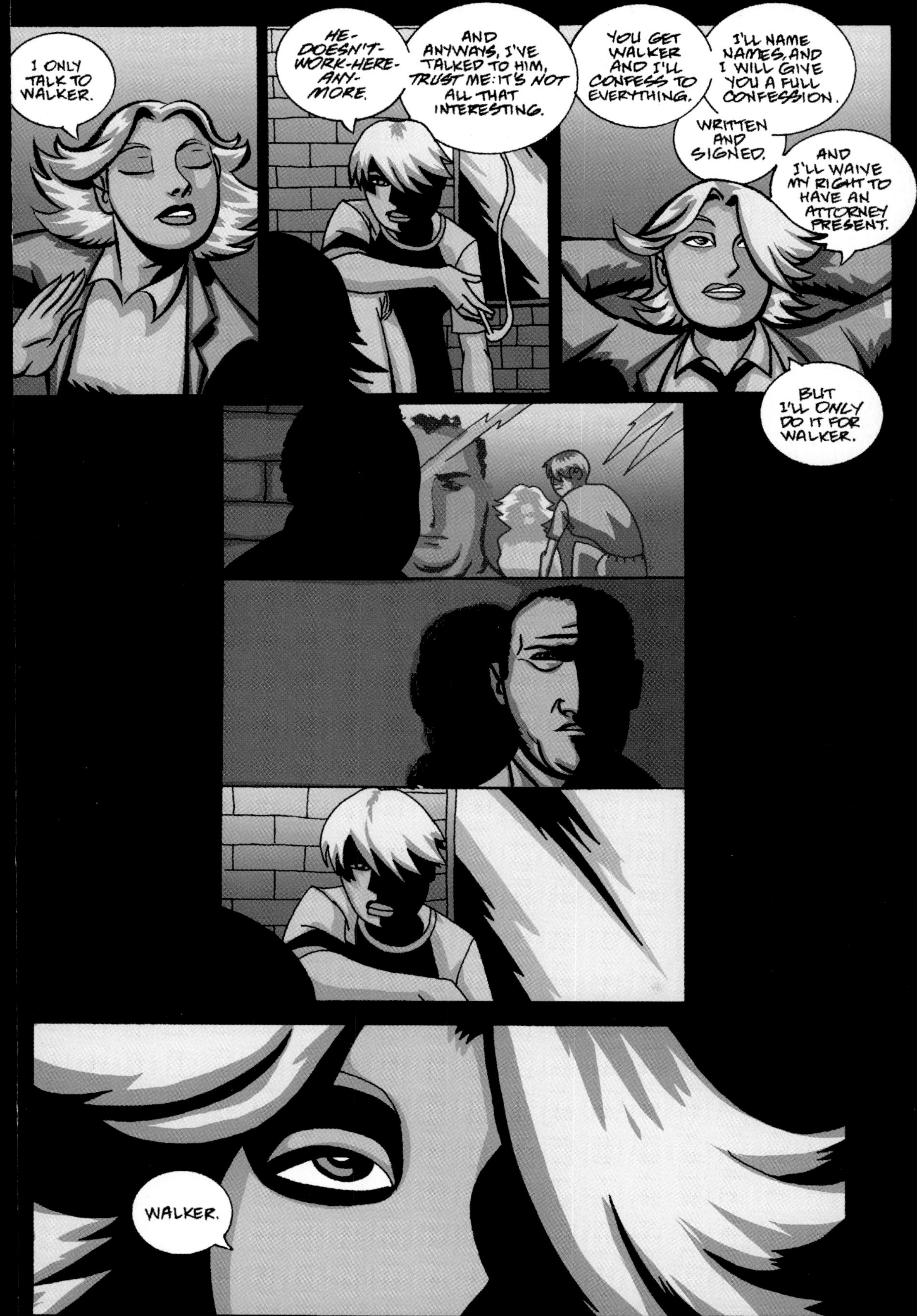
I ONLY TALK TO WALKER.
HE-DOESN'T-WORK-HERE-ANY-MORE.
AND ANYWAYS, I'VE TALKED TO HIM, TRUST ME: IT'S NOT ALL THAT INTERESTING.
YOU GET WALKER AND I'LL CONFESS TO EVERYTHING.
I'LL NAME NAMES, AND I WILL GIVE YOU A FULL CONFESSION.
WRITTEN AND SIGNED.
AND I'LL WAIVE MY RIGHT TO HAVE AN ATTORNEY PRESENT.
BUT I'LL ONLY DO IT FOR WALKER.
WALKER.

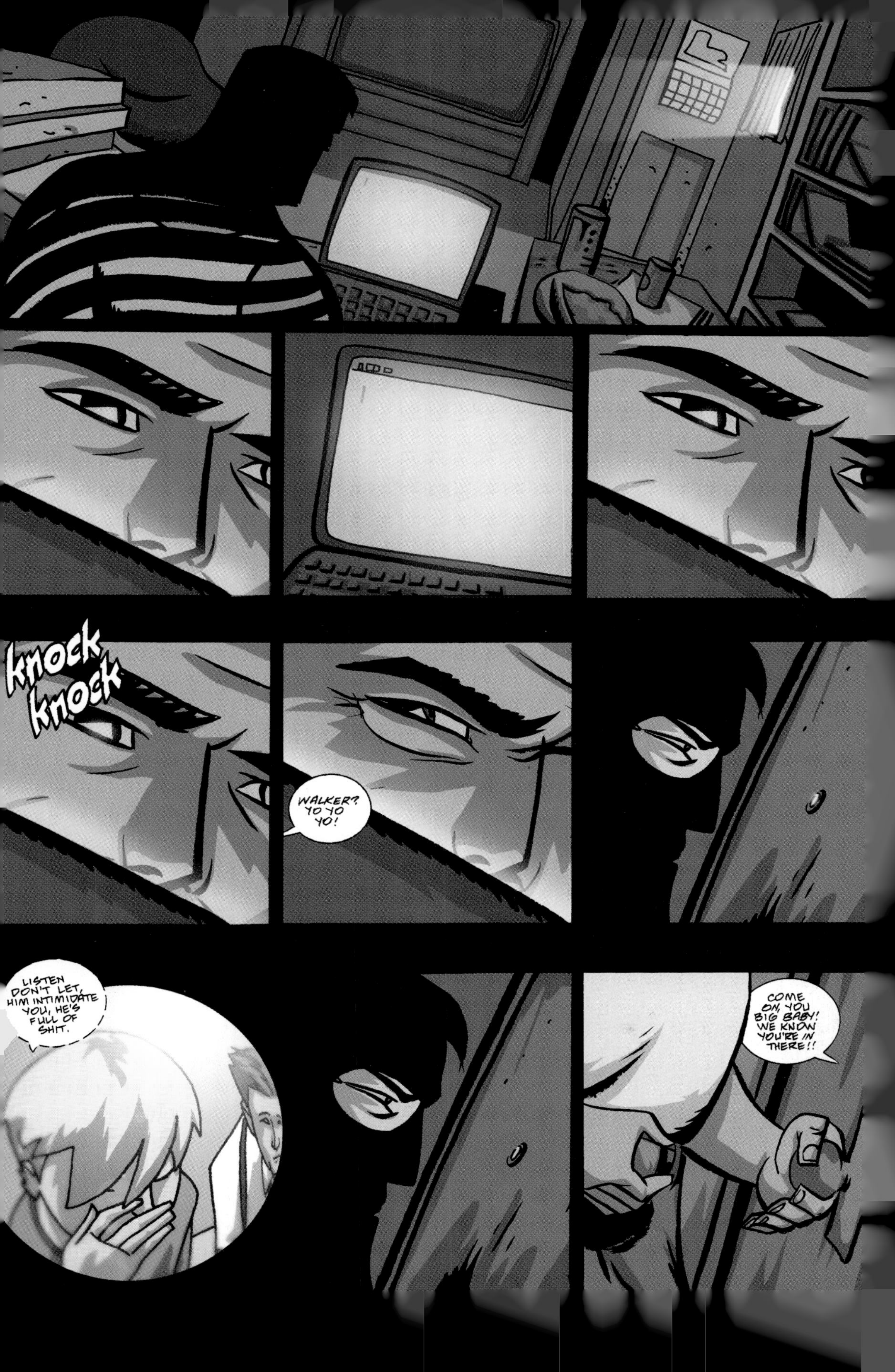

knock knock
WALKER? YO YO YO!
LISTEN DON'T LET, HIM INTIMIDATE YOU, HE'S FULL OF SHIT.
COME ON, YOU BIG BABY! WE KNOW YOU'RE IN THERE!!

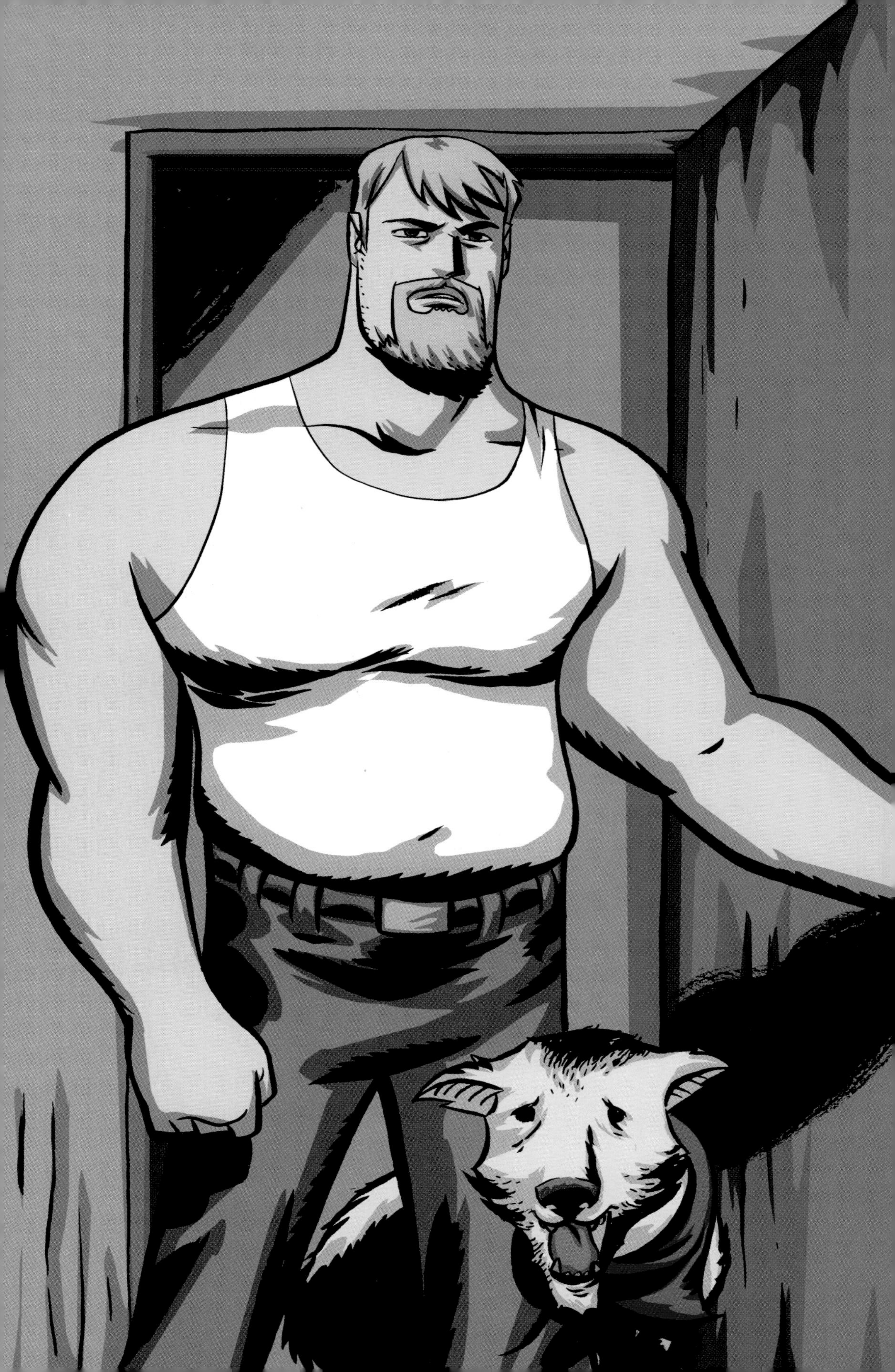

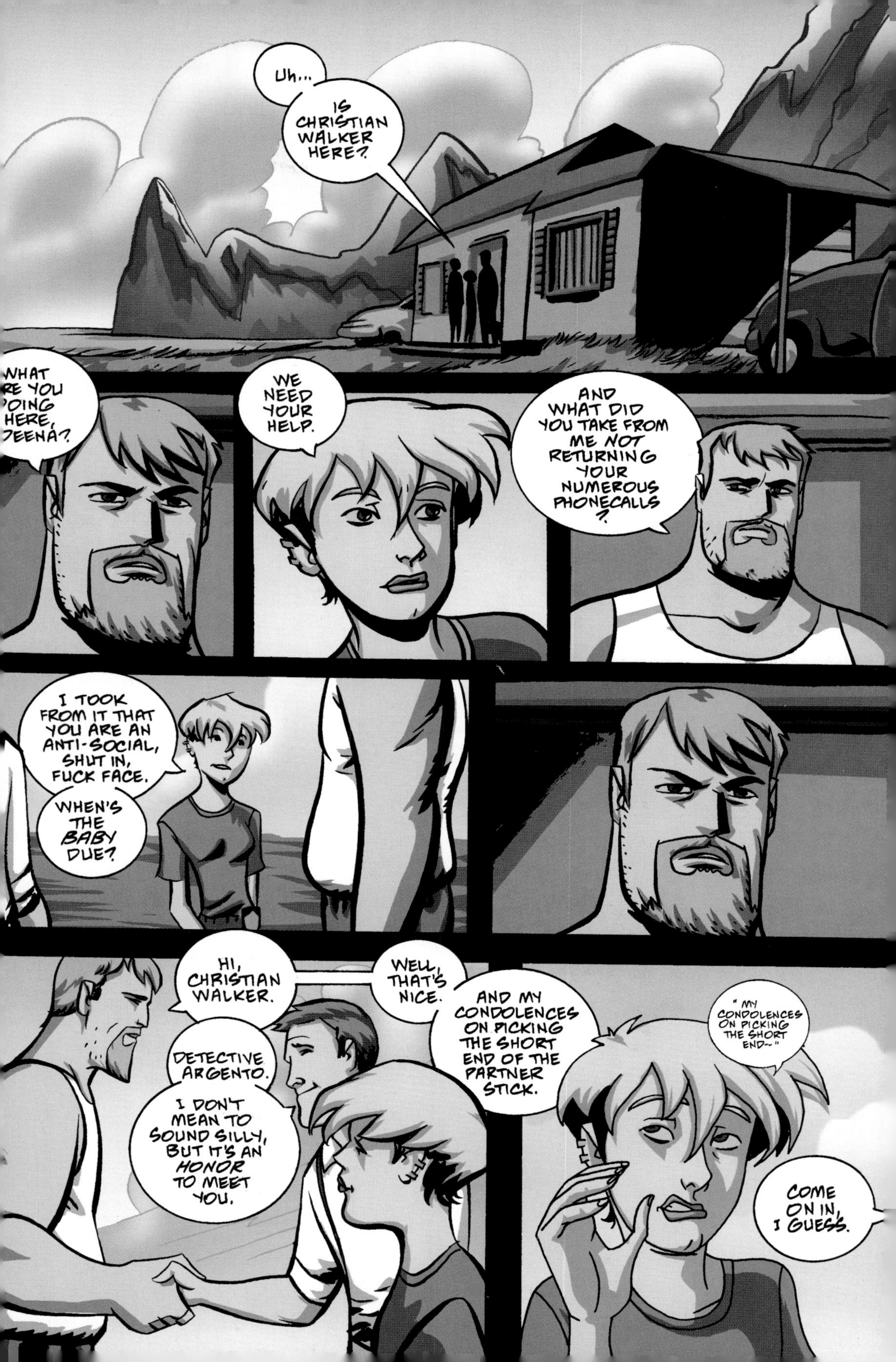
Uh...
IS CHRISTIAN WALKER HERE?
WHAT ARE YOU DOING HERE, DEENA?
WE NEED YOUR HELP.
AND WHAT DID YOU TAKE FROM ME *NOT* RETURNING YOUR NUMEROUS PHONECALLS?
I TOOK FROM IT THAT YOU ARE AN ANTI-SOCIAL, SHUT IN, FUCK FACE.
WHEN'S THE *BABY* DUE?
HI, CHRISTIAN WALKER.
WELL, THAT'S NICE.
DETECTIVE ARGENTO.
I DON'T MEAN TO SOUND SILLY, BUT IT'S AN *HONOR* TO MEET YOU.
AND MY CONDOLENCES ON PICKING THE SHORT END OF THE PARTNER STICK.
" MY CONDOLENCES ON PICKING THE SHORT END-- "
COME ON IN, I GUESS.

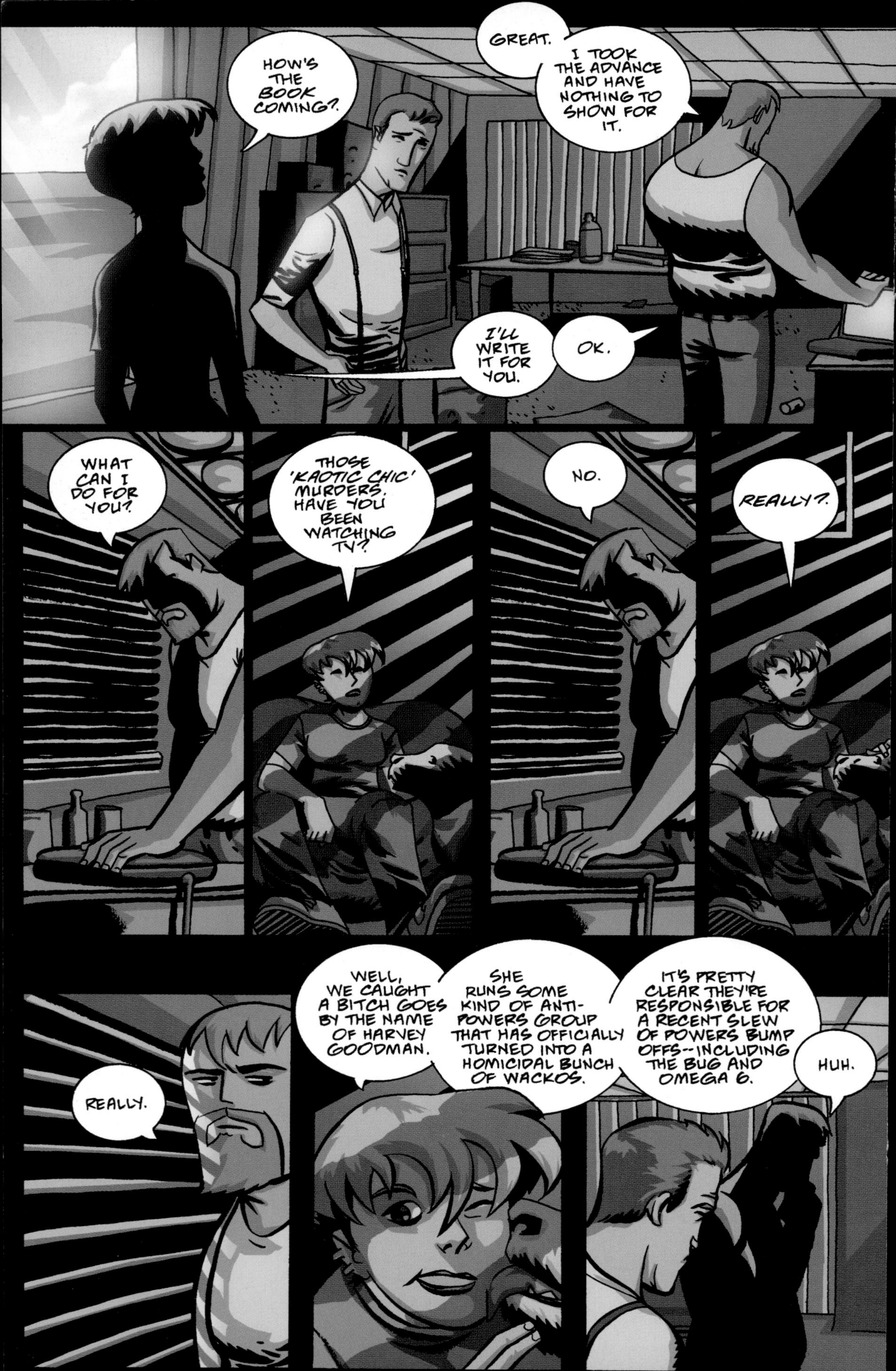
HOW'S THE BOOK COMING?
GREAT.
I TOOK THE ADVANCE AND HAVE NOTHING TO SHOW FOR IT.
I'LL WRITE IT FOR YOU.
OK.
WHAT CAN I DO FOR YOU?
THOSE 'KAOTIC CHIC' MURDERS. HAVE YOU BEEN WATCHING TV?
NO.
REALLY?.
REALLY.
WELL, WE CAUGHT A BITCH GOES BY THE NAME OF HARVEY GOODMAN.
SHE RUNS SOME KIND OF ANTI-POWERS GROUP THAT HAS OFFICIALLY TURNED INTO A HOMICIDAL BUNCH OF WACKOS.
IT'S PRETTY CLEAR THEY'RE RESPONSIBLE FOR A RECENT SLEW OF POWERS BUMP OFFS--INCLUDING THE BUG AND OMEGA 6.
HUH.

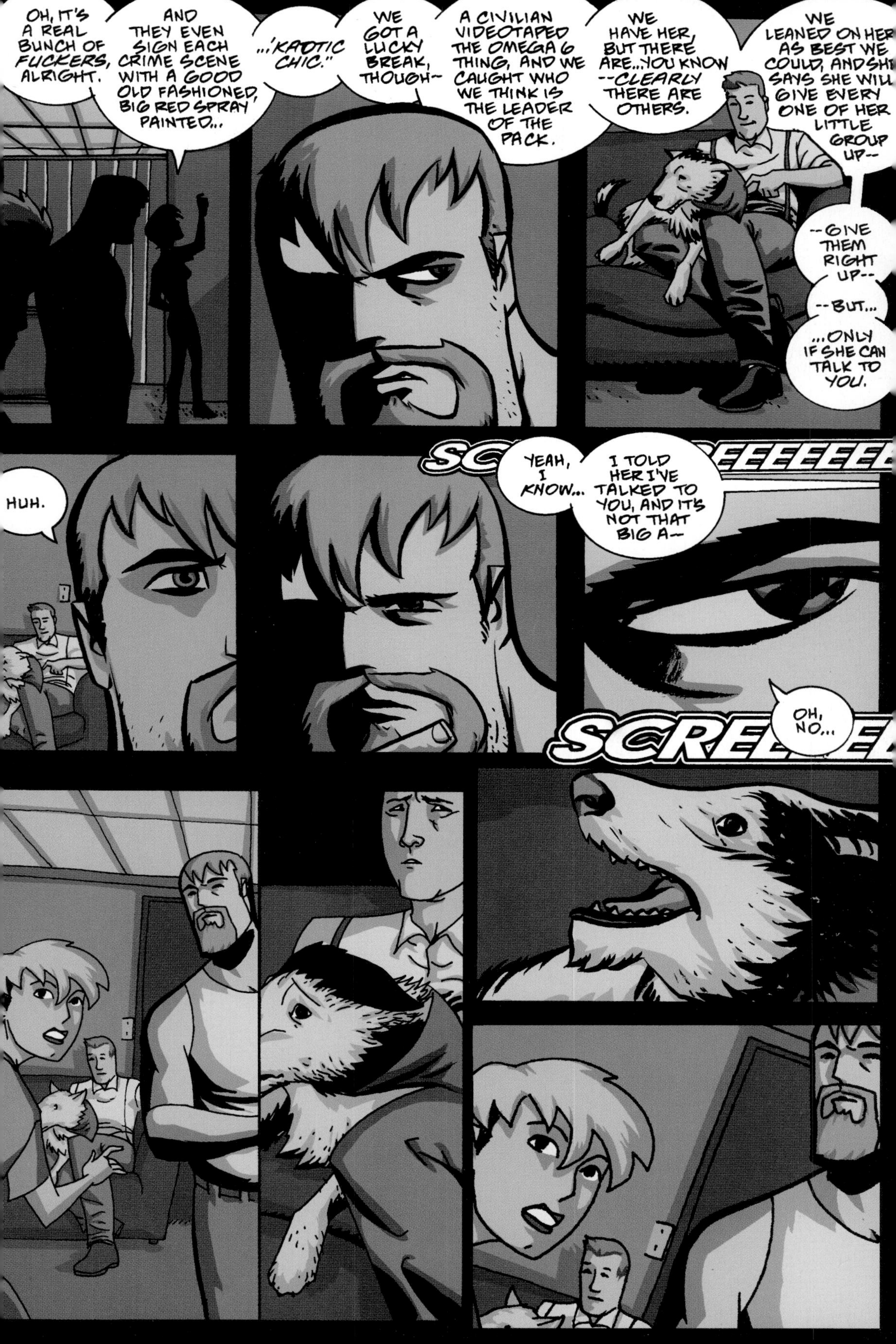

OH, IT'S A REAL BUNCH OF FUCKERS, ALRIGHT.
AND THEY EVEN SIGN EACH CRIME SCENE WITH A GOOD OLD FASHIONED, BIG RED SPRAY PAINTED...
...'KAOTIC CHIC.'
WE GOT A LUCKY BREAK, THOUGH--
A CIVILIAN VIDEOTAPED THE OMEGA 6 THING, AND WE CAUGHT WHO WE THINK IS THE LEADER OF THE PACK.
WE HAVE HER, BUT THERE ARE...YOU KNOW --CLEARLY THERE ARE OTHERS.
WE LEANED ON HER AS BEST WE COULD, AND SHE SAYS SHE WILL GIVE EVERY ONE OF HER LITTLE GROUP UP--
--GIVE THEM RIGHT UP--
--BUT...
...ONLY IF SHE CAN TALK TO YOU.
HUH.
SCREEEEEEEE
YEAH, I KNOW...
I TOLD HER I'VE TALKED TO YOU, AND IT'S NOT THAT BIG A--
OH, NO...
SCREEEE

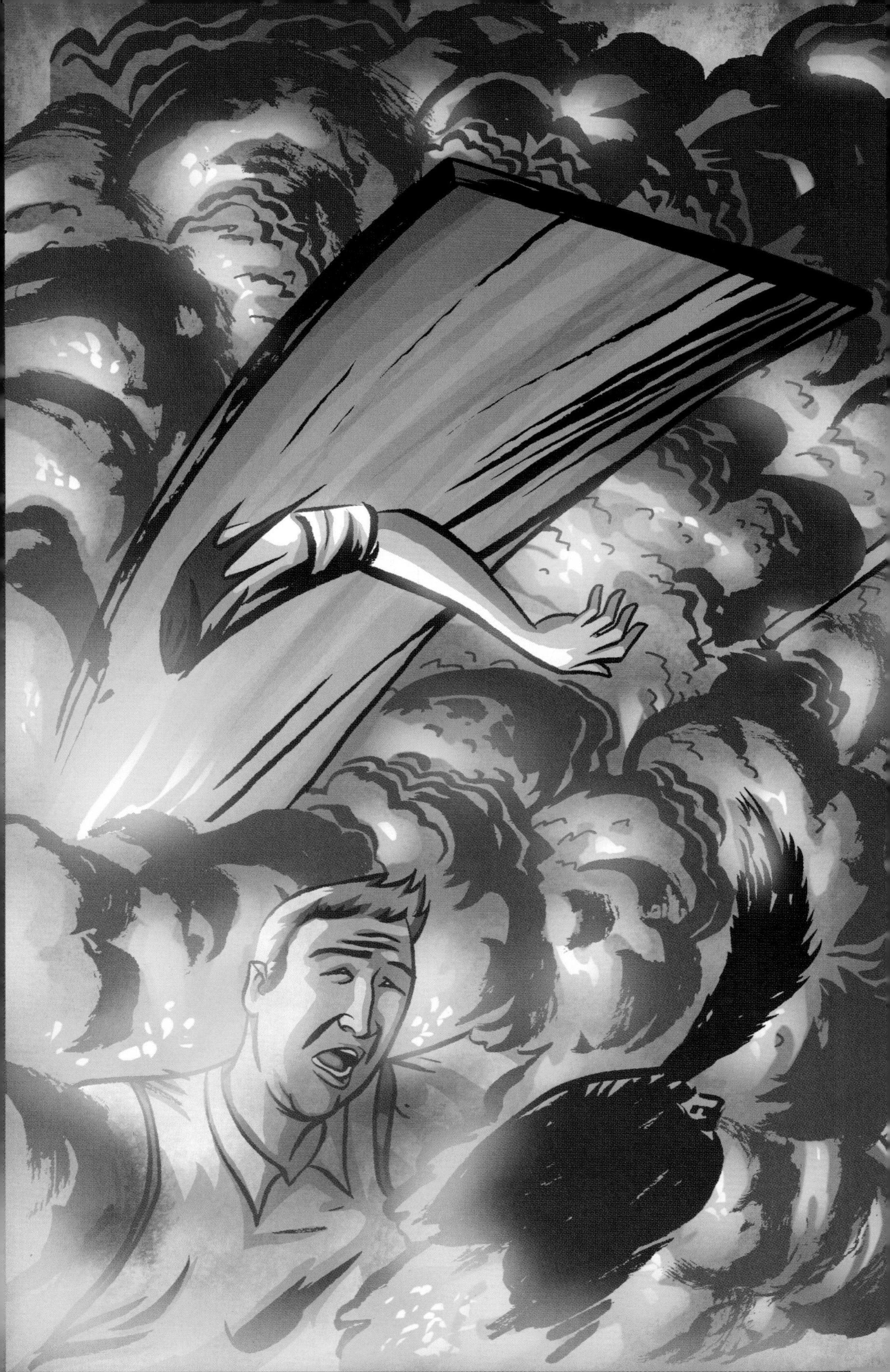

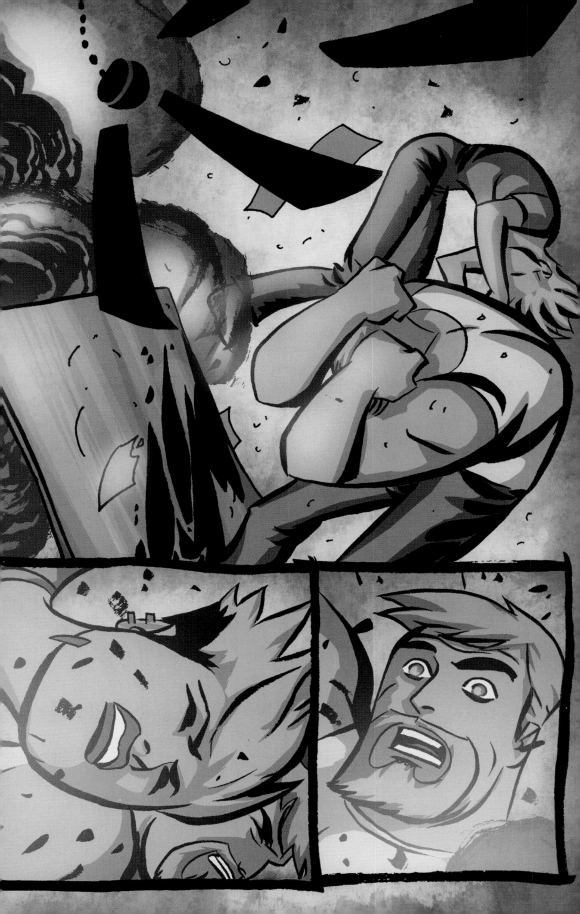

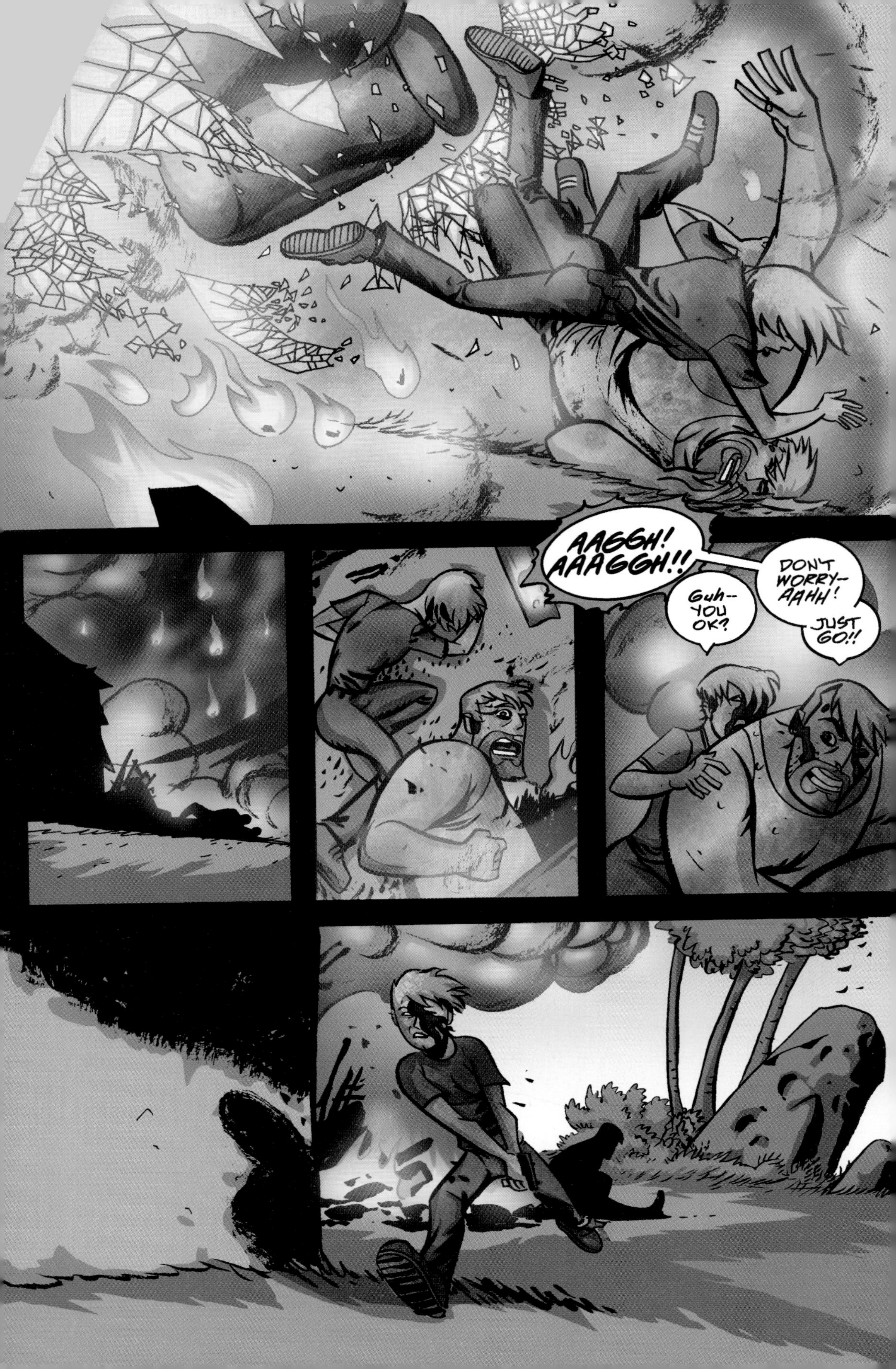
AAGGH! AAAGGH!!
Guh-- YOU OK?
DON'T WORRY-- AAHH!
JUST GO!!

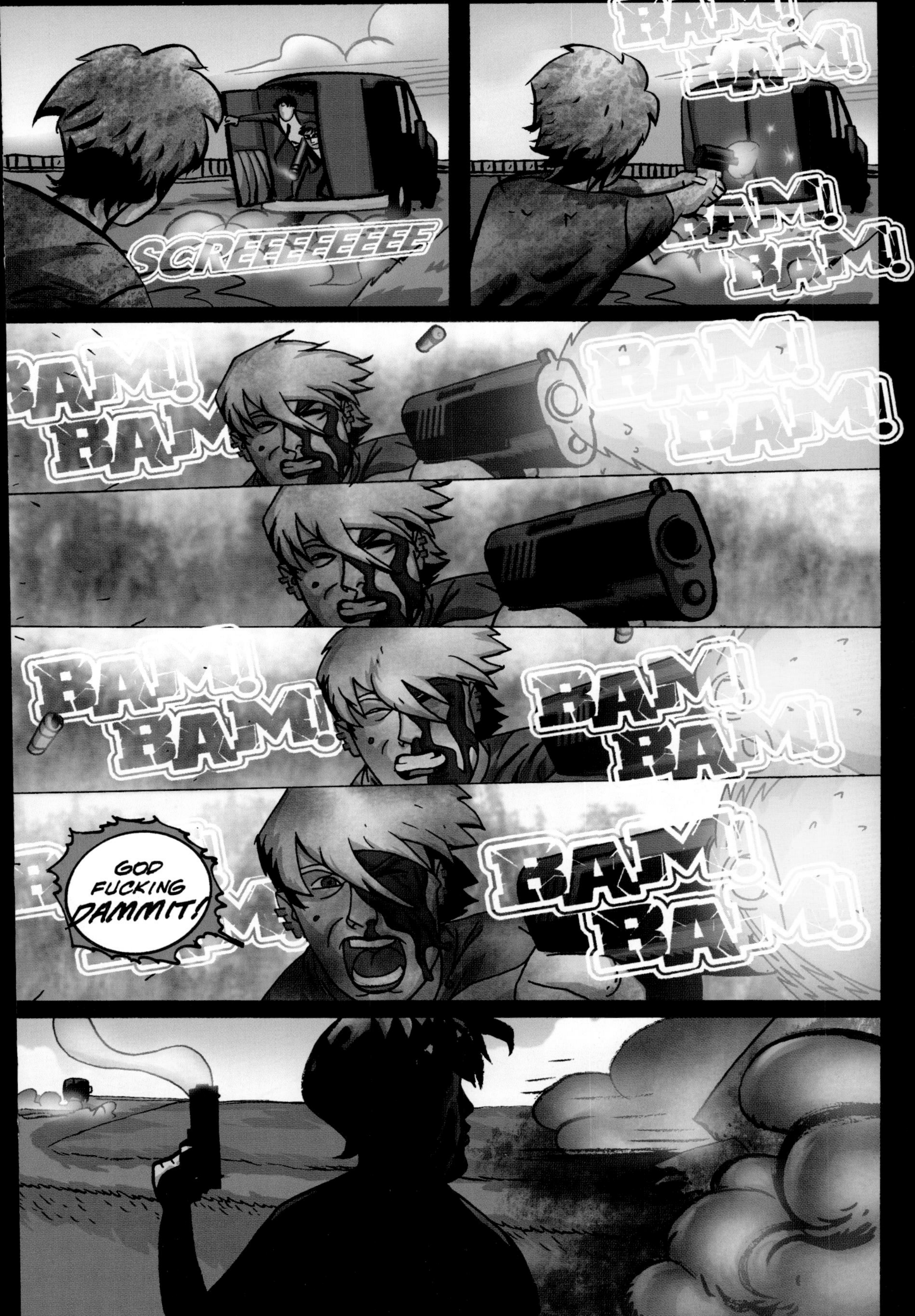
SCREEEEEEEE
BAM! BAM!
BAM! BAM!
BAM! BAM!
BAM! BAM!
BAM! BAM!
BAM! BAM!
GOD FUCKING DAMMIT!
BAM! BAM!

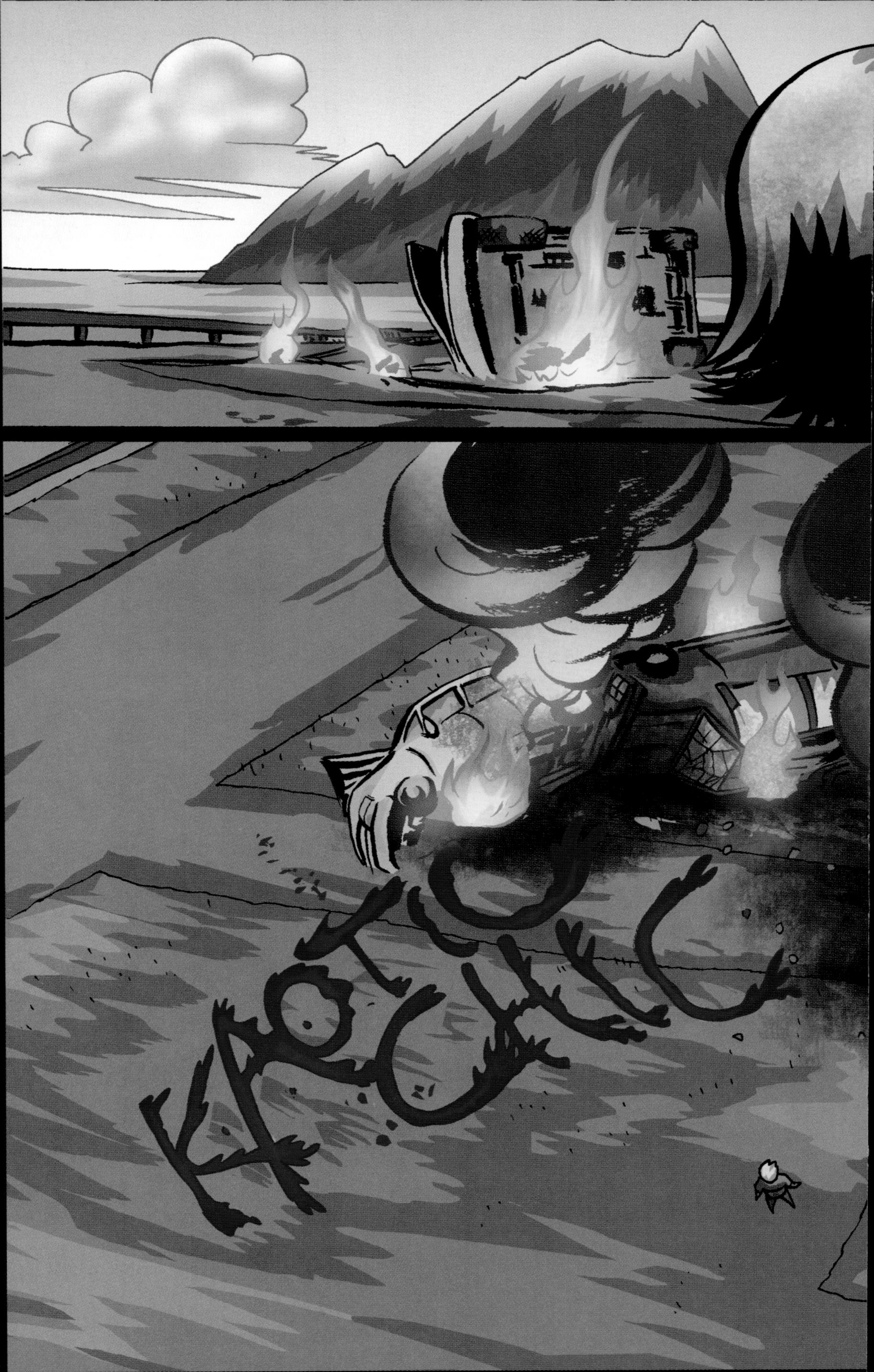

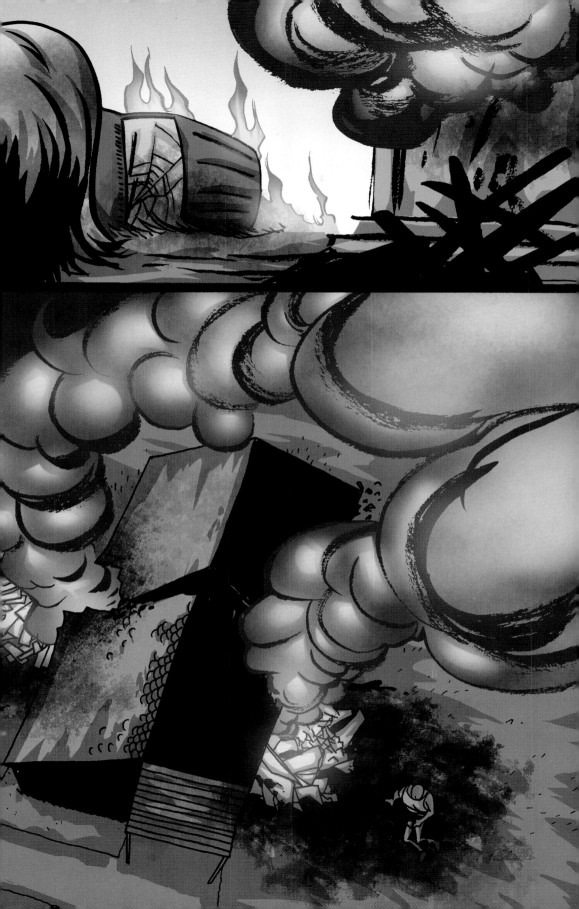

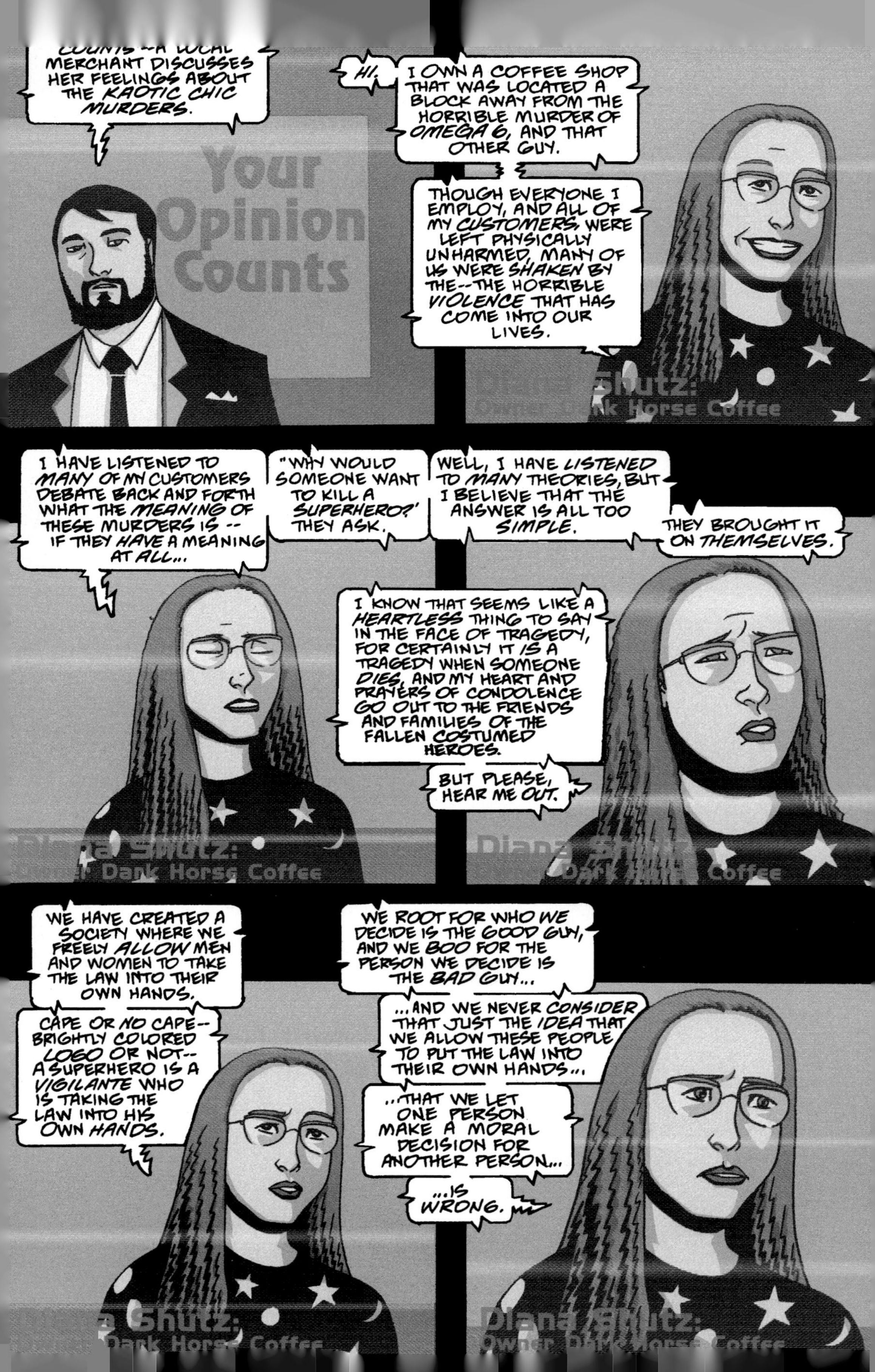
COUNTS--A LOCAL MERCHANT DISCUSSES HER FEELINGS ABOUT THE KAOTIC CHIC MURDERS.
Your Opinion Counts
HI.
I OWN A COFFEE SHOP THAT WAS LOCATED A BLOCK AWAY FROM THE HORRIBLE MURDER OF OMEGA 6, AND THAT OTHER GUY.
THOUGH EVERYONE I EMPLOY, AND ALL OF MY CUSTOMERS, WERE LEFT PHYSICALLY UNHARMED, MANY OF US WERE SHAKEN BY THE--THE HORRIBLE VIOLENCE THAT HAS COME INTO OUR LIVES.
Diana Shutz:
Owner Dark Horse Coffee
I HAVE LISTENED TO MANY OF MY CUSTOMERS DEBATE BACK AND FORTH WHAT THE MEANING OF THESE MURDERS IS -- IF THEY HAVE A MEANING AT ALL...
"WHY WOULD SOMEONE WANT TO KILL A SUPERHERO?' THEY ASK.
WELL, I HAVE LISTENED TO MANY THEORIES, BUT I BELIEVE THAT THE ANSWER IS ALL TOO SIMPLE.
THEY BROUGHT IT ON THEMSELVES.
I KNOW THAT SEEMS LIKE A HEARTLESS THING TO SAY IN THE FACE OF TRAGEDY, FOR CERTAINLY IT IS A TRAGEDY WHEN SOMEONE DIES, AND MY HEART AND PRAYERS OF CONDOLENCE GO OUT TO THE FRIENDS AND FAMILIES OF THE FALLEN COSTUMED HEROES.
BUT PLEASE, HEAR ME OUT.
WE HAVE CREATED A SOCIETY WHERE WE FREELY ALLOW MEN AND WOMEN TO TAKE THE LAW INTO THEIR OWN HANDS.
CAPE OR NO CAPE-- BRIGHTLY COLORED LOGO OR NOT-- A SUPERHERO IS A VIGILANTE WHO IS TAKING THE LAW INTO HIS OWN HANDS.
WE ROOT FOR WHO WE DECIDE IS THE GOOD GUY, AND WE BOO FOR THE PERSON WE DECIDE IS THE BAD GUY...
...AND WE NEVER CONSIDER THAT JUST THE IDEA THAT WE ALLOW THESE PEOPLE TO PUT THE LAW INTO THEIR OWN HANDS...
...THAT WE LET ONE PERSON MAKE A MORAL DECISION FOR ANOTHER PERSON...
...IS WRONG.

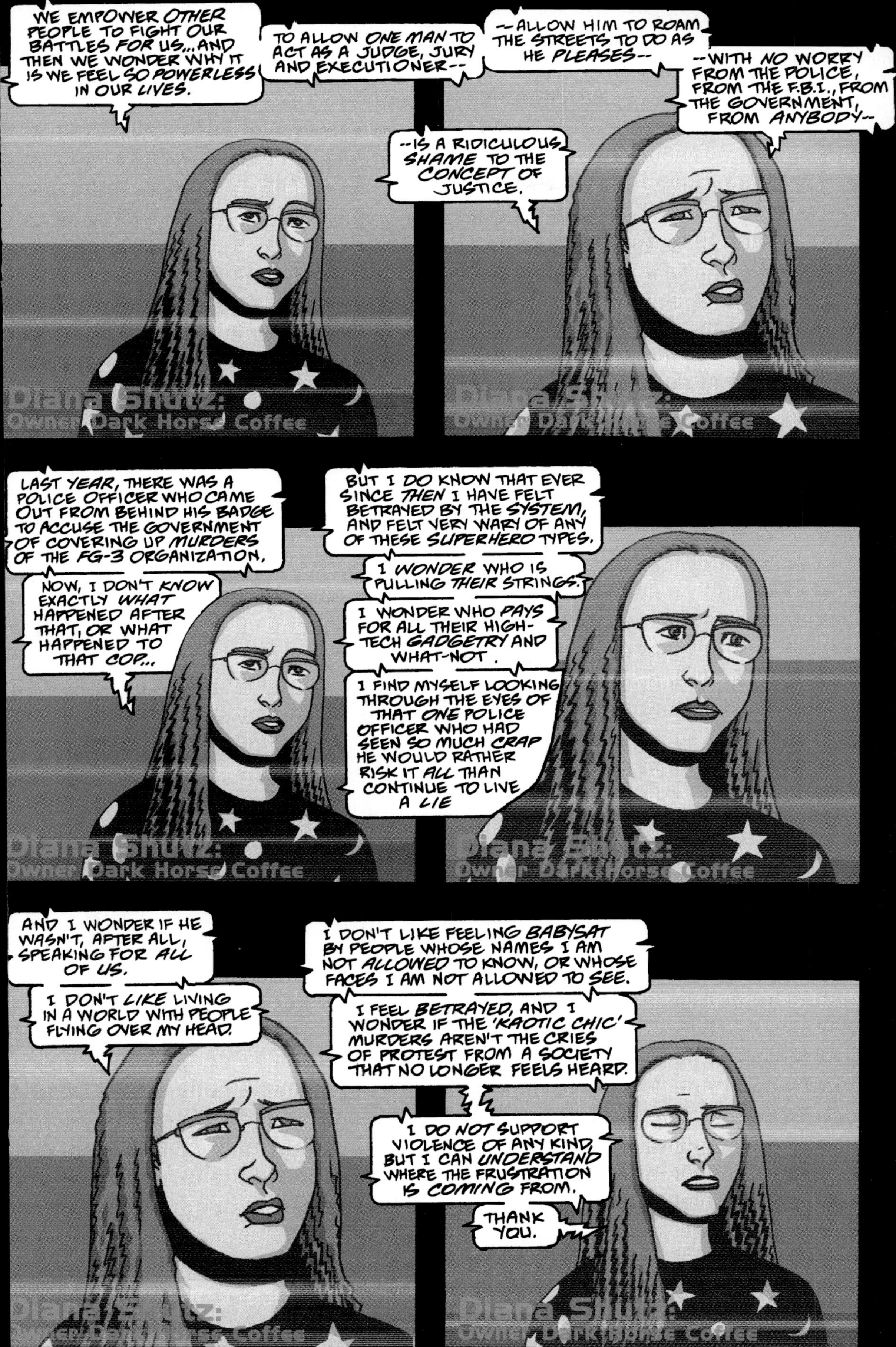
WE EMPOWER OTHER PEOPLE TO FIGHT OUR BATTLES FOR US... AND THEN WE WONDER WHY IT IS WE FEEL SO POWERLESS IN OUR LIVES.
TO ALLOW ONE MAN TO ACT AS A JUDGE, JURY AND EXECUTIONER--
--ALLOW HIM TO ROAM THE STREETS TO DO AS HE PLEASES--
--WITH NO WORRY FROM THE POLICE, FROM THE F.B.I., FROM THE GOVERNMENT, FROM ANYBODY--
--IS A RIDICULOUS SHAME TO THE CONCEPT OF JUSTICE.
Diana Shutz:
Owner Dark Horse Coffee
Diana Shutz:
Owner Dark Horse Coffee
LAST YEAR, THERE WAS A POLICE OFFICER WHO CAME OUT FROM BEHIND HIS BADGE TO ACCUSE THE GOVERNMENT OF COVERING UP MURDERS OF THE FG-3 ORGANIZATION.
NOW, I DON'T KNOW EXACTLY WHAT HAPPENED AFTER THAT, OR WHAT HAPPENED TO THAT COP...
BUT I DO KNOW THAT EVER SINCE THEN I HAVE FELT BETRAYED BY THE SYSTEM, AND FELT VERY WARY OF ANY OF THESE SUPERHERO TYPES.
I WONDER WHO IS PULLING THEIR STRINGS.
I WONDER WHO PAYS FOR ALL THEIR HIGH-TECH GADGETRY AND WHAT-NOT.
I FIND MYSELF LOOKING THROUGH THE EYES OF THAT ONE POLICE OFFICER WHO HAD SEEN SO MUCH CRAP HE WOULD RATHER RISK IT ALL THAN CONTINUE TO LIVE A LIE
Diana Shutz:
Owner Dark Horse Coffee
Diana Shutz:
Owner Dark Horse Coffee
AND I WONDER IF HE WASN'T, AFTER ALL, SPEAKING FOR ALL OF US.
I DON'T LIKE LIVING IN A WORLD WITH PEOPLE FLYING OVER MY HEAD.
I DON'T LIKE FEELING BABYSAT BY PEOPLE WHOSE NAMES I AM NOT ALLOWED TO KNOW, OR WHOSE FACES I AM NOT ALLOWED TO SEE.
I FEEL BETRAYED, AND I WONDER IF THE 'KAOTIC CHIC' MURDERS AREN'T THE CRIES OF PROTEST FROM A SOCIETY THAT NO LONGER FEELS HEARD.
I DO NOT SUPPORT VIOLENCE OF ANY KIND, BUT I CAN UNDERSTAND WHERE THE FRUSTRATION IS COMING FROM.
THANK YOU.
Diana Shutz:
Owner Dark Horse Coffee
Diana Shutz:
Owner Dark Horse Coffee

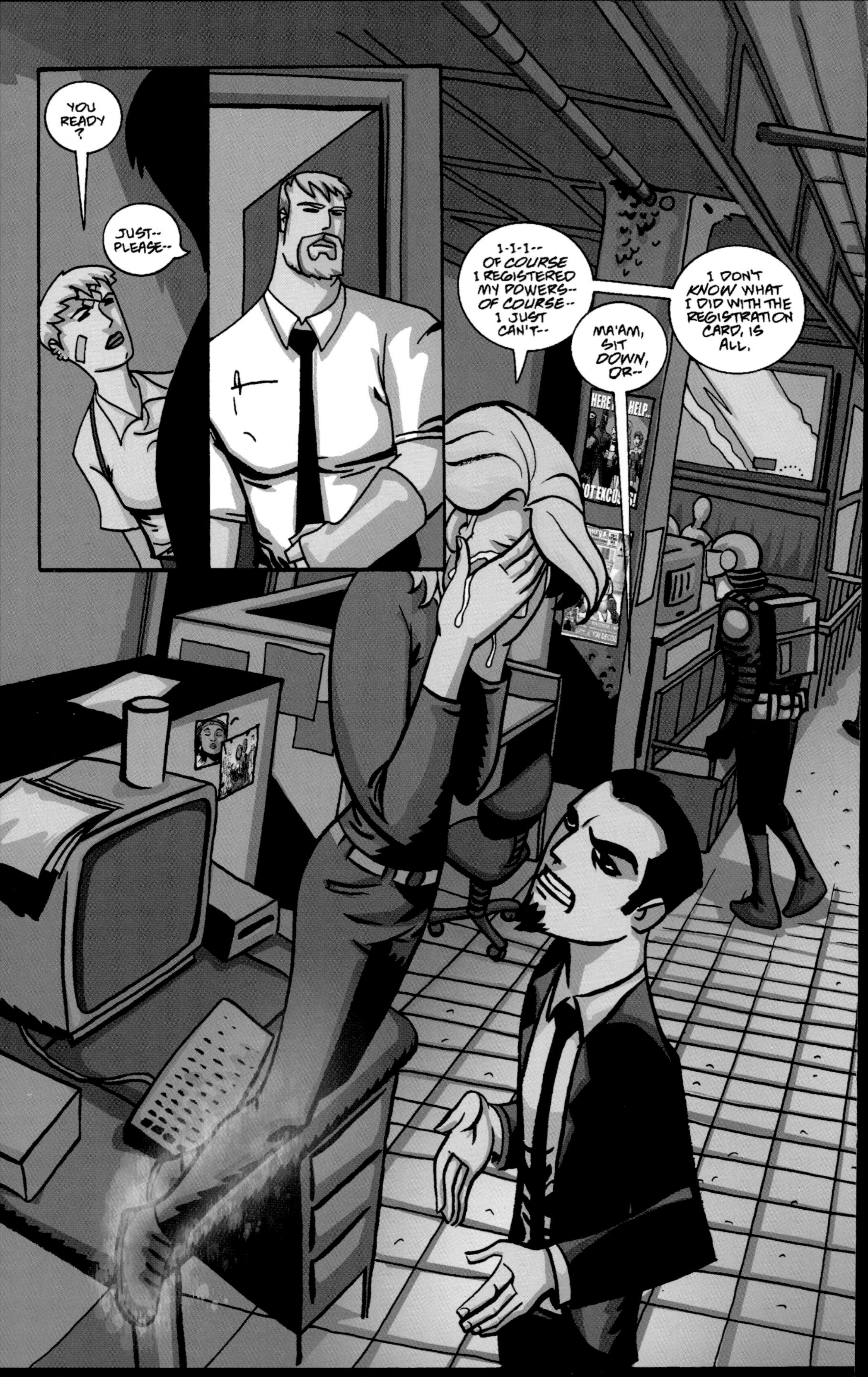
YOU READY ?
JUST-- PLEASE--
I-I-I-- OF COURSE I REGISTERED MY POWERS-- OF COURSE-- I JUST CAN'T--
I DON'T KNOW WHAT I DID WITH THE REGISTRATION CARD, IS ALL.
MA'AM, SIT DOWN, OR--

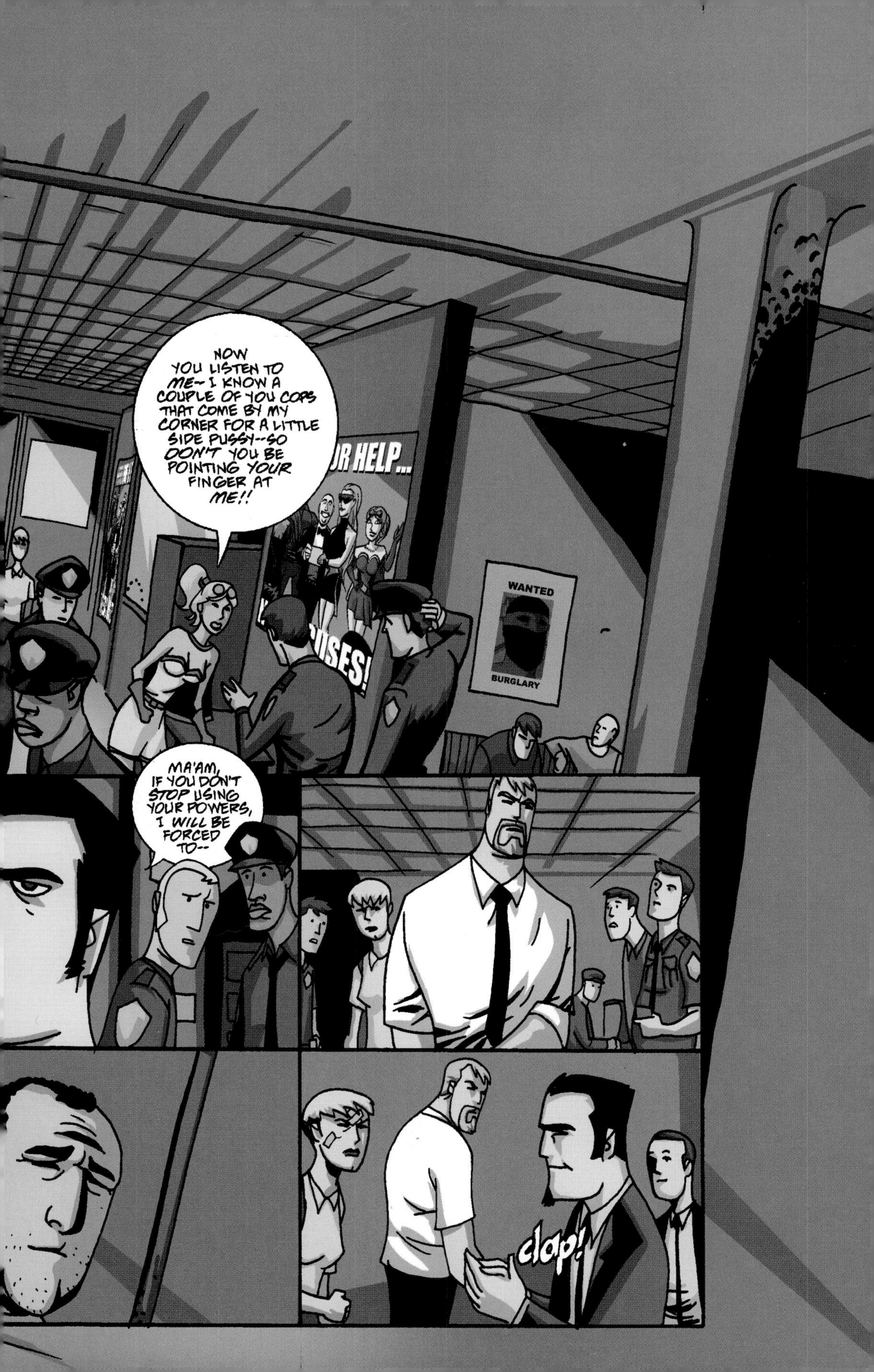
NOW YOU LISTEN TO ME-- I KNOW A COUPLE OF YOU COPS THAT COME BY MY CORNER FOR A LITTLE SIDE PUSSY--SO DON'T YOU BE POINTING YOUR FINGER AT ME!!
WANTED
BURGLARY
MA'AM, IF YOU DON'T STOP USING YOUR POWERS, I WILL BE FORCED TO--
clap!

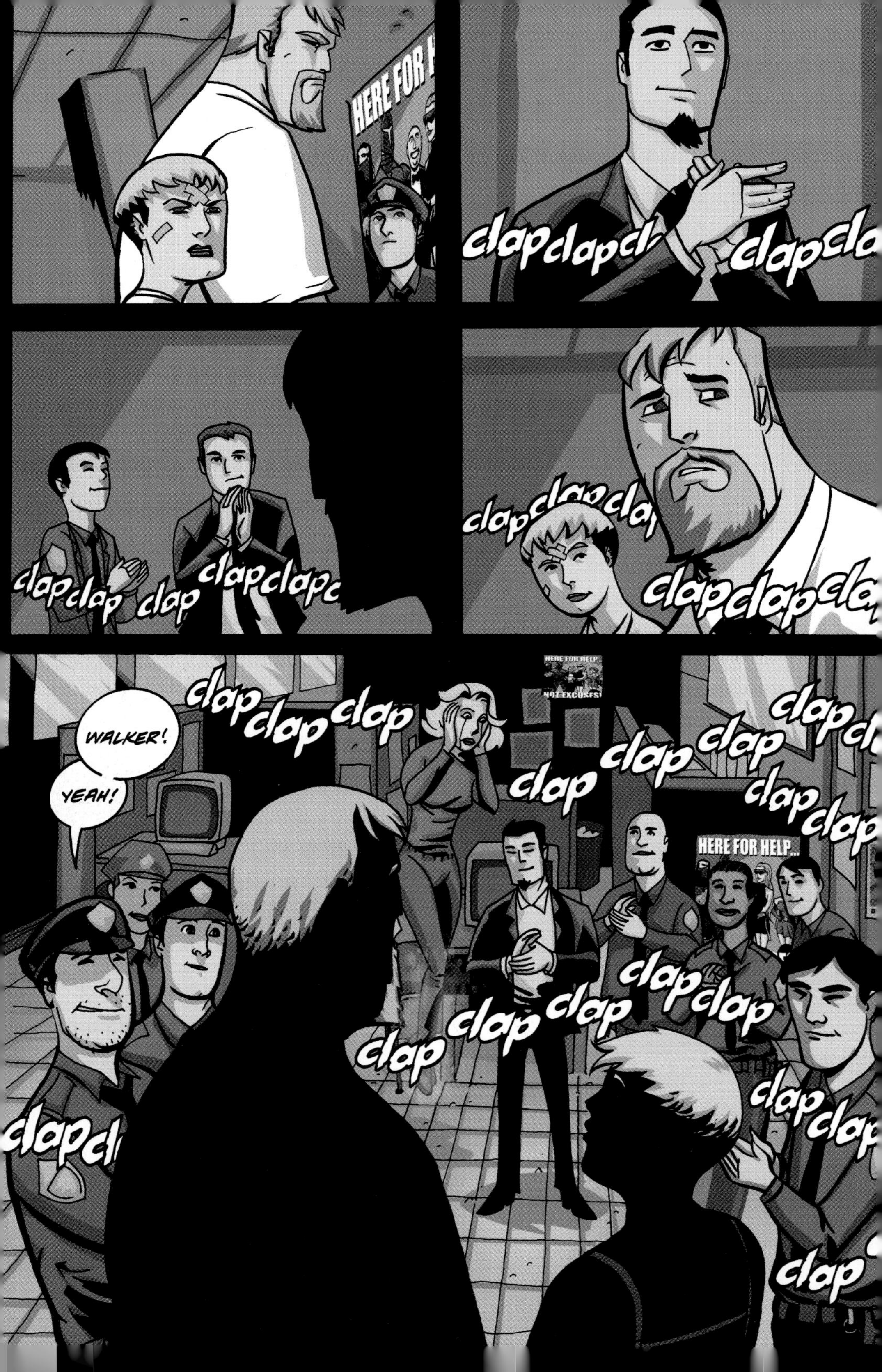

HERE FOR H
clap clap cl
clap cla
clap clap
clap
clap clap c
clap clap cl
clap clap cla
clap clap clap
WALKER!
YEAH!
HERE FOR HELP...
NOT EXCUSES!
clap clap clap clap
clap clap
HERE FOR HELP...
clap clap clap clap clap
clap cl
clap clap
clap
clap

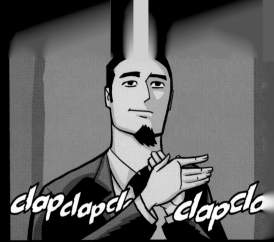

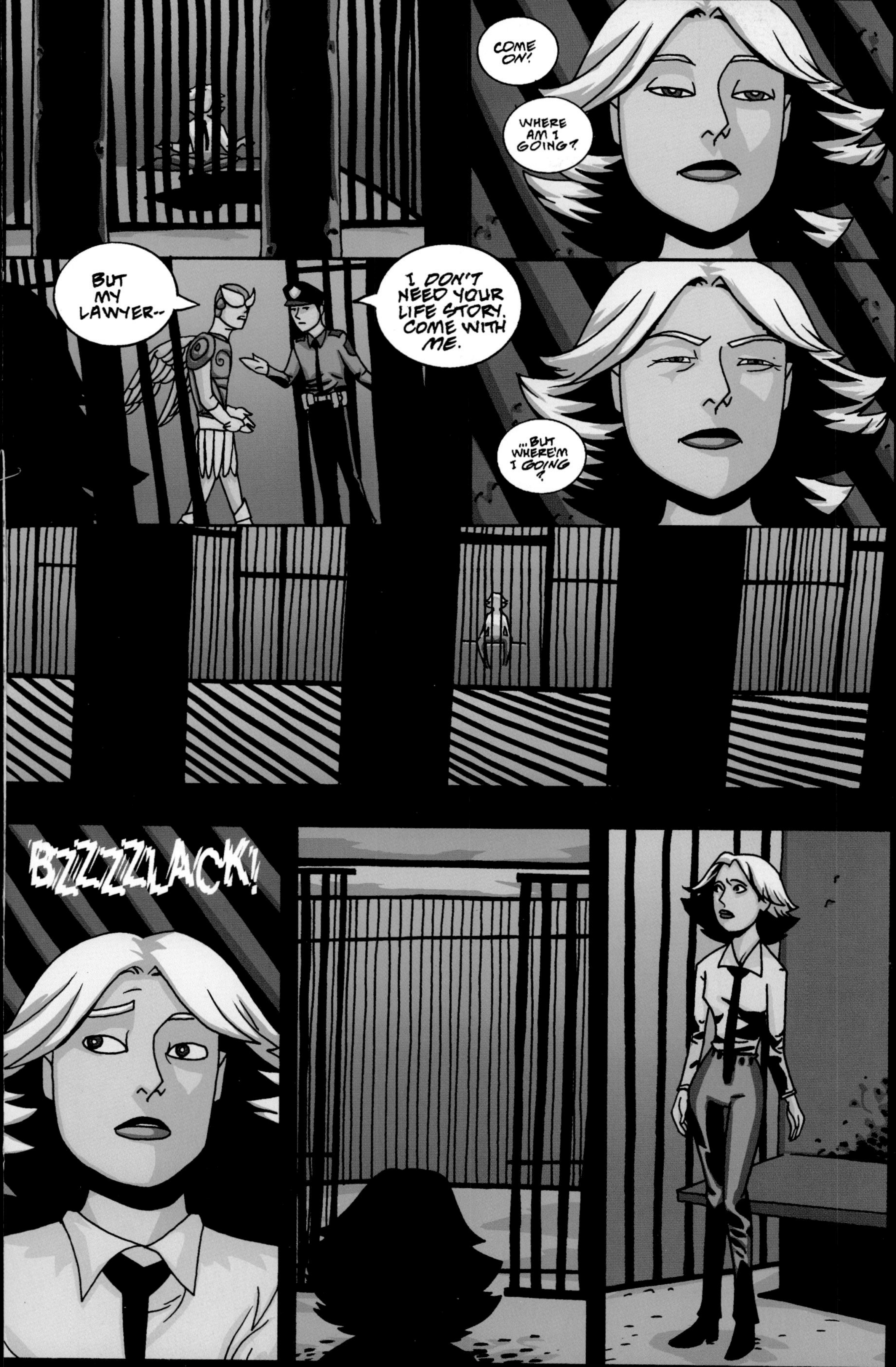
COME ON!
WHERE AM I GOING?
BUT MY LAWYER--
I DON'T NEED YOUR LIFE STORY. COME WITH ME.
...BUT WHERE'M I GOING?
BZZZLACK!

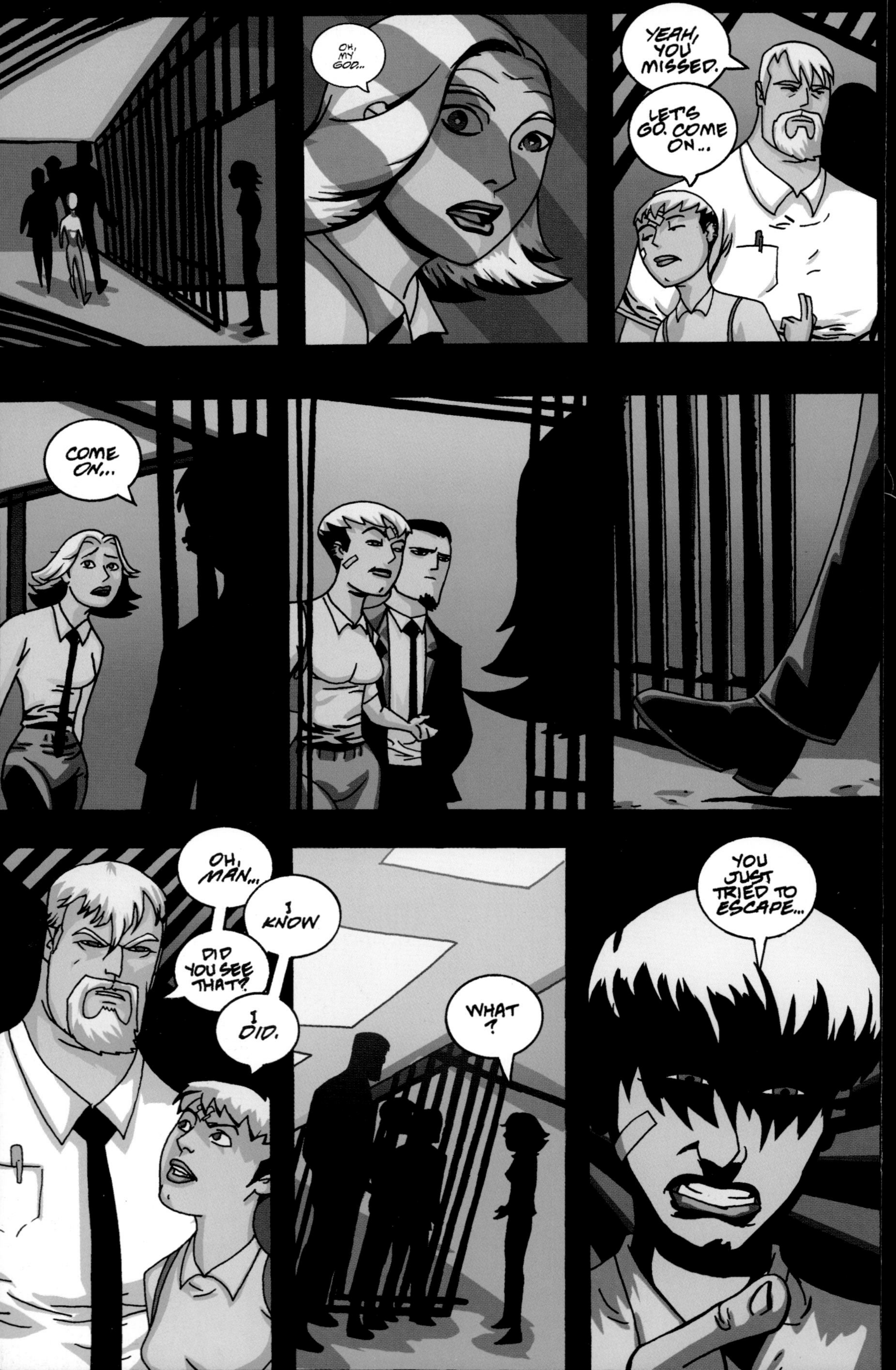
OH, MY GOD...
YEAH, YOU MISSED.
LET'S GO. COME ON...
COME ON...
OH, MAN...
I KNOW
DID YOU SEE THAT?
I DID.
WHAT?
YOU JUST TRIED TO ESCAPE...

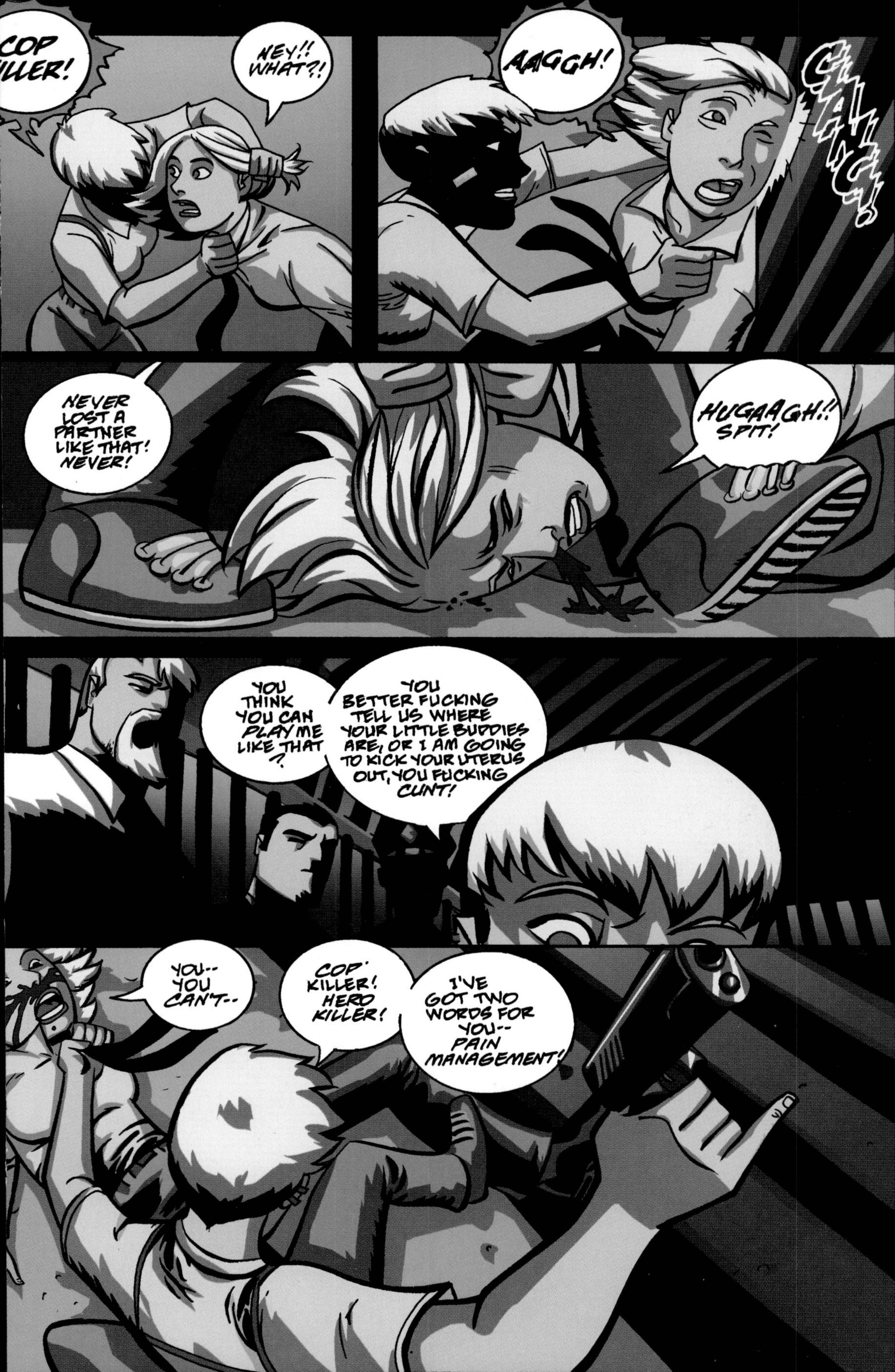
COP ILLER!
HEY!! WHAT?!
AAGGH!
NEVER LOST A PARTNER LIKE THAT! NEVER!
HUGAAGH!! SPIT!
YOU THINK YOU CAN PLAY ME LIKE THAT ?
YOU BETTER FUCKING TELL US WHERE YOUR LITTLE BUDDIES ARE, OR I AM GOING TO KICK YOUR UTERUS OUT, YOU FUCKING CUNT!
YOU-- YOU CAN'T--
COP KILLER! HERO KILLER!
I'VE GOT TWO WORDS FOR YOU-- PAIN MANAGEMENT!

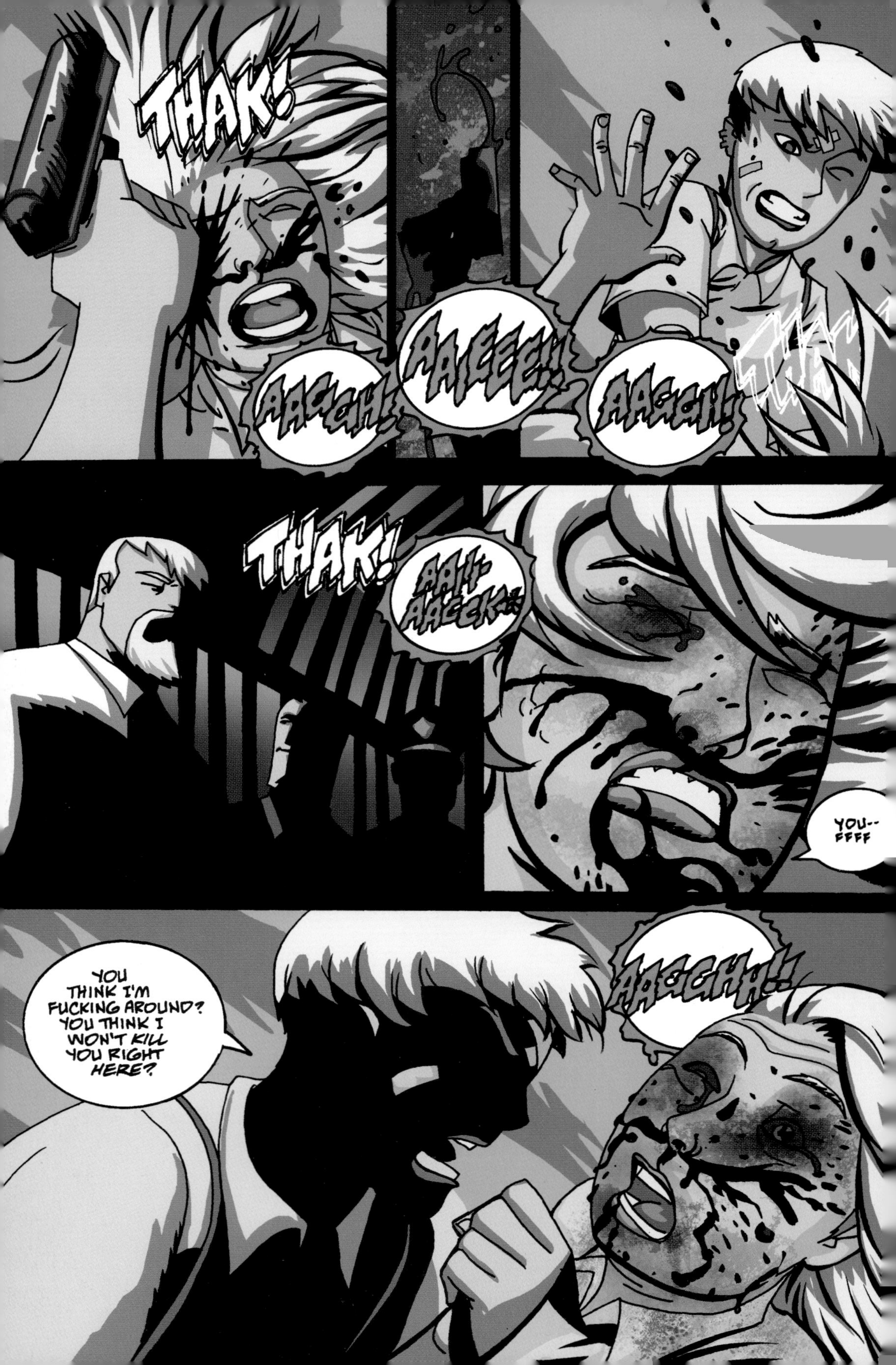
THAK!
AAGGH!
AAIEEE!!
AAGGH!!
THAK
THAK!
AAH-AAGGK--!
YOU--
FFFF
YOU THINK I'M FUCKING AROUND? YOU THINK I WON'T KILL YOU RIGHT HERE?
AAGGHH!

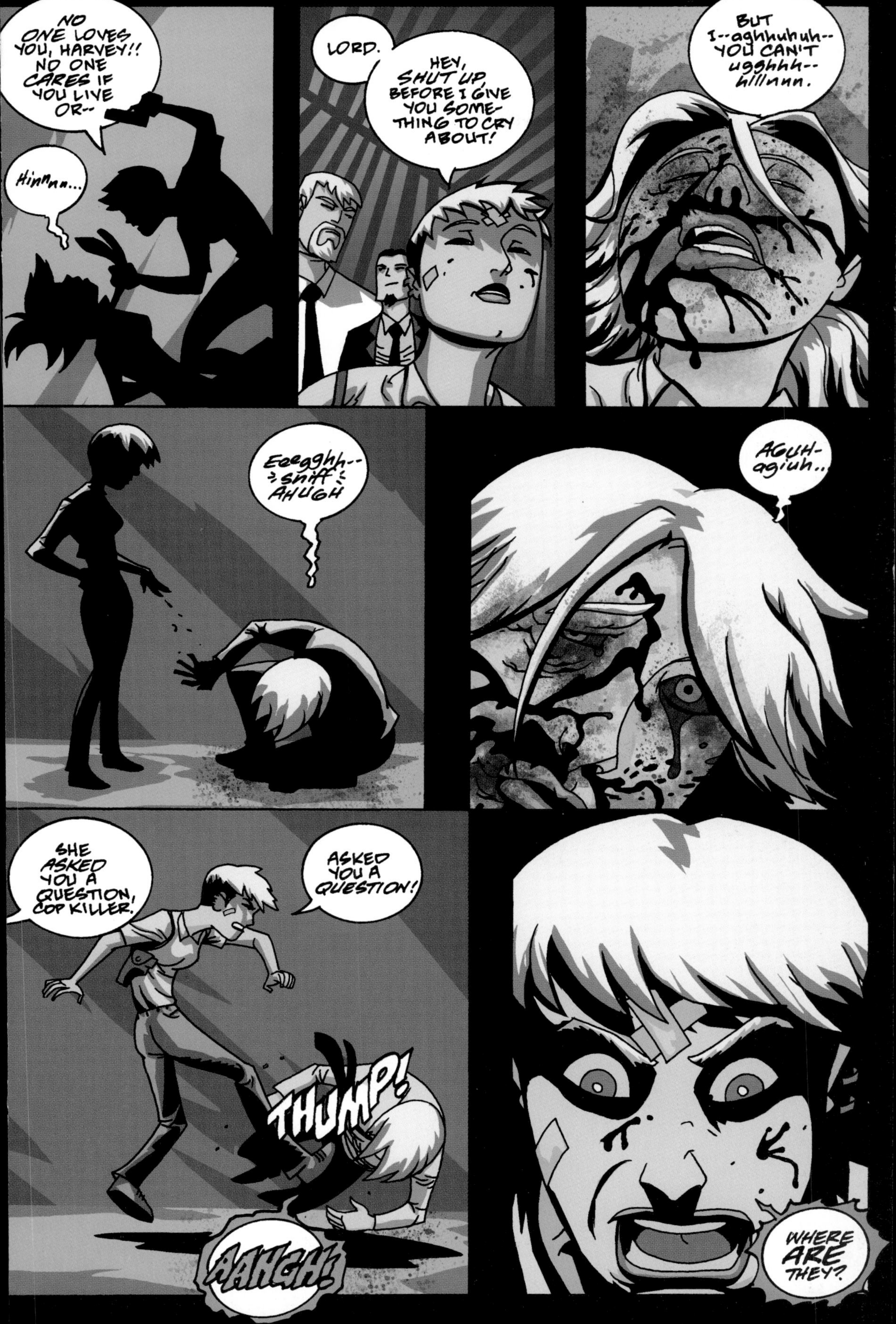
NO ONE LOVES YOU, HARVEY!! NO ONE CARES IF YOU LIVE OR--
Hinnnn...
LORD.
HEY, SHUT UP, BEFORE I GIVE YOU SOME-THING TO CRY ABOUT!
BUT I--aghhuhuh-- YOU CAN'T ugghhh-- hlllnnn.
Eeegghh-- sniff AHUGH
AGUH-agiuh...
SHE ASKED YOU A QUESTION, COP KILLER!
ASKED YOU A QUESTION!
THUMP!
AAHGH!
WHERE ARE THEY?

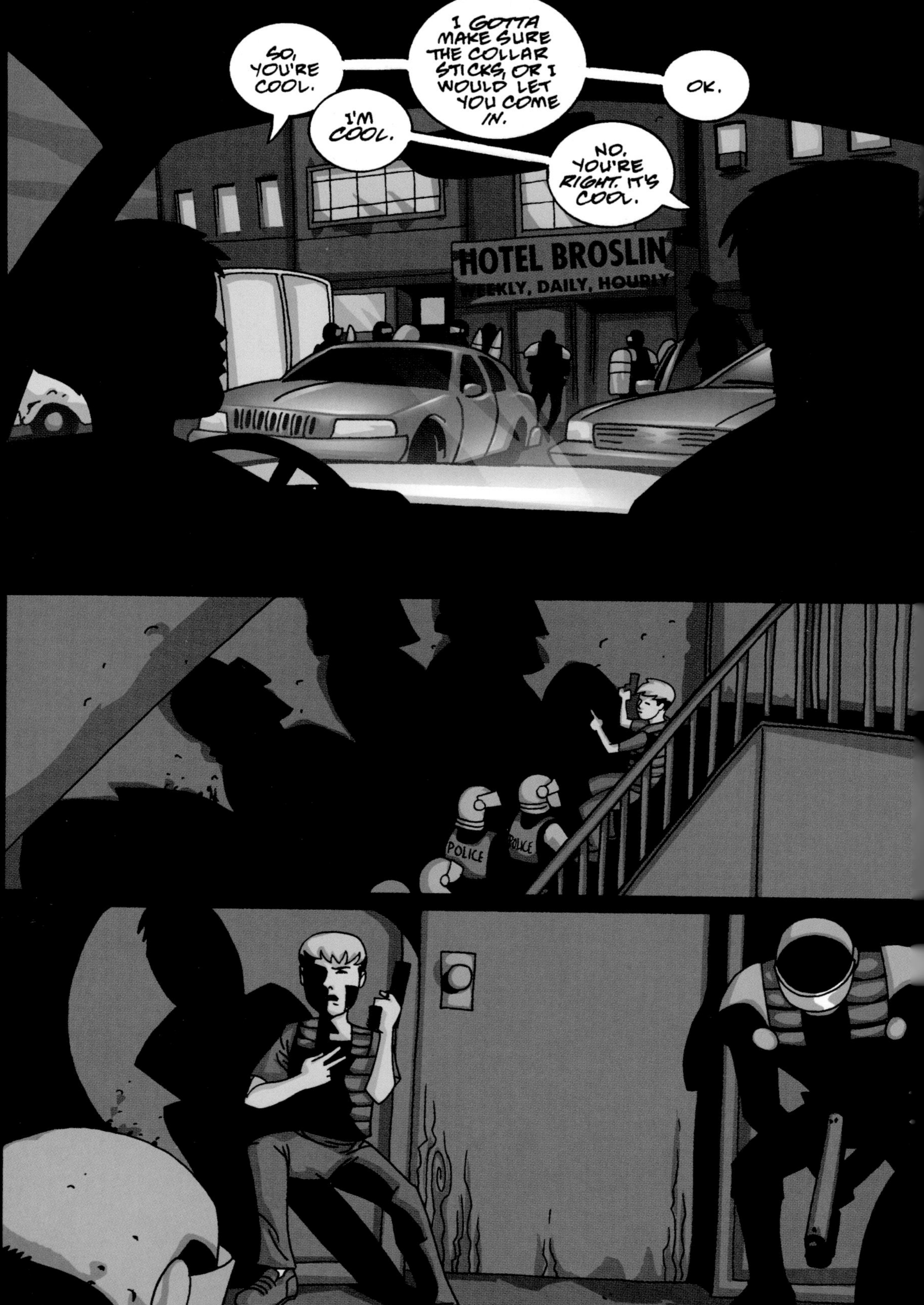
SO, YOU'RE COOL.
I GOTTA MAKE SURE THE COLLAR STICKS, OR I WOULD LET YOU COME IN.
OK.
I'M COOL.
NO, YOU'RE RIGHT. IT'S COOL.
HOTEL BROSLIN
WEEKLY, DAILY, HOURLY
POLICE
POLICE

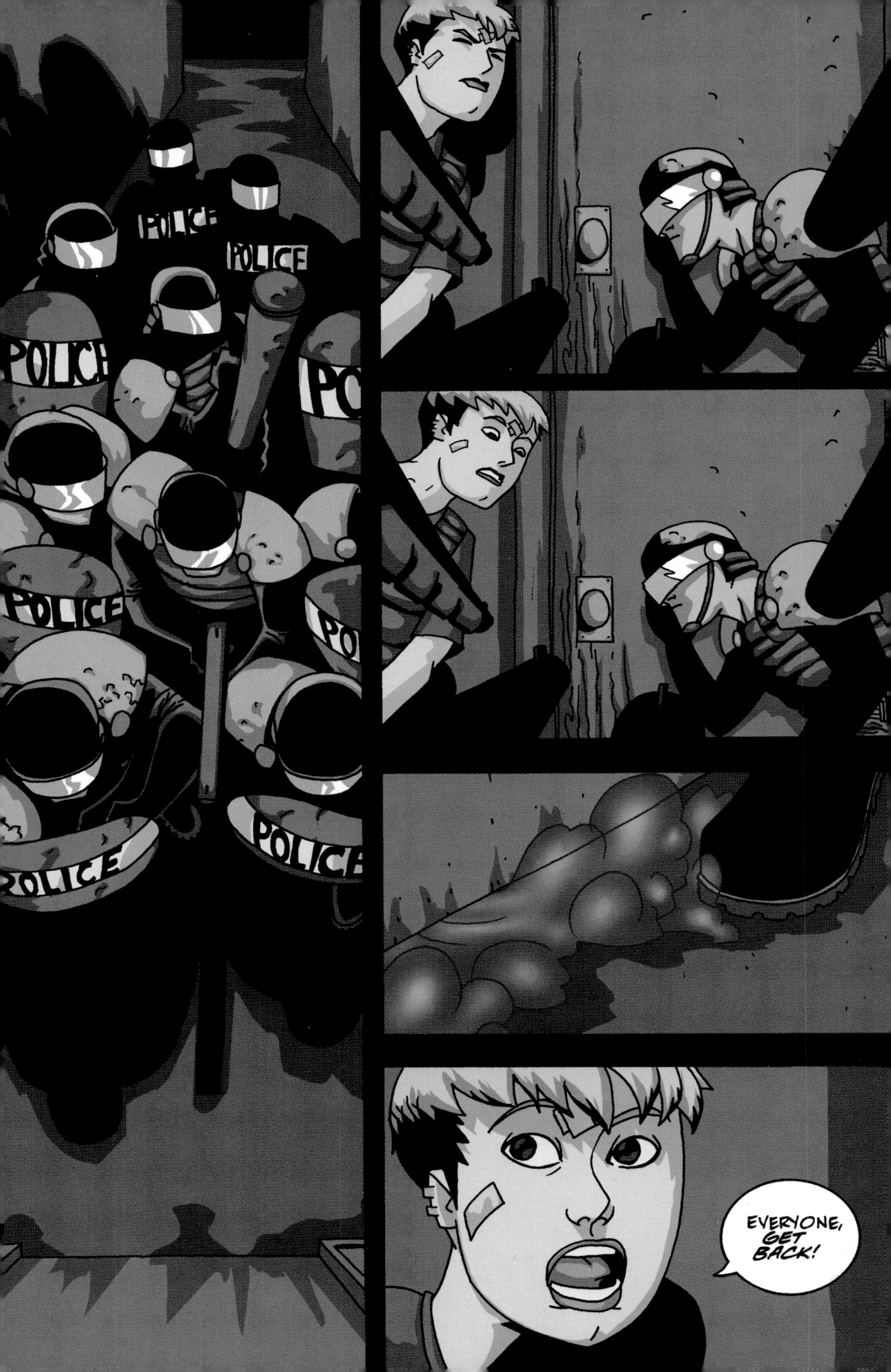
POLICE
POLICE
POLICE
POLICE
POLICE
POLICE
EVERYONE, GET BACK!

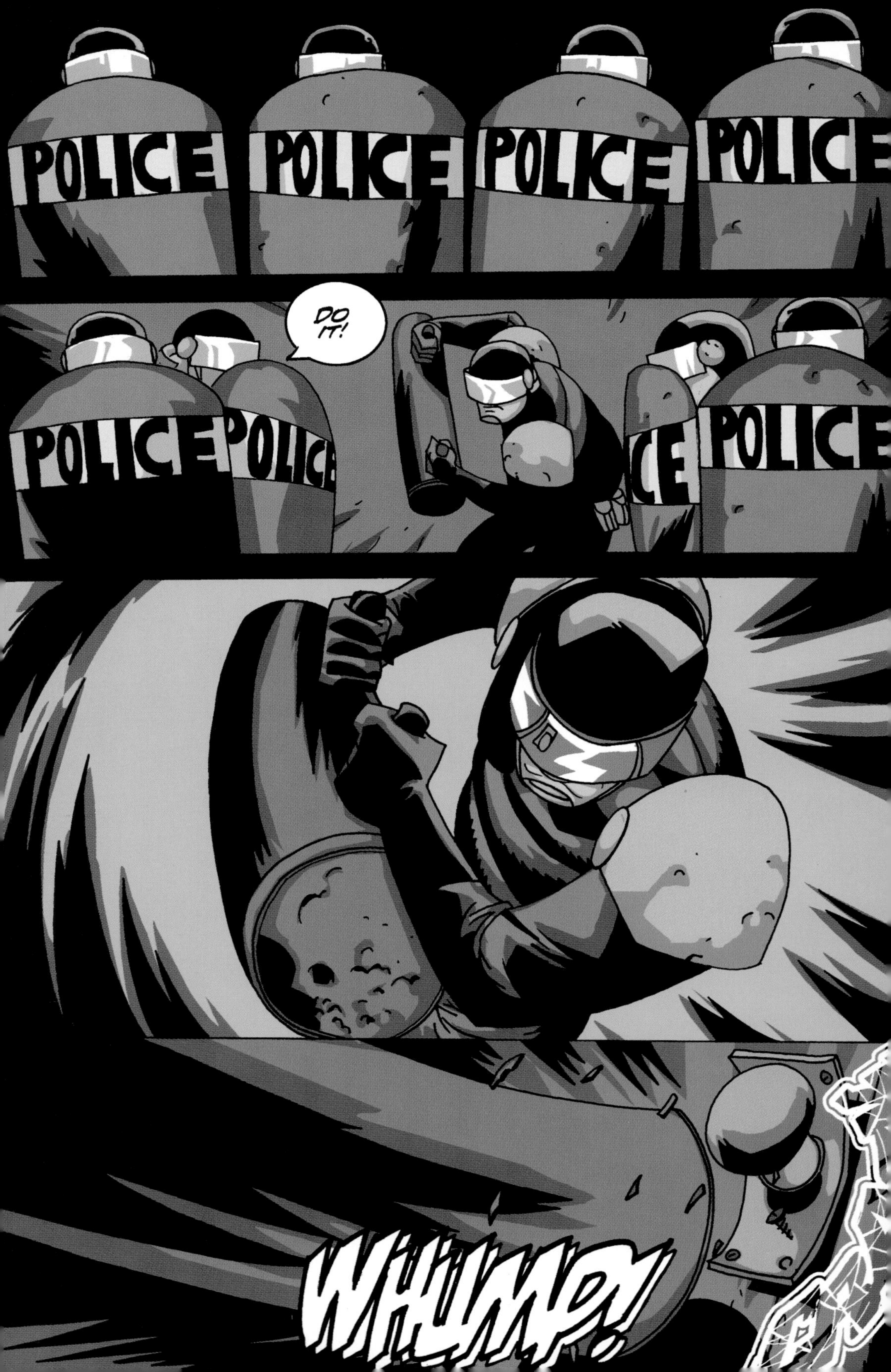
POLICE
POLICE
POLICE
POLICE
POLICE
POLICE
DO IT!
POLICE
WHUMP!

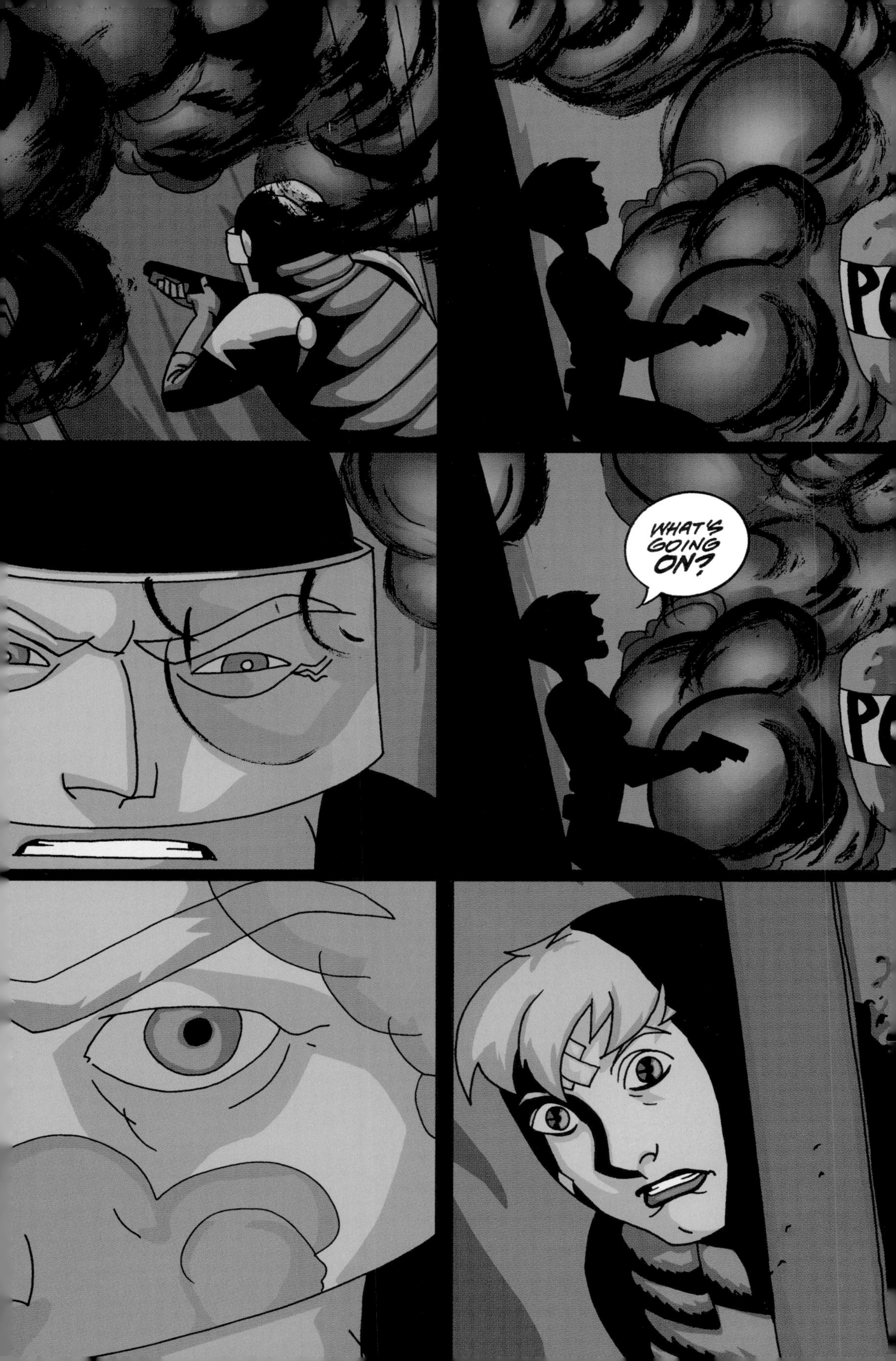
PO
PO
WHAT'S GOING ON?

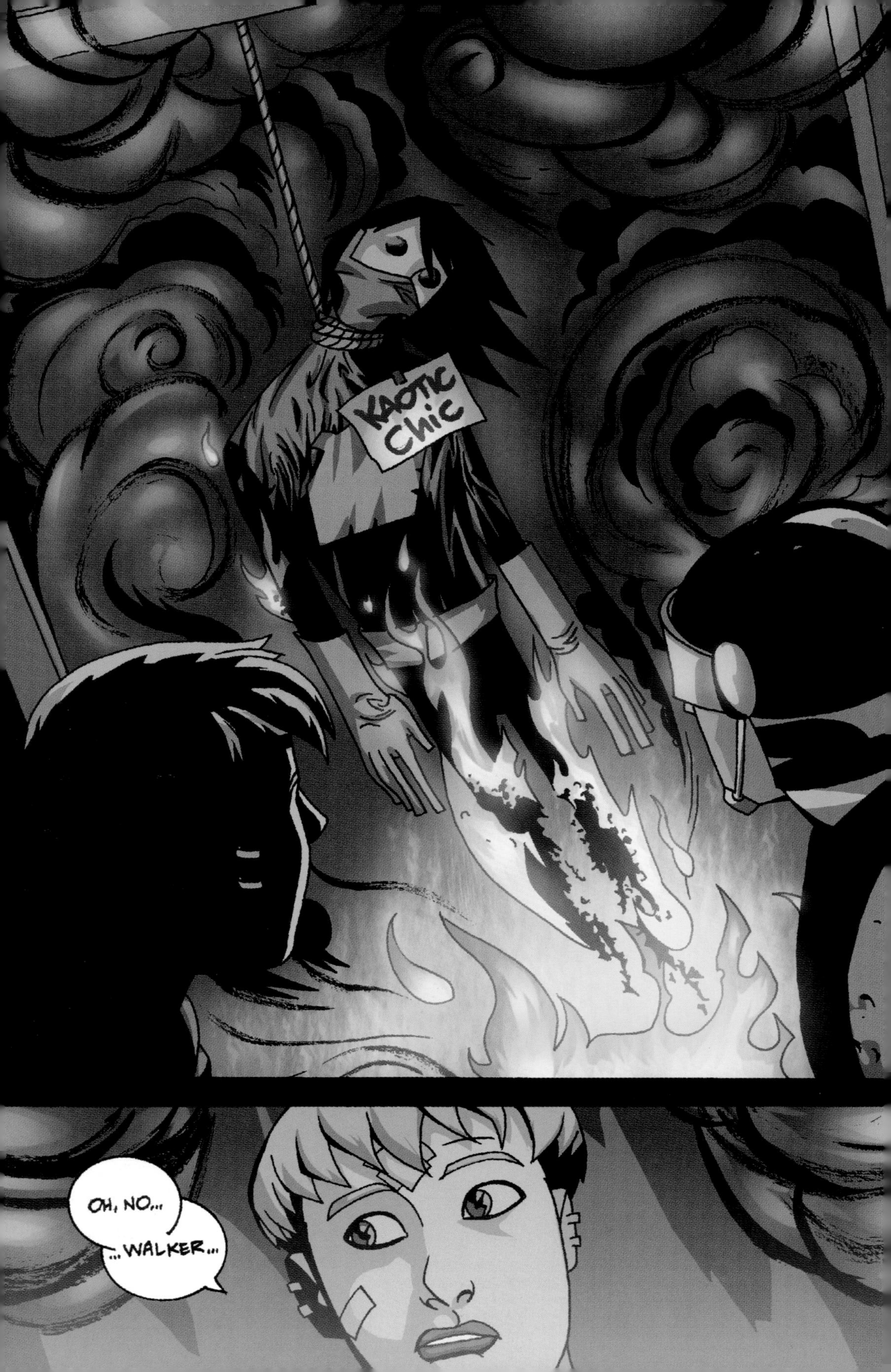
KAOTIC Chic
OH, NO...
...WALKER...

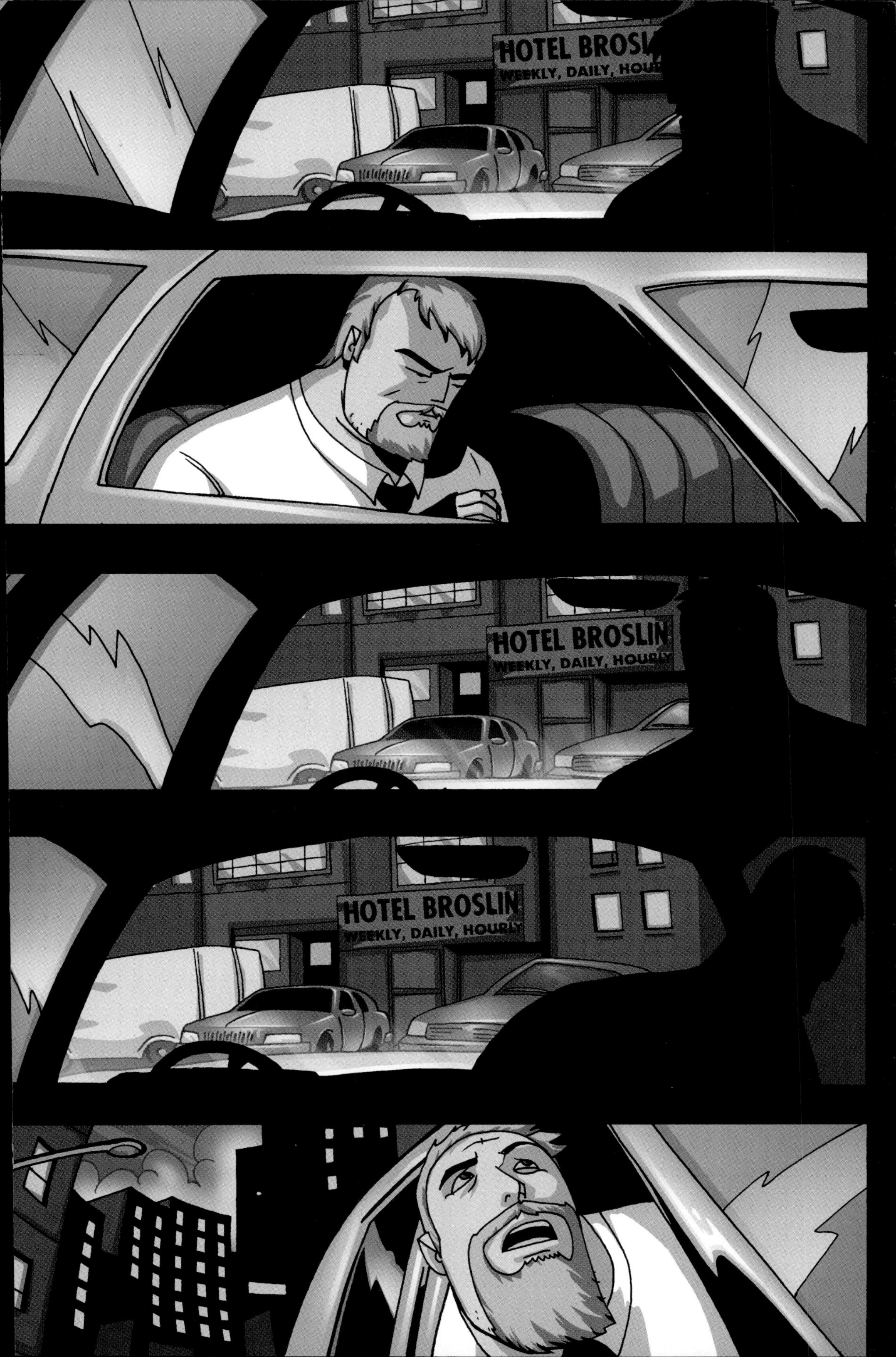
HOTEL BROSLIN
WEEKLY, DAILY, HOURLY
HOTEL BROSLIN
WEEKLY, DAILY, HOURLY
HOTEL BROSLIN
WEEKLY, DAILY, HOURLY

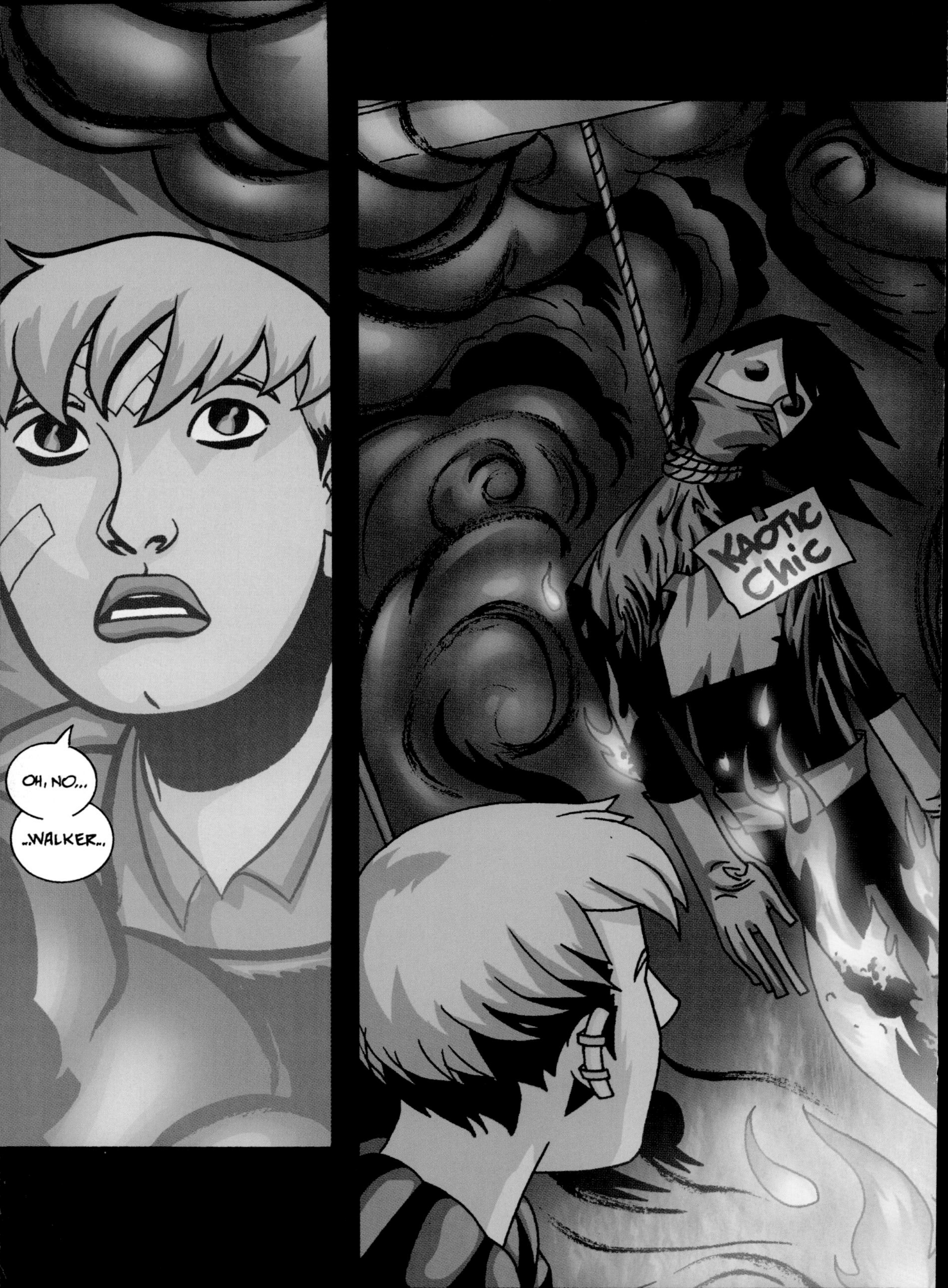

OH, NO...
...WALKER...
KAOTIC CHIC

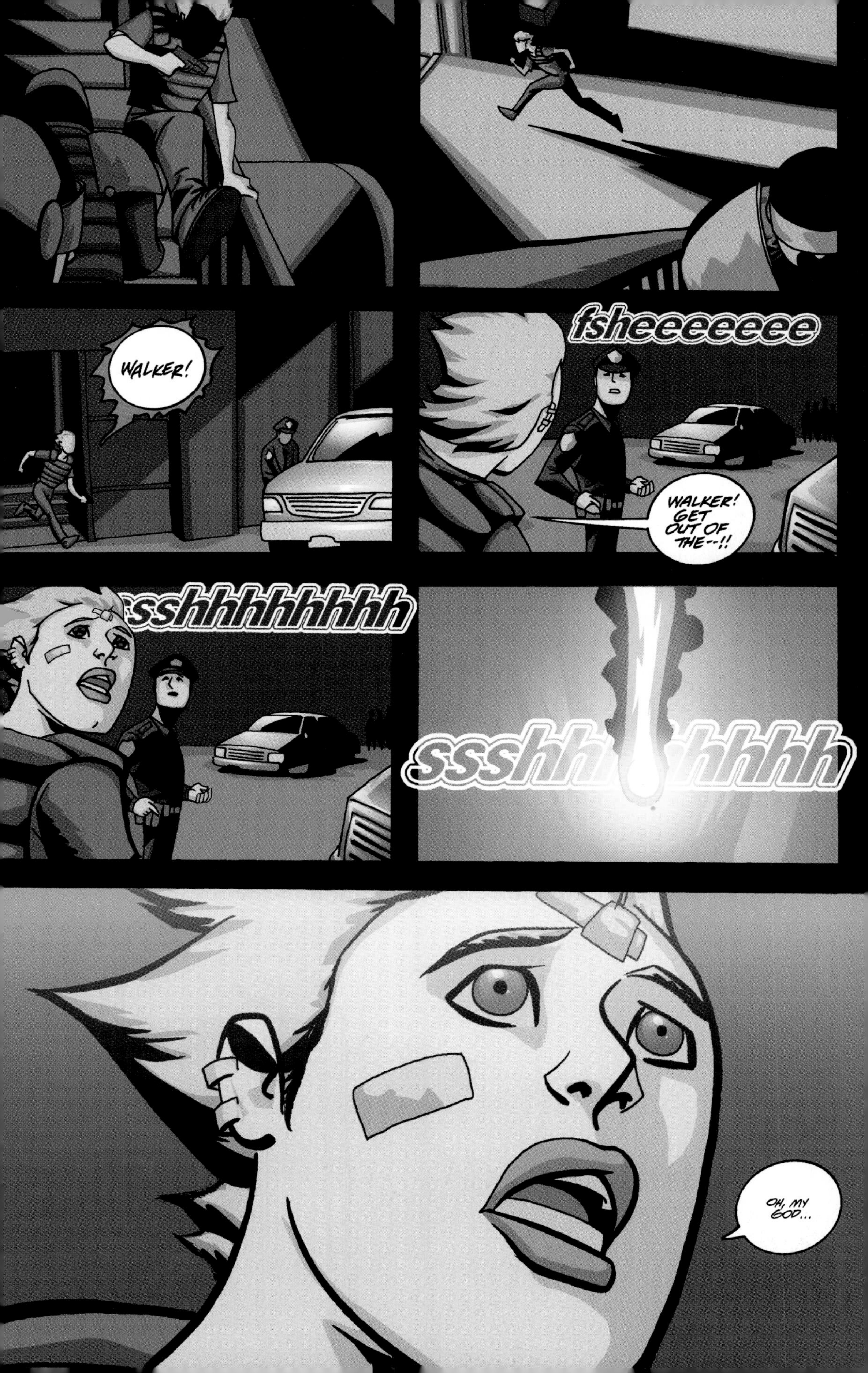
WALKER!
fsheeeeeeee
WALKER! GET OUT OF THE--!!
ssshhhhhhhh
OH, MY GOD...

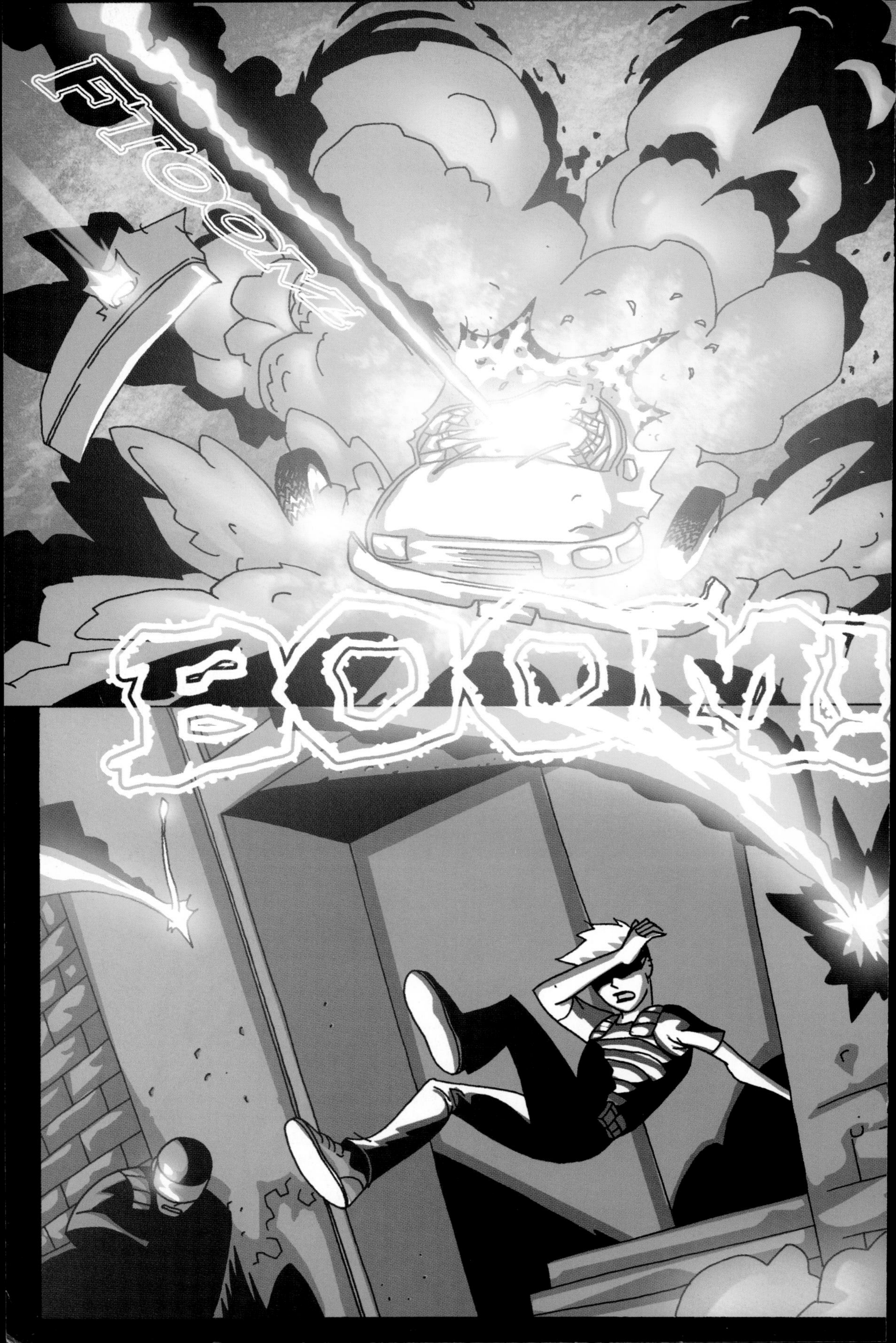
FTOOM
BOOM!

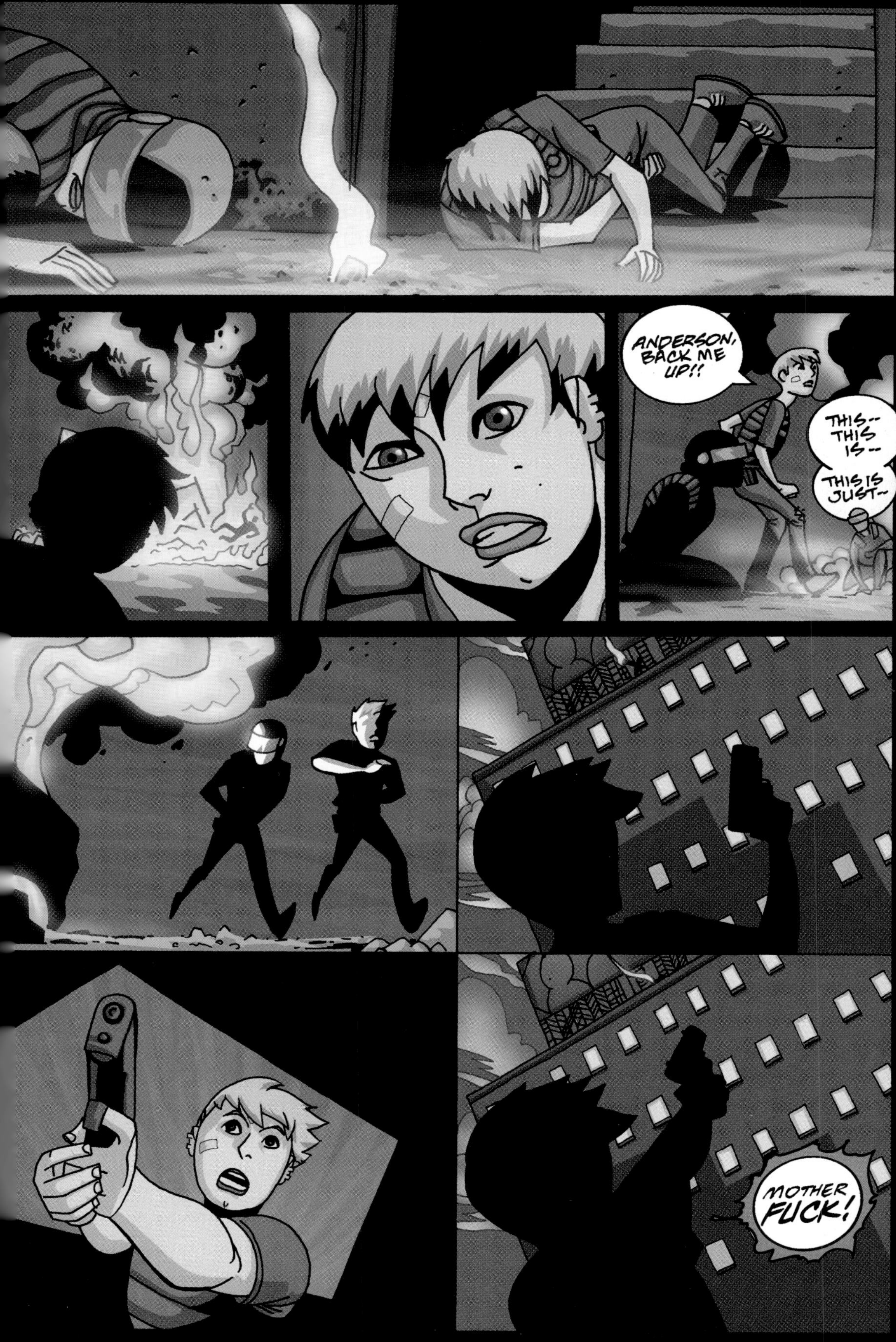
ANDERSON, BACK ME UP!!
THIS-- THIS IS--
THIS IS JUST--
MOTHER FUCK!

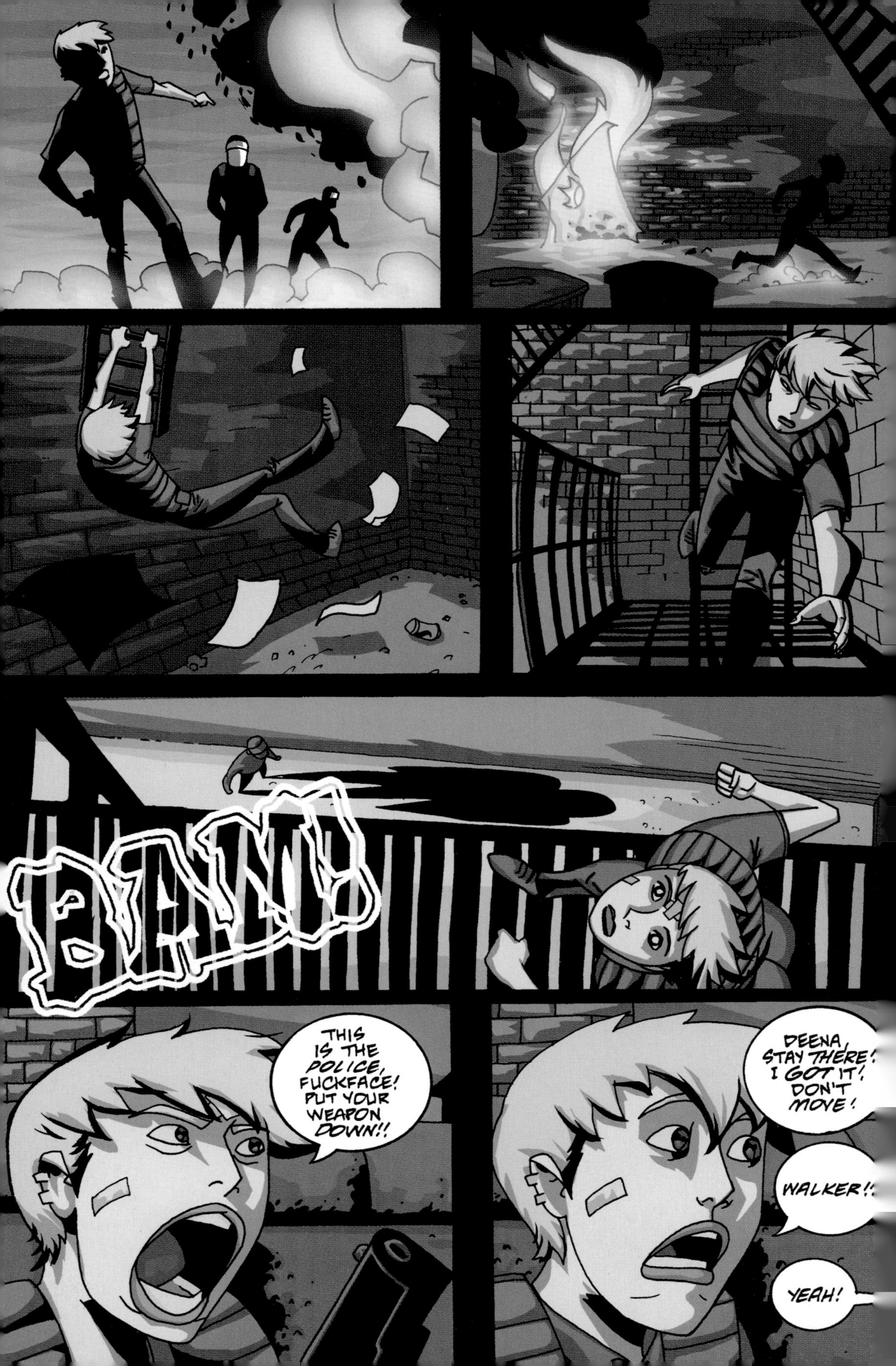
BLAM!
THIS IS THE POLICE, FUCKFACE! PUT YOUR WEAPON DOWN!!
DEENA, STAY THERE! I GOT IT! DON'T MOVE!
WALKER!!
YEAH!

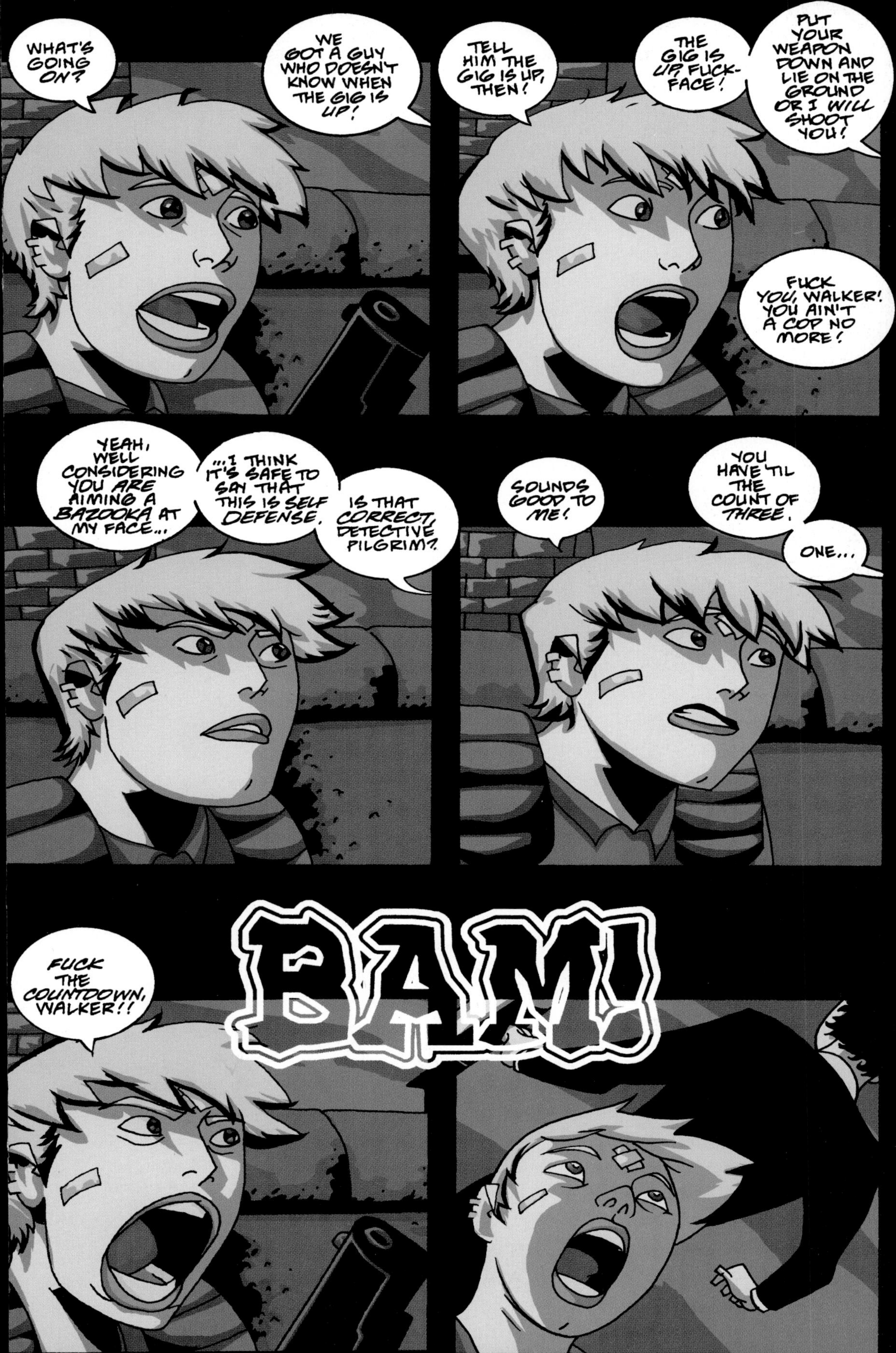
WHAT'S GOING ON?
WE GOT A GUY WHO DOESN'T KNOW WHEN THE GIG IS UP!
TELL HIM THE GIG IS UP, THEN!
THE GIG IS UP, FUCK-FACE!
PUT YOUR WEAPON DOWN AND LIE ON THE GROUND OR I WILL SHOOT YOU!
FUCK YOU, WALKER! YOU AIN'T A COP NO MORE!
YEAH, WELL CONSIDERING YOU ARE AIMING A BAZOOKA AT MY FACE...
...I THINK IT'S SAFE TO SAY THAT THIS IS SELF DEFENSE.
IS THAT CORRECT, DETECTIVE PILGRIM?
SOUNDS GOOD TO ME!
YOU HAVE 'TIL THE COUNT OF THREE.
ONE...
FUCK THE COUNTDOWN, WALKER!!
BAM!

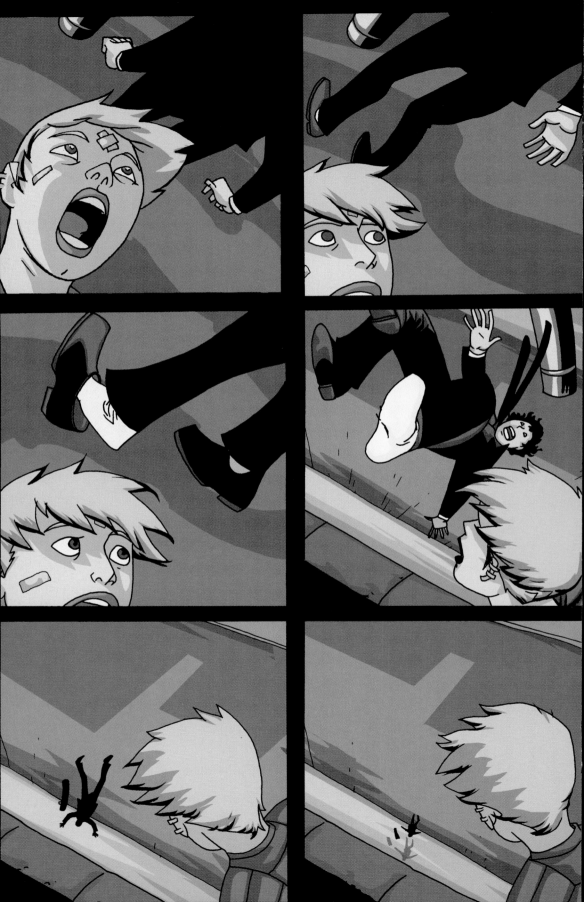

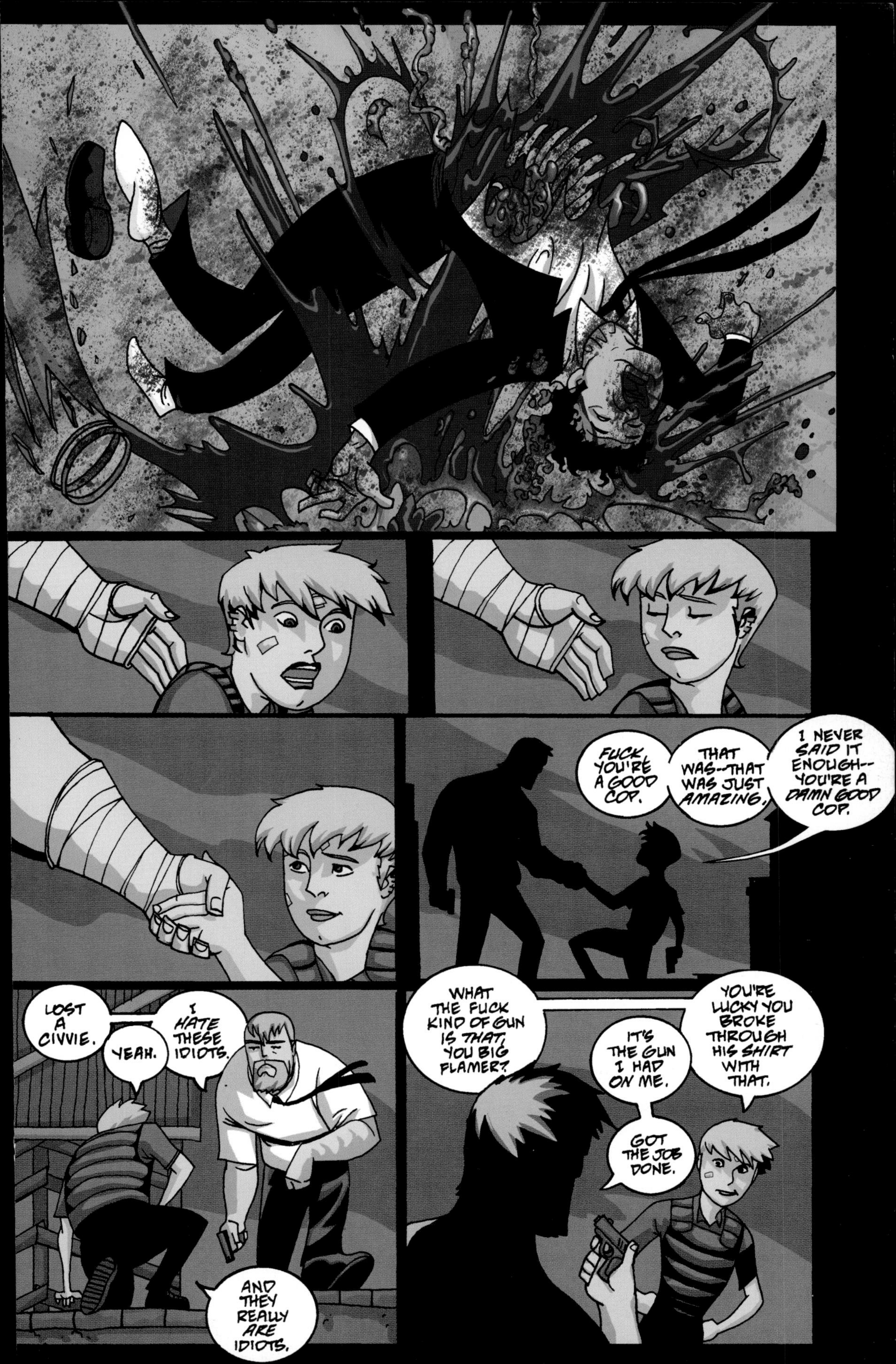
FUCK, YOU'RE A GOOD COP.
THAT WAS--THAT WAS JUST AMAZING.
I NEVER SAID IT ENOUGH-- YOU'RE A DAMN GOOD COP.
LOST A CIVVIE.
YEAH.
I HATE THESE IDIOTS.
AND THEY REALLY ARE IDIOTS.
WHAT THE FUCK KIND OF GUN IS THAT, YOU BIG FLAMER?
IT'S THE GUN I HAD ON ME.
GOT THE JOB DONE.
YOU'RE LUCKY YOU BROKE THROUGH HIS SHIRT WITH THAT.

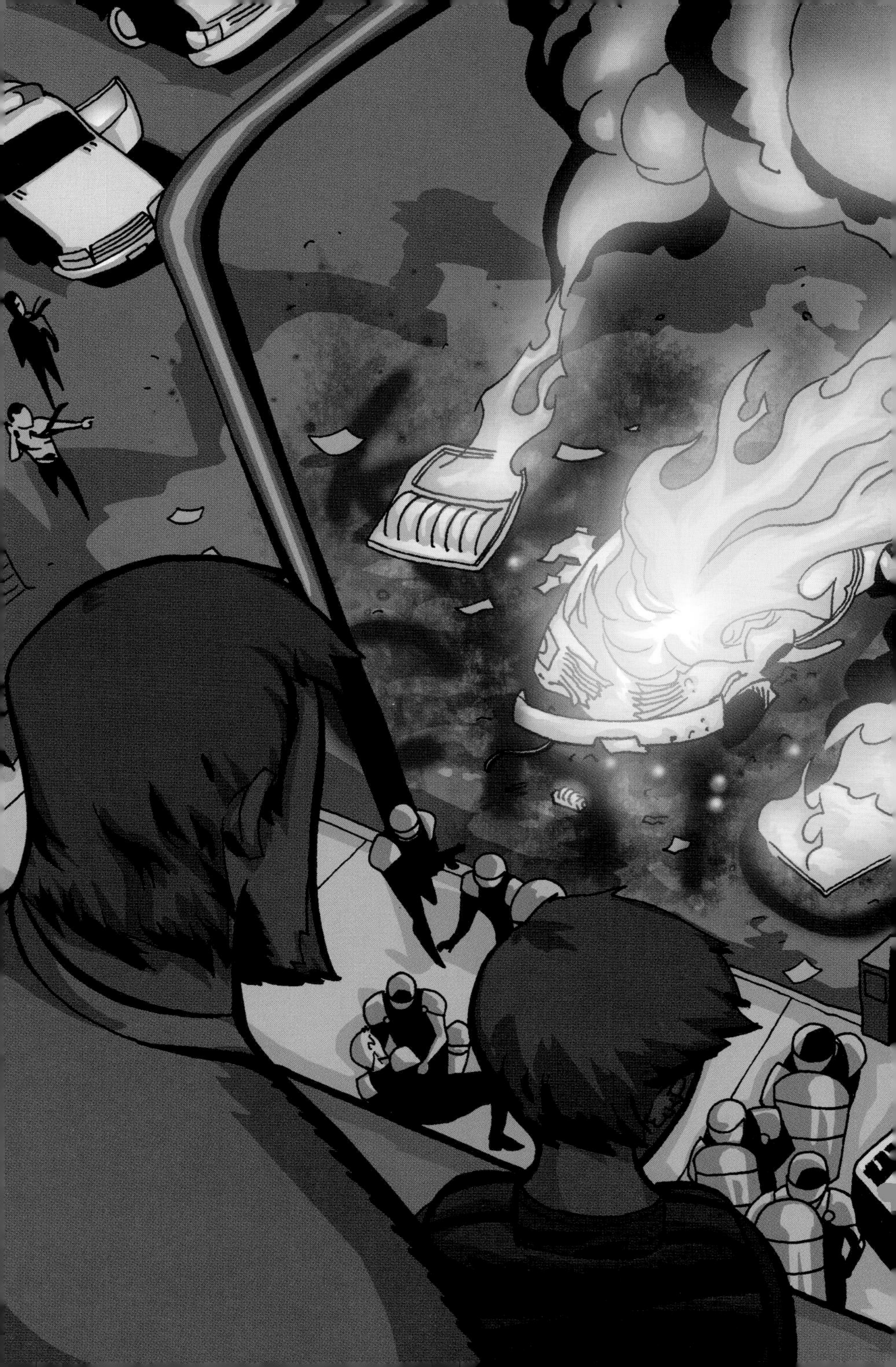

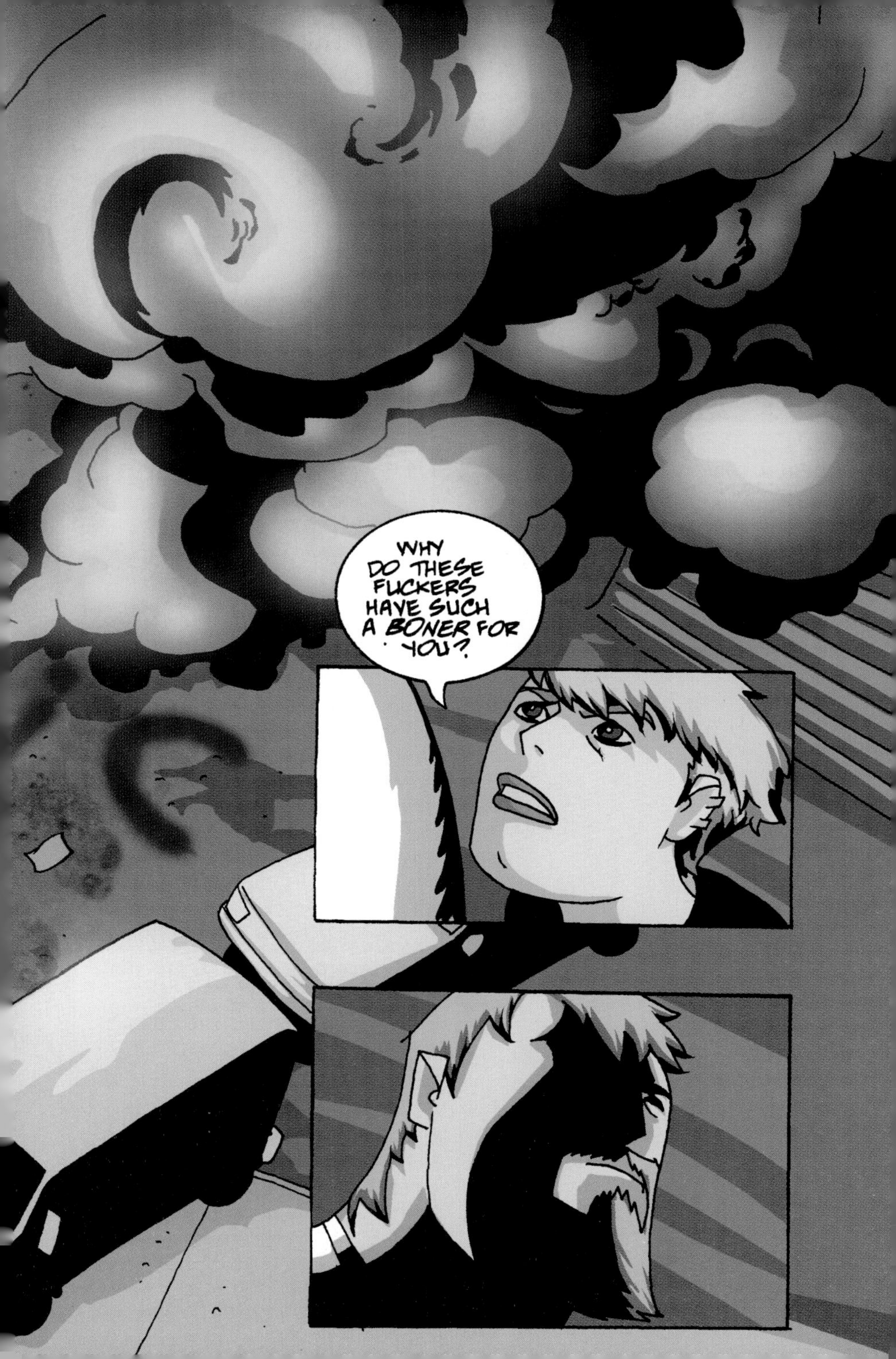
WHY DO THESE FUCKERS HAVE SUCH A BONER FOR YOU?

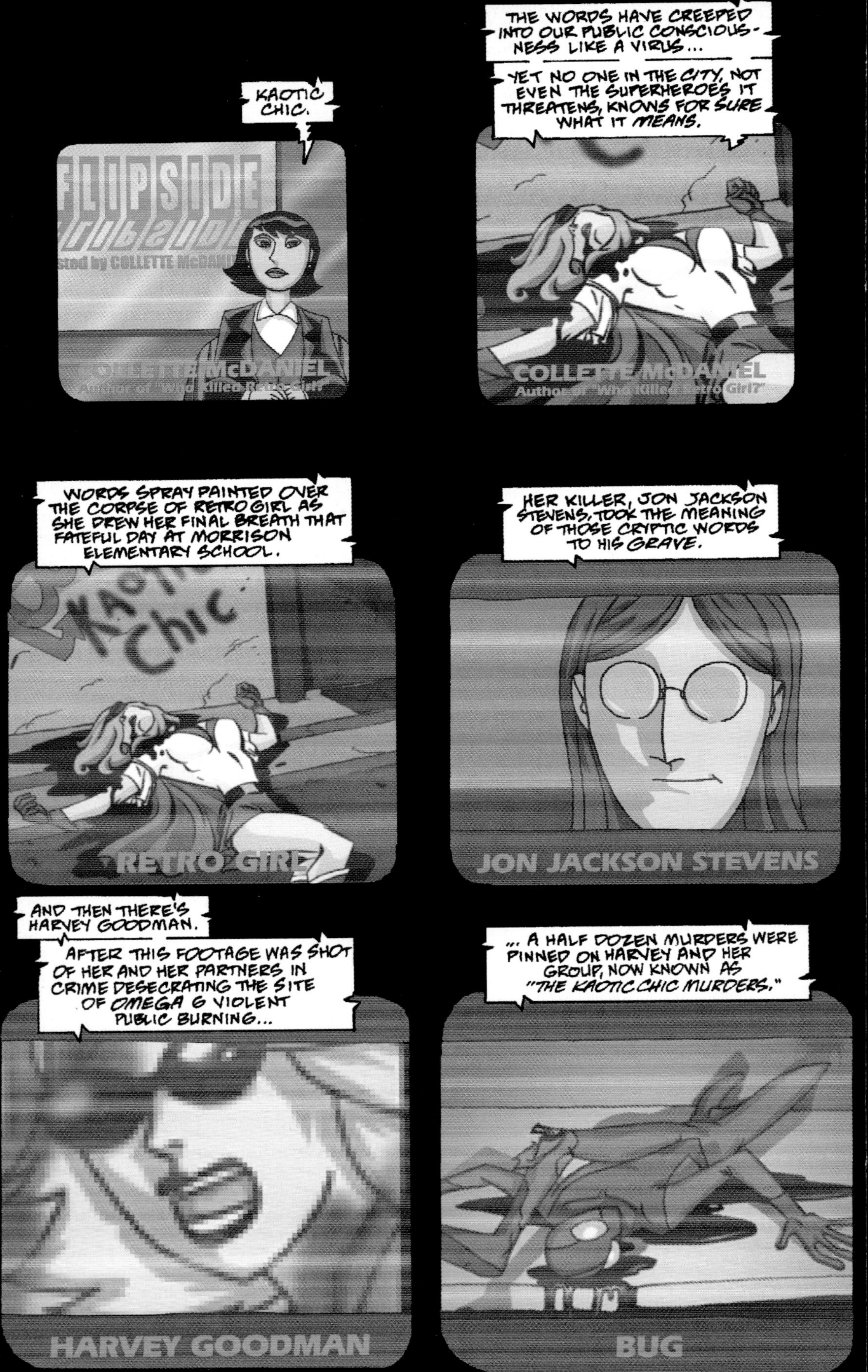
KAOTIC CHIC.
FLIPSIDE
Hosted by COLLETTE McDANIEL
COLLETTE McDANIEL
Author of "Who Killed Retro Girl?"
THE WORDS HAVE CREEPED INTO OUR PUBLIC CONSCIOUS-NESS LIKE A VIRUS...
YET NO ONE IN THE CITY, NOT EVEN THE SUPERHEROES IT THREATENS, KNOWS FOR SURE WHAT IT MEANS.
COLLETTE McDANIEL
Author of "Who Killed Retro Girl?"
WORDS SPRAY PAINTED OVER THE CORPSE OF RETRO GIRL AS SHE DREW HER FINAL BREATH THAT FATEFUL DAY AT MORRISON ELEMENTARY SCHOOL.
Chic
RETRO GIRL
HER KILLER, JON JACKSON STEVENS, TOOK THE MEANING OF THOSE CRYPTIC WORDS TO HIS GRAVE.
JON JACKSON STEVENS
AND THEN THERE'S HARVEY GOODMAN.
AFTER THIS FOOTAGE WAS SHOT OF HER AND HER PARTNERS IN CRIME DESECRATING THE SITE OF OMEGA 6 VIOLENT PUBLIC BURNING...
HARVEY GOODMAN
... A HALF DOZEN MURDERS WERE PINNED ON HARVEY AND HER GROUP, NOW KNOWN AS "THE KAOTIC CHIC MURDERS."
BUG

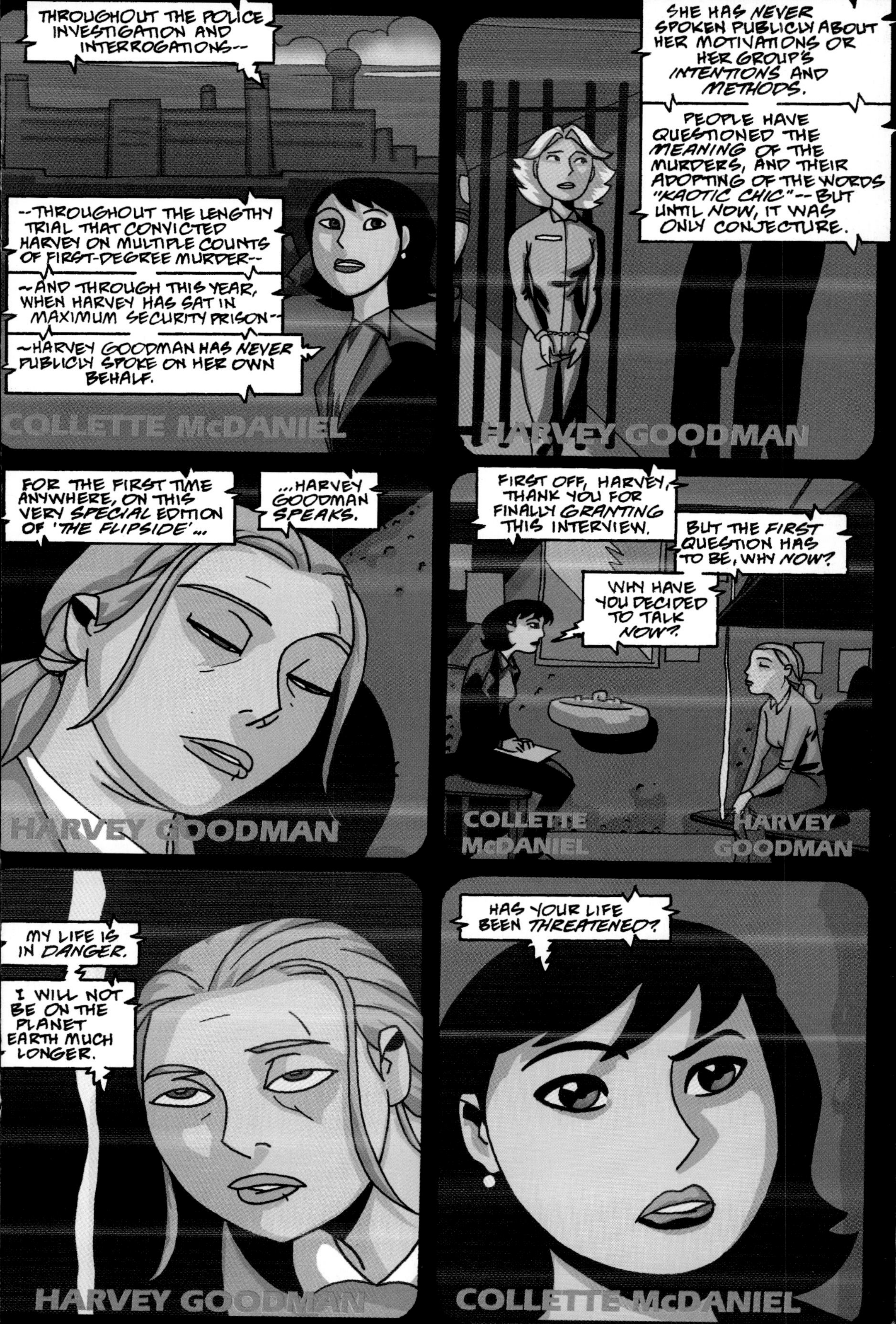
THROUGHOUT THE POLICE INVESTIGATION AND INTERROGATIONS--
--THROUGHOUT THE LENGTHY TRIAL THAT CONVICTED HARVEY ON MULTIPLE COUNTS OF FIRST-DEGREE MURDER--
--AND THROUGH THIS YEAR, WHEN HARVEY HAS SAT IN MAXIMUM SECURITY PRISON--
--HARVEY GOODMAN HAS NEVER PUBLICLY SPOKE ON HER OWN BEHALF.
COLLETTE McDANIEL
SHE HAS NEVER SPOKEN PUBLICLY ABOUT HER MOTIVATIONS OR HER GROUP'S INTENTIONS AND METHODS.
PEOPLE HAVE QUESTIONED THE MEANING OF THE MURDERS, AND THEIR ADOPTING OF THE WORDS "KAOTIC CHIC"-- BUT UNTIL NOW, IT WAS ONLY CONJECTURE.
HARVEY GOODMAN
FOR THE FIRST TIME ANYWHERE, ON THIS VERY SPECIAL EDITION OF 'THE FLIPSIDE'...
...HARVEY GOODMAN SPEAKS.
HARVEY GOODMAN
FIRST OFF, HARVEY, THANK YOU FOR FINALLY GRANTING THIS INTERVIEW.
BUT THE FIRST QUESTION HAS TO BE, WHY NOW?
WHY HAVE YOU DECIDED TO TALK NOW?
COLLETTE McDANIEL
HARVEY GOODMAN
MY LIFE IS IN DANGER.
I WILL NOT BE ON THE PLANET EARTH MUCH LONGER.
HARVEY GOODMAN
HAS YOUR LIFE BEEN THREATENED?
COLLETTE McDANIEL

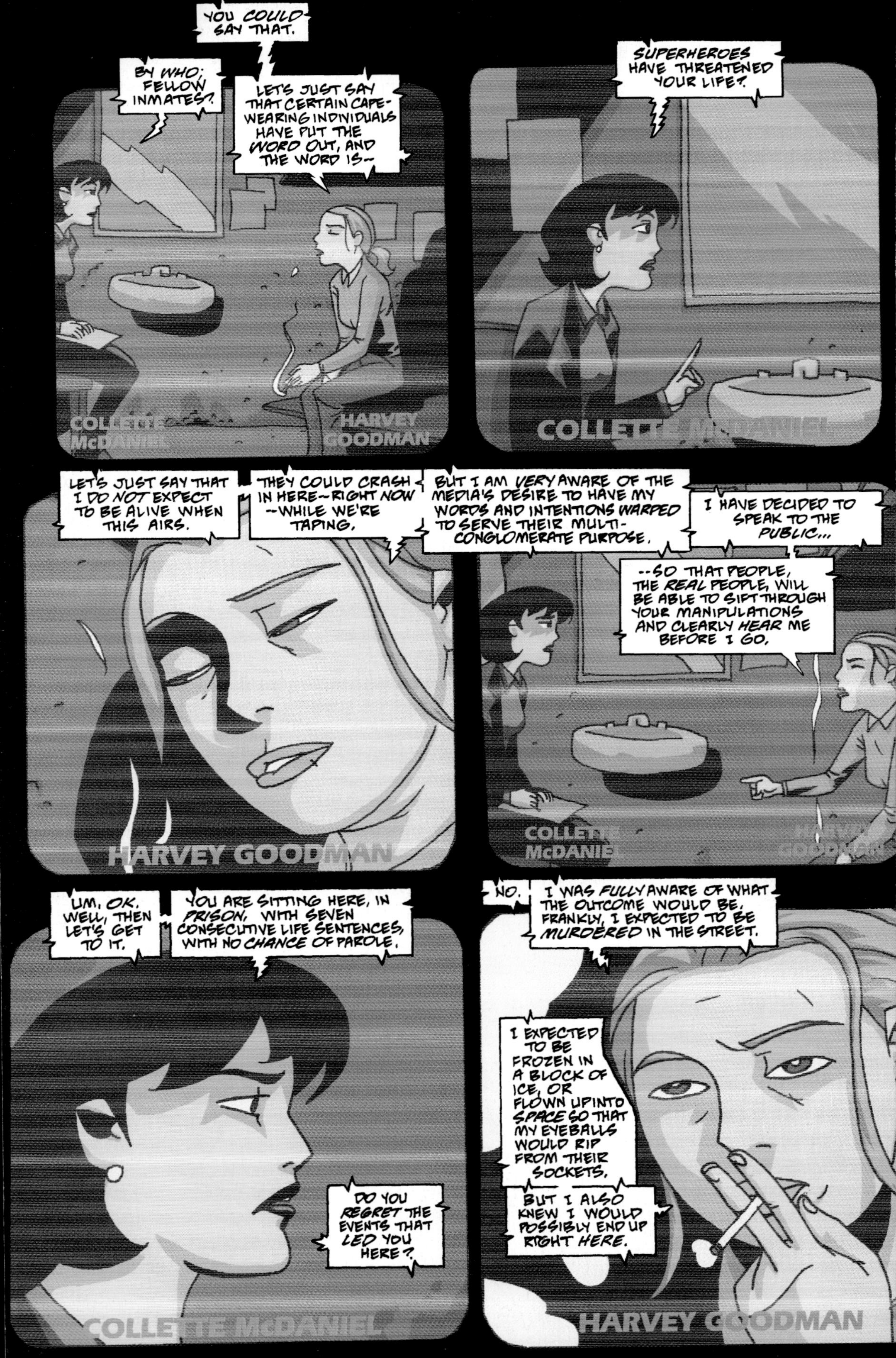
BY WHO; FELLOW INMATES?
YOU COULD SAY THAT.
LET'S JUST SAY THAT CERTAIN CAPE-WEARING INDIVIDUALS HAVE PUT THE WORD OUT, AND THE WORD IS--
COLLETTE McDANIEL
HARVEY GOODMAN
SUPERHEROES HAVE THREATENED YOUR LIFE?
COLLETTE McDANIEL
LET'S JUST SAY THAT I DO NOT EXPECT TO BE ALIVE WHEN THIS AIRS.
THEY COULD CRASH IN HERE--RIGHT NOW --WHILE WE'RE TAPING.
HARVEY GOODMAN
BUT I AM VERY AWARE OF THE MEDIA'S DESIRE TO HAVE MY WORDS AND INTENTIONS WARPED TO SERVE THEIR MULTI-CONGLOMERATE PURPOSE.
I HAVE DECIDED TO SPEAK TO THE PUBLIC...
--SO THAT PEOPLE, THE REAL PEOPLE, WILL BE ABLE TO SIFT THROUGH YOUR MANIPULATIONS AND CLEARLY HEAR ME BEFORE I GO.
COLLETTE McDANIEL
HARVEY GOODMAN
UM, OK. WELL, THEN LET'S GET TO IT.
YOU ARE SITTING HERE, IN PRISON, WITH SEVEN CONSECUTIVE LIFE SENTENCES, WITH NO CHANCE OF PAROLE.
DO YOU REGRET THE EVENTS THAT LED YOU HERE?
COLLETTE McDANIEL
NO.
I WAS FULLY AWARE OF WHAT THE OUTCOME WOULD BE. FRANKLY, I EXPECTED TO BE MURDERED IN THE STREET.
I EXPECTED TO BE FROZEN IN A BLOCK OF ICE, OR FLOWN UP INTO SPACE SO THAT MY EYEBALLS WOULD RIP FROM THEIR SOCKETS.
BUT I ALSO KNEW I WOULD POSSIBLY END UP RIGHT HERE.
HARVEY GOODMAN

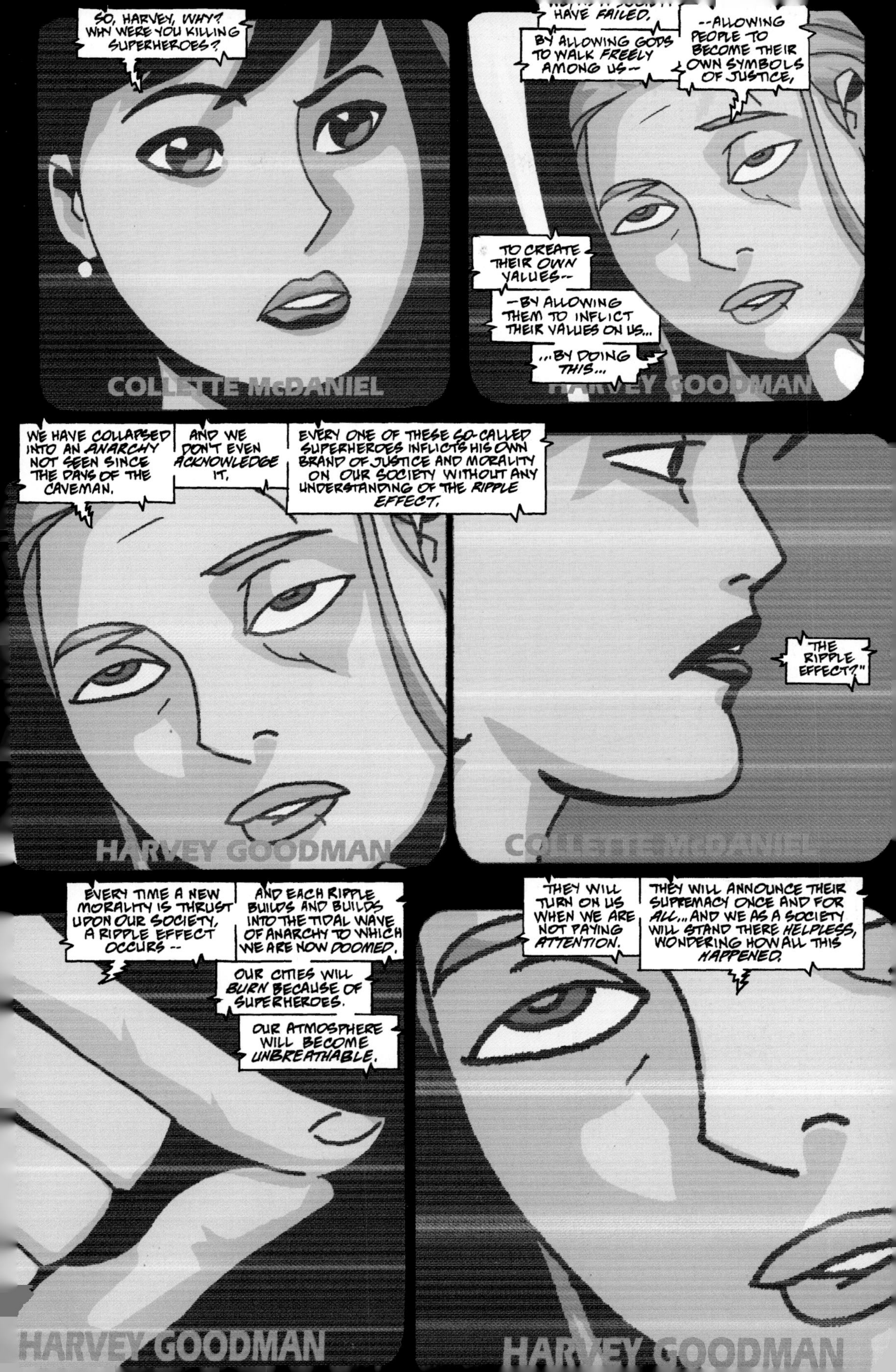

SO, HARVEY, WHY? WHY WERE YOU KILLING SUPERHEROES?
COLLETTE McDANIEL
HAVE FAILED,
BY ALLOWING GODS TO WALK FREELY AMONG US--
--ALLOWING PEOPLE TO BECOME THEIR OWN SYMBOLS OF JUSTICE,
TO CREATE THEIR OWN VALUES--
--BY ALLOWING THEM TO INFLICT THEIR VALUES ON US...
...BY DOING THIS...
HARVEY GOODMAN
WE HAVE COLLAPSED INTO AN ANARCHY NOT SEEN SINCE THE DAYS OF THE CAVEMAN.
AND WE DON'T EVEN ACKNOWLEDGE IT,
EVERY ONE OF THESE SO-CALLED SUPERHEROES INFLICTS HIS OWN BRAND OF JUSTICE AND MORALITY ON OUR SOCIETY WITHOUT ANY UNDERSTANDING OF THE RIPPLE EFFECT,
HARVEY GOODMAN
"THE RIPPLE EFFECT?"
COLLETTE McDANIEL
EVERY TIME A NEW MORALITY IS THRUST UPON OUR SOCIETY, A RIPPLE EFFECT OCCURS --
AND EACH RIPPLE BUILDS AND BUILDS INTO THE TIDAL WAVE OF ANARCHY TO WHICH WE ARE NOW DOOMED.
OUR CITIES WILL BURN BECAUSE OF SUPERHEROES.
OUR ATMOSPHERE WILL BECOME UNBREATHABLE.
HARVEY GOODMAN
THEY WILL TURN ON US WHEN WE ARE NOT PAYING ATTENTION.
THEY WILL ANNOUNCE THEIR SUPREMACY ONCE AND FOR ALL... AND WE AS A SOCIETY WILL STAND THERE HELPLESS, WONDERING HOW ALL THIS HAPPENED.
HARVEY GOODMAN

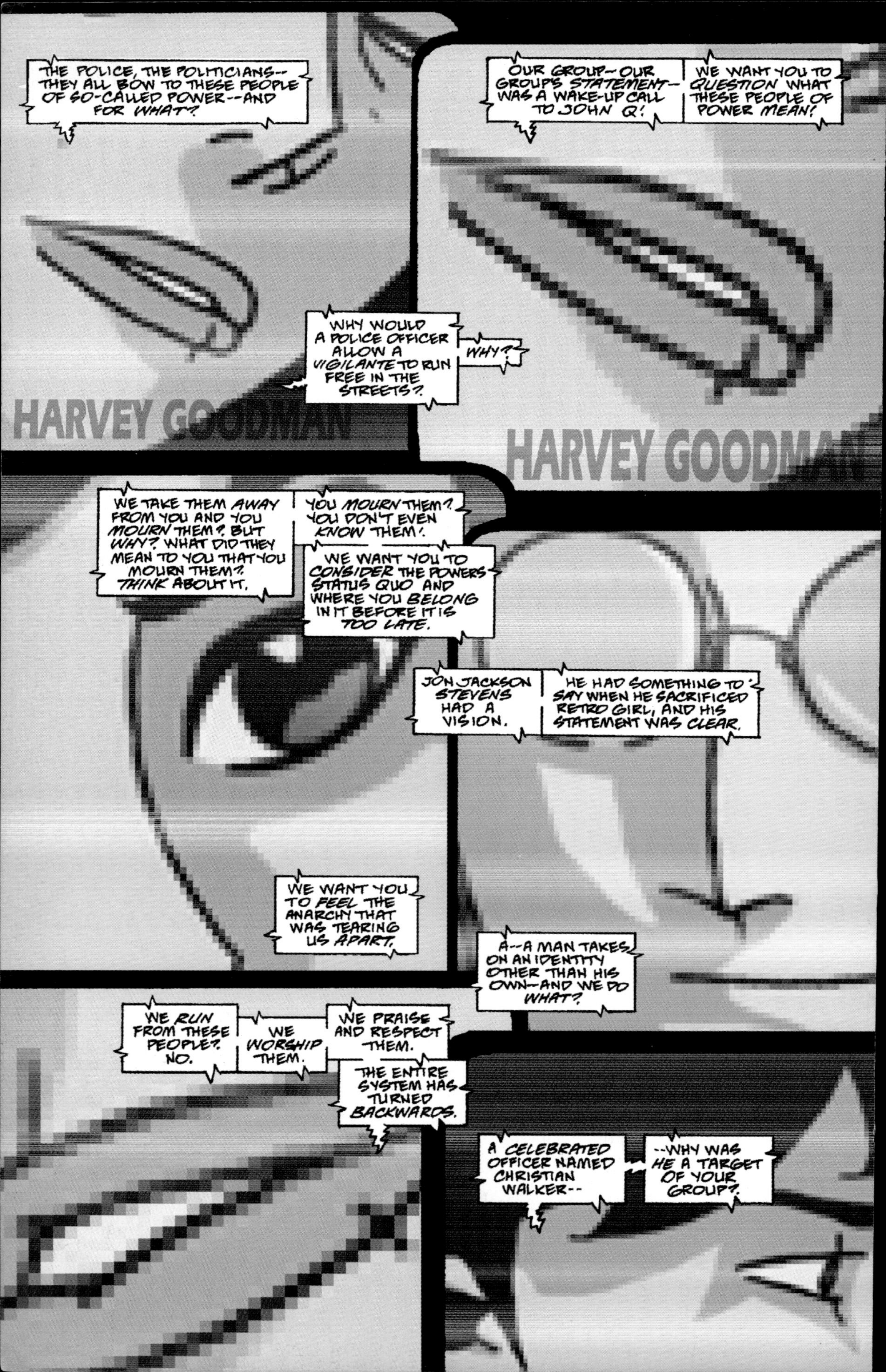
THE POLICE, THE POLITICIANS-- THEY ALL BOW TO THESE PEOPLE OF SO-CALLED POWER--AND FOR WHAT?
OUR GROUP-- OUR GROUP'S STATEMENT-- WAS A WAKE-UP CALL TO JOHN Q!
WE WANT YOU TO QUESTION WHAT THESE PEOPLE OF POWER MEAN!
WHY WOULD A POLICE OFFICER ALLOW A VIGILANTE TO RUN FREE IN THE STREETS?
WHY?
HARVEY GOODMAN
HARVEY GOODMAN
WE TAKE THEM AWAY FROM YOU AND YOU MOURN THEM? BUT WHY? WHAT DID THEY MEAN TO YOU THAT YOU MOURN THEM? THINK ABOUT IT.
YOU MOURN THEM? YOU DON'T EVEN KNOW THEM!
WE WANT YOU TO CONSIDER THE POWERS STATUS QUO AND WHERE YOU BELONG IN IT BEFORE IT IS TOO LATE.
JON JACKSON STEVENS HAD A VISION.
HE HAD SOMETHING TO SAY WHEN HE SACRIFICED RETRO GIRL, AND HIS STATEMENT WAS CLEAR.
WE WANT YOU TO FEEL THE ANARCHY THAT WAS TEARING US APART.
A--A MAN TAKES ON AN IDENTITY OTHER THAN HIS OWN--AND WE DO WHAT?
WE RUN FROM THESE PEOPLE? NO.
WE WORSHIP THEM.
WE PRAISE AND RESPECT THEM.
THE ENTIRE SYSTEM HAS TURNED BACKWARDS.
A CELEBRATED OFFICER NAMED CHRISTIAN WALKER--
--WHY WAS HE A TARGET OF YOUR GROUP?

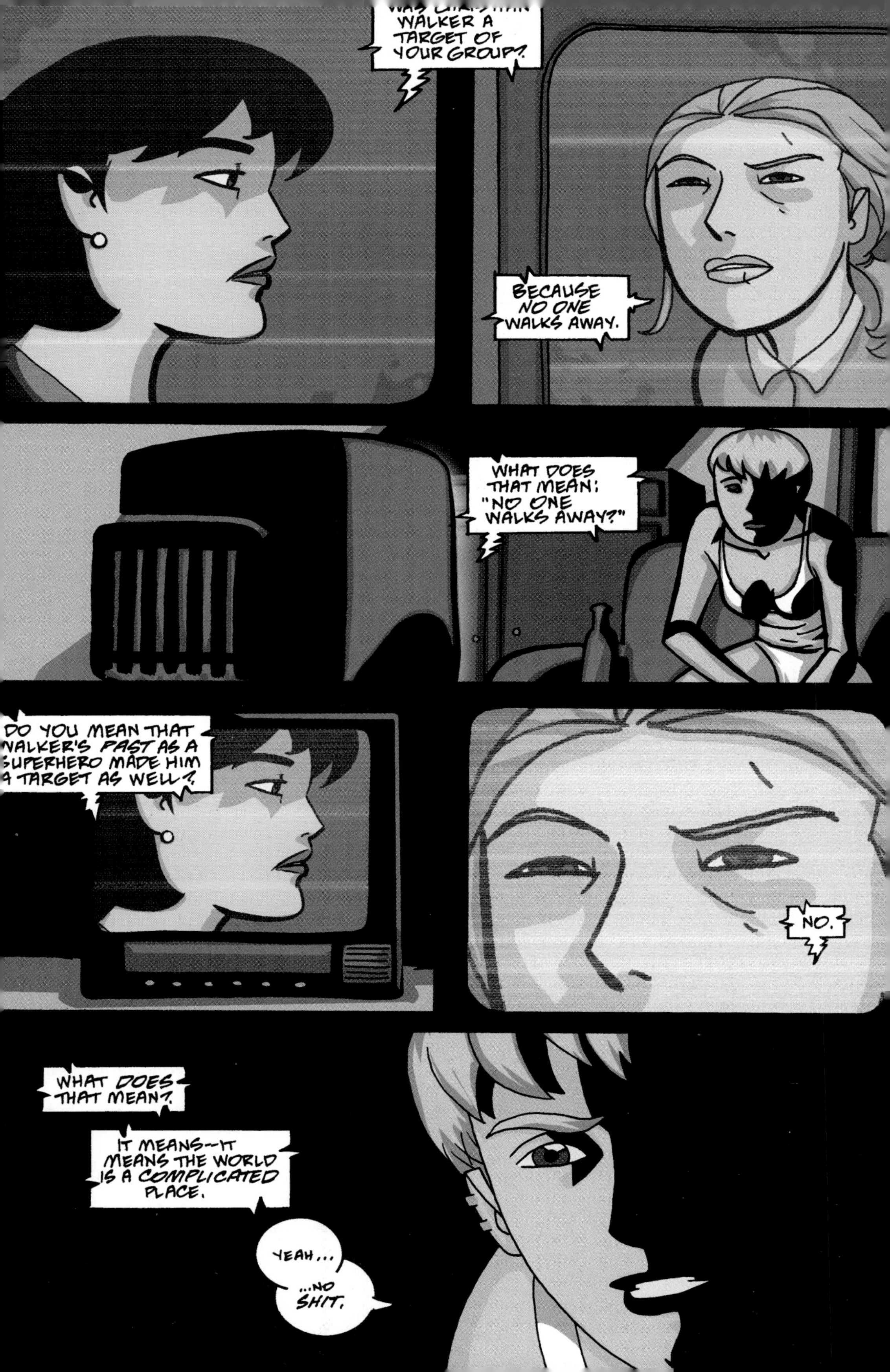
WALKER A TARGET OF YOUR GROUP?
BECAUSE NO ONE WALKS AWAY.
WHAT DOES THAT MEAN: "NO ONE WALKS AWAY?"
DO YOU MEAN THAT WALKER'S *PAST* AS A SUPERHERO MADE HIM A TARGET AS WELL?
NO.
WHAT *DOES* THAT MEAN?
IT MEANS--IT MEANS THE WORLD IS A *COMPLICATED* PLACE.
YEAH...
...NO *SHIT.*

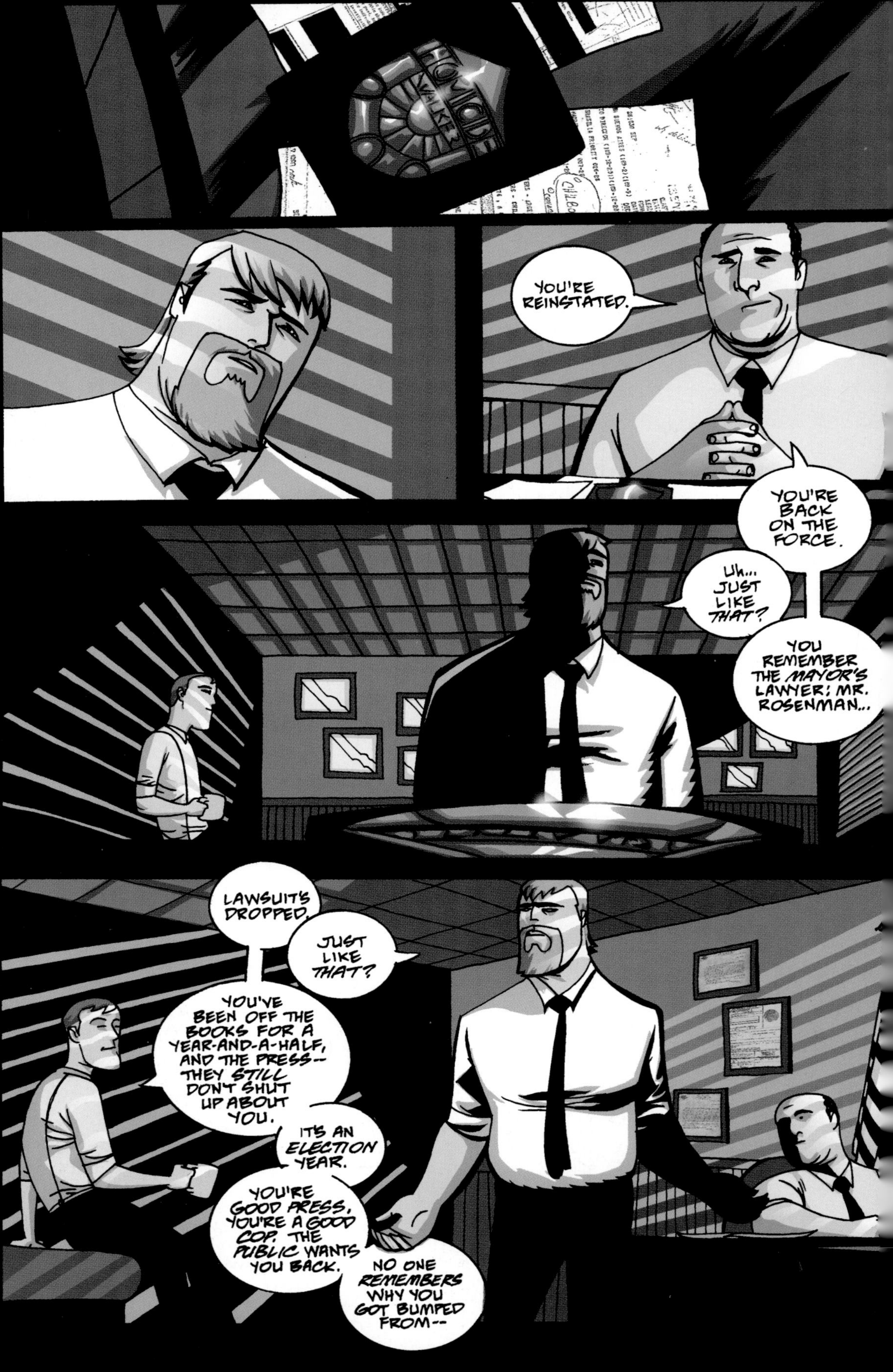
YOU'RE REINSTATED.
YOU'RE BACK ON THE FORCE.
Uh... JUST LIKE THAT?
YOU REMEMBER THE MAYOR'S LAWYER; MR. ROSENMAN...
LAWSUIT'S DROPPED.
JUST LIKE THAT?
YOU'VE BEEN OFF THE BOOKS FOR A YEAR-AND-A-HALF, AND THE PRESS-- THEY STILL DON'T SHUT UP ABOUT YOU.
IT'S AN ELECTION YEAR.
YOU'RE GOOD PRESS, YOU'RE A GOOD COP. THE PUBLIC WANTS YOU BACK.
NO ONE REMEMBERS WHY YOU GOT BUMPED FROM--

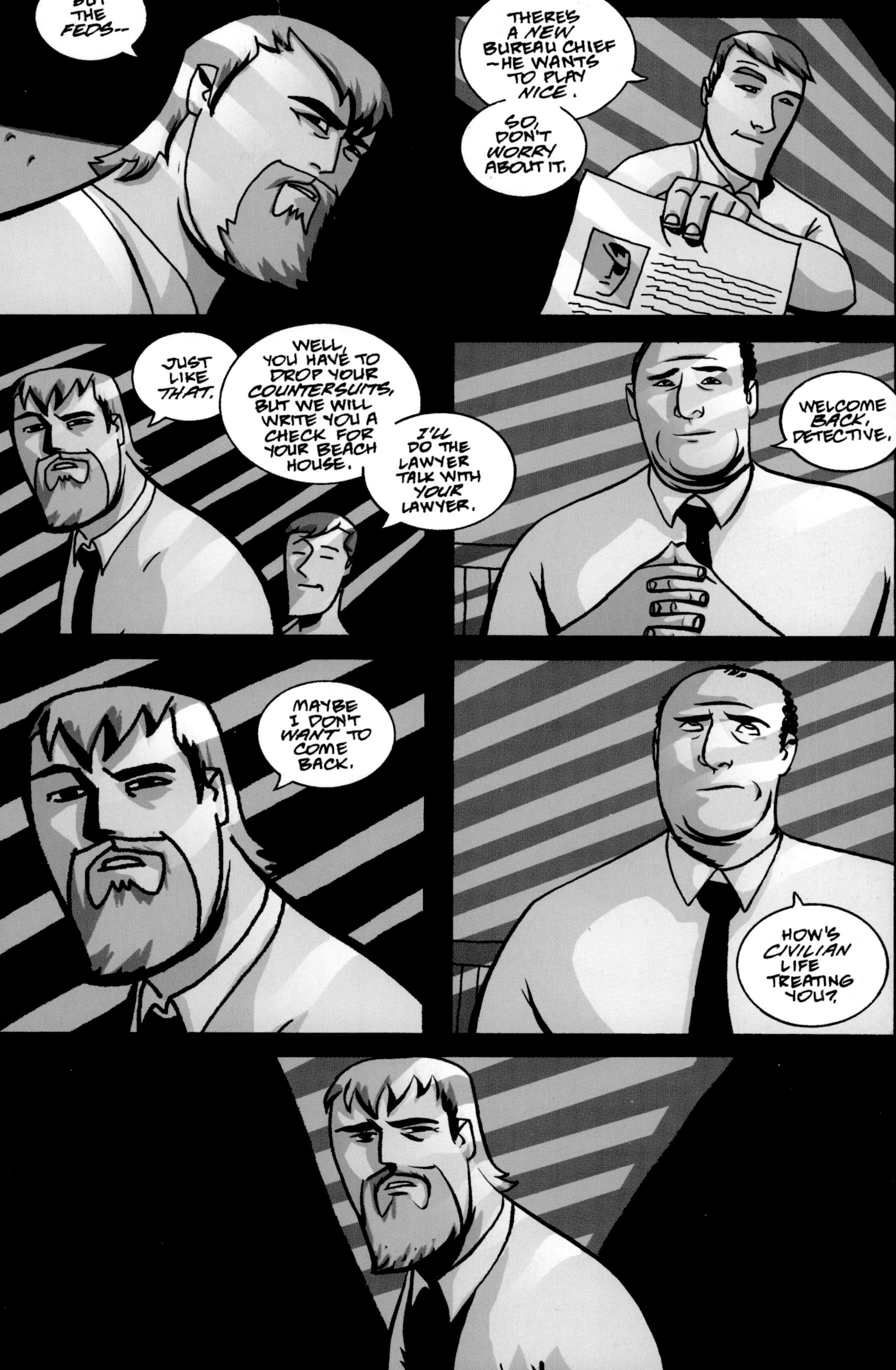
BUT THE FEDS--
THERE'S A NEW BUREAU CHIEF --HE WANTS TO PLAY NICE.
SO, DON'T WORRY ABOUT IT.
JUST LIKE THAT.
WELL, YOU HAVE TO DROP YOUR COUNTERSUITS, BUT WE WILL WRITE YOU A CHECK FOR YOUR BEACH HOUSE.
I'LL DO THE LAWYER TALK WITH YOUR LAWYER.
WELCOME BACK, DETECTIVE.
MAYBE I DON'T WANT TO COME BACK.
HOW'S CIVILIAN LIFE TREATING YOU?

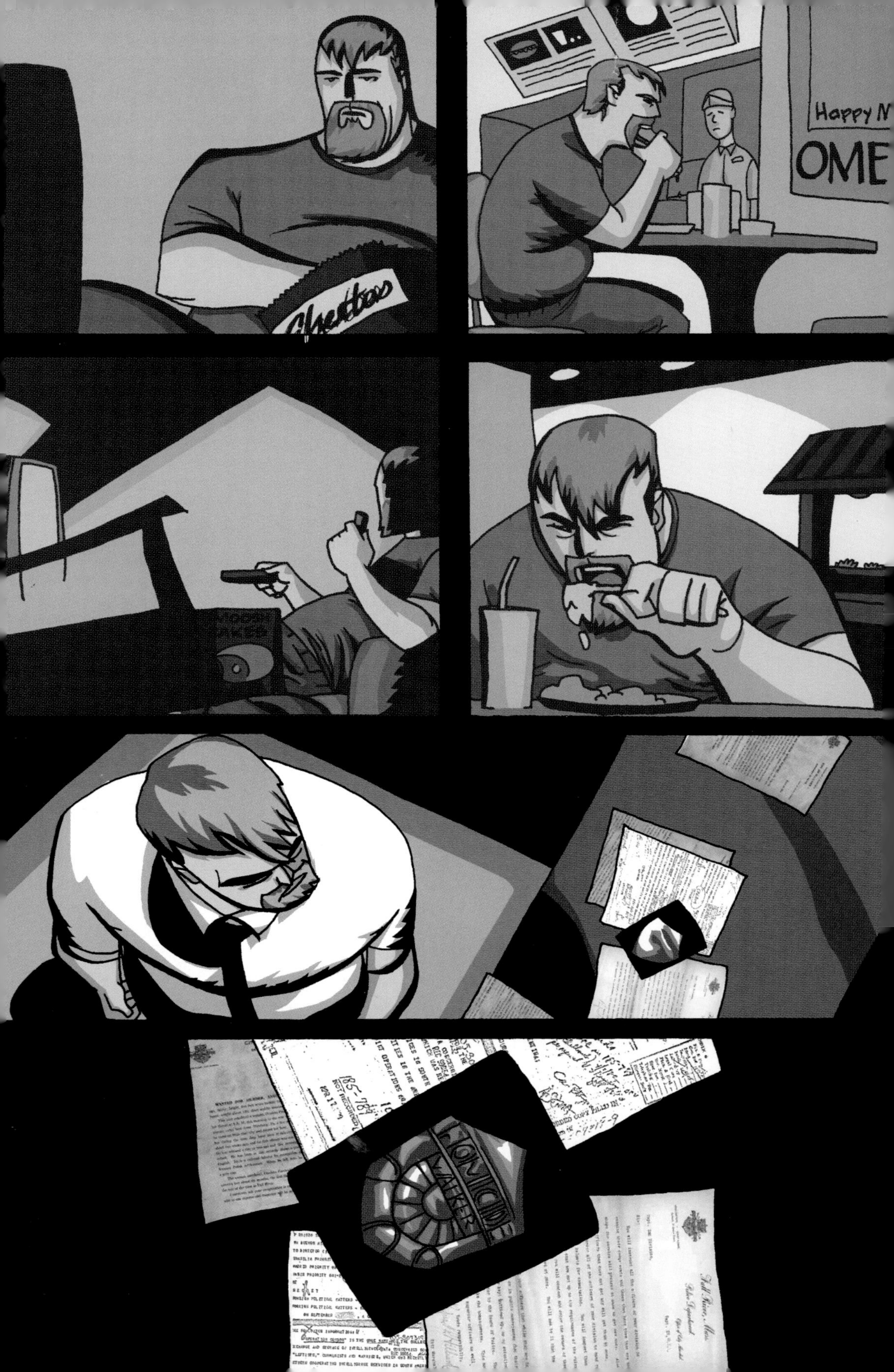
Happy N
OME

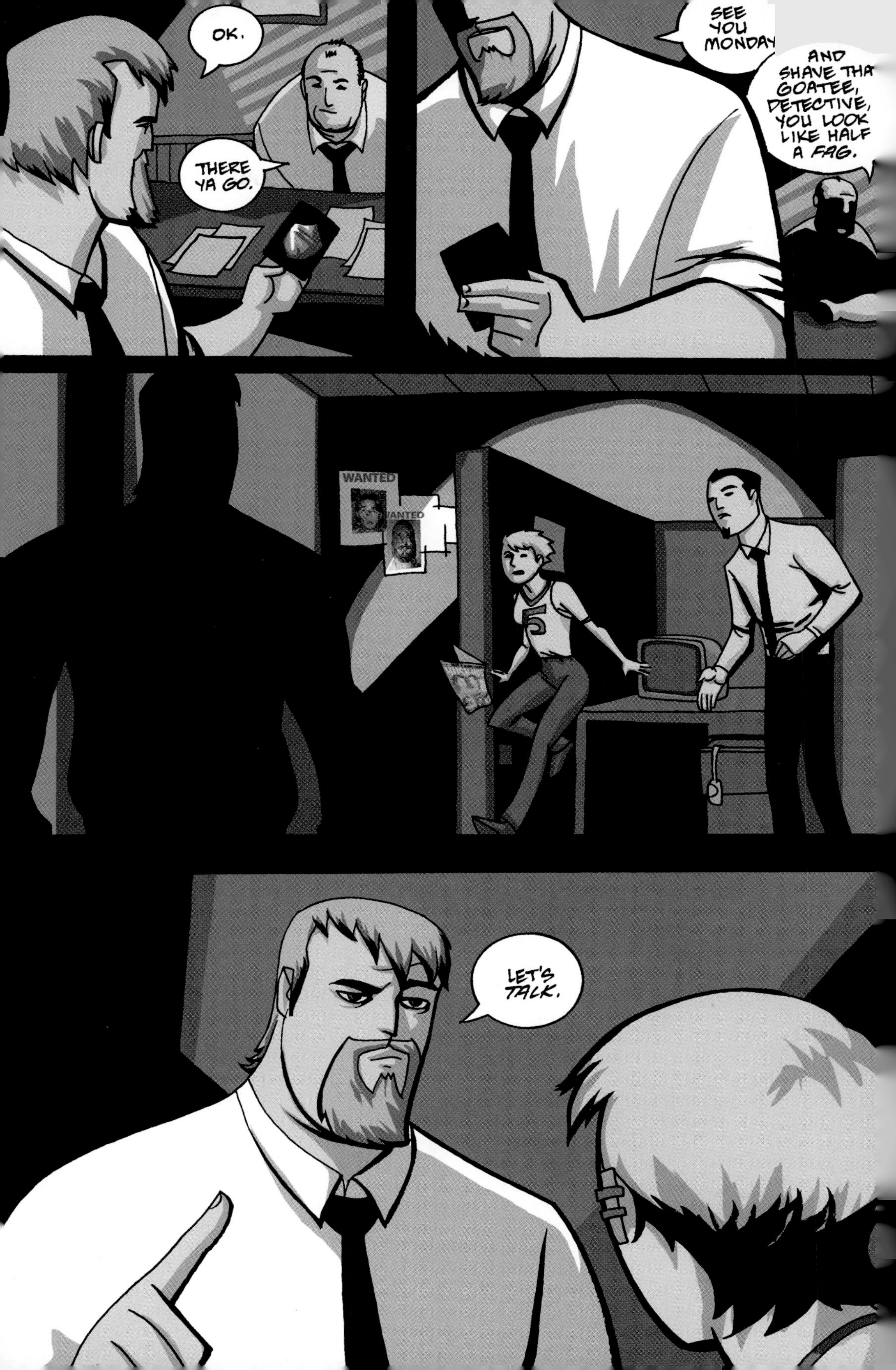
OK.
THERE YA GO.
SEE YOU MONDAY
AND SHAVE THA GOATEE, DETECTIVE, YOU LOOK LIKE HALF A FAG.
WANTED
WANTED
LET'S TALK.

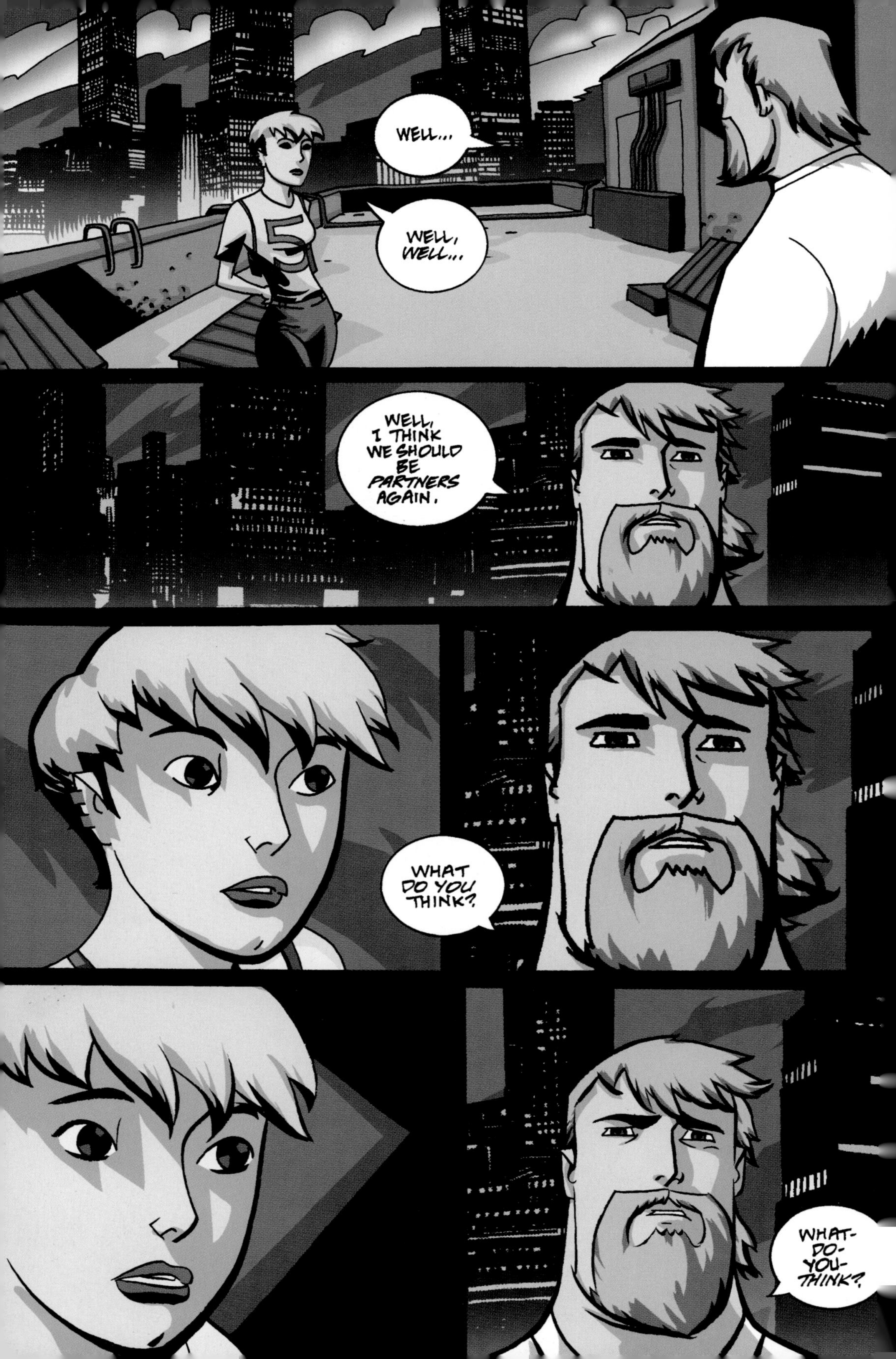
WELL...
WELL, WELL...
WELL, I THINK WE SHOULD BE PARTNERS AGAIN.
WHAT DO YOU THINK?
WHAT-DO-YOU-THINK?

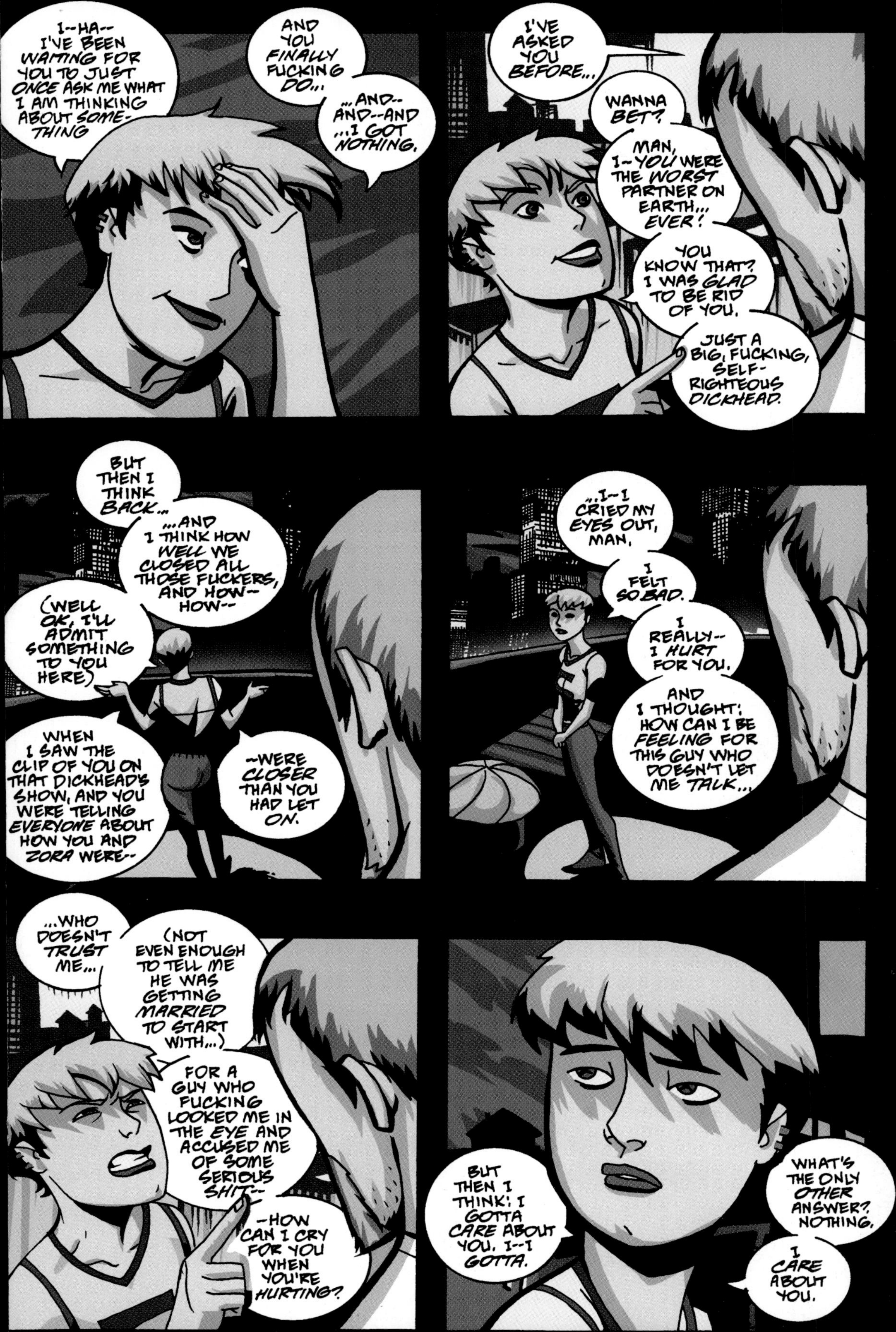
I--HA-- I'VE BEEN WAITING FOR YOU TO JUST ONCE ASK ME WHAT I AM THINKING ABOUT SOME-THING
AND YOU FINALLY FUCKING DO...
...AND-- AND--AND ...I GOT NOTHING.
I'VE ASKED YOU BEFORE...
WANNA BET?
MAN, I--YOU WERE THE WORST PARTNER ON EARTH... EVER!
YOU KNOW THAT? I WAS GLAD TO BE RID OF YOU.
JUST A BIG, FUCKING, SELF-RIGHTEOUS DICKHEAD.
BUT THEN I THINK BACK...
...AND I THINK HOW WELL WE CLOSED ALL THOSE FUCKERS, AND HOW--HOW--
(WELL OK, I'LL ADMIT SOMETHING TO YOU HERE)
WHEN I SAW THE CLIP OF YOU ON THAT DICKHEAD'S SHOW, AND YOU WERE TELLING EVERYONE ABOUT HOW YOU AND ZORA WERE--
--WERE CLOSER THAN YOU HAD LET ON.
...I--I CRIED MY EYES OUT, MAN.
I FELT SO BAD.
I REALLY-- I HURT FOR YOU.
AND I THOUGHT: HOW CAN I BE FEELING FOR THIS GUY WHO DOESN'T LET ME TALK...
...WHO DOESN'T TRUST ME...
(NOT EVEN ENOUGH TO TELL ME HE WAS GETTING MARRIED TO START WITH...)
FOR A GUY WHO FUCKING LOOKED ME IN THE EYE AND ACCUSED ME OF SOME SERIOUS SHIT--
--HOW CAN I CRY FOR YOU WHEN YOU'RE HURTING?
BUT THEN I THINK: I GOTTA CARE ABOUT YOU. I--I GOTTA.
WHAT'S THE ONLY OTHER ANSWER? NOTHING.
I CARE ABOUT YOU.

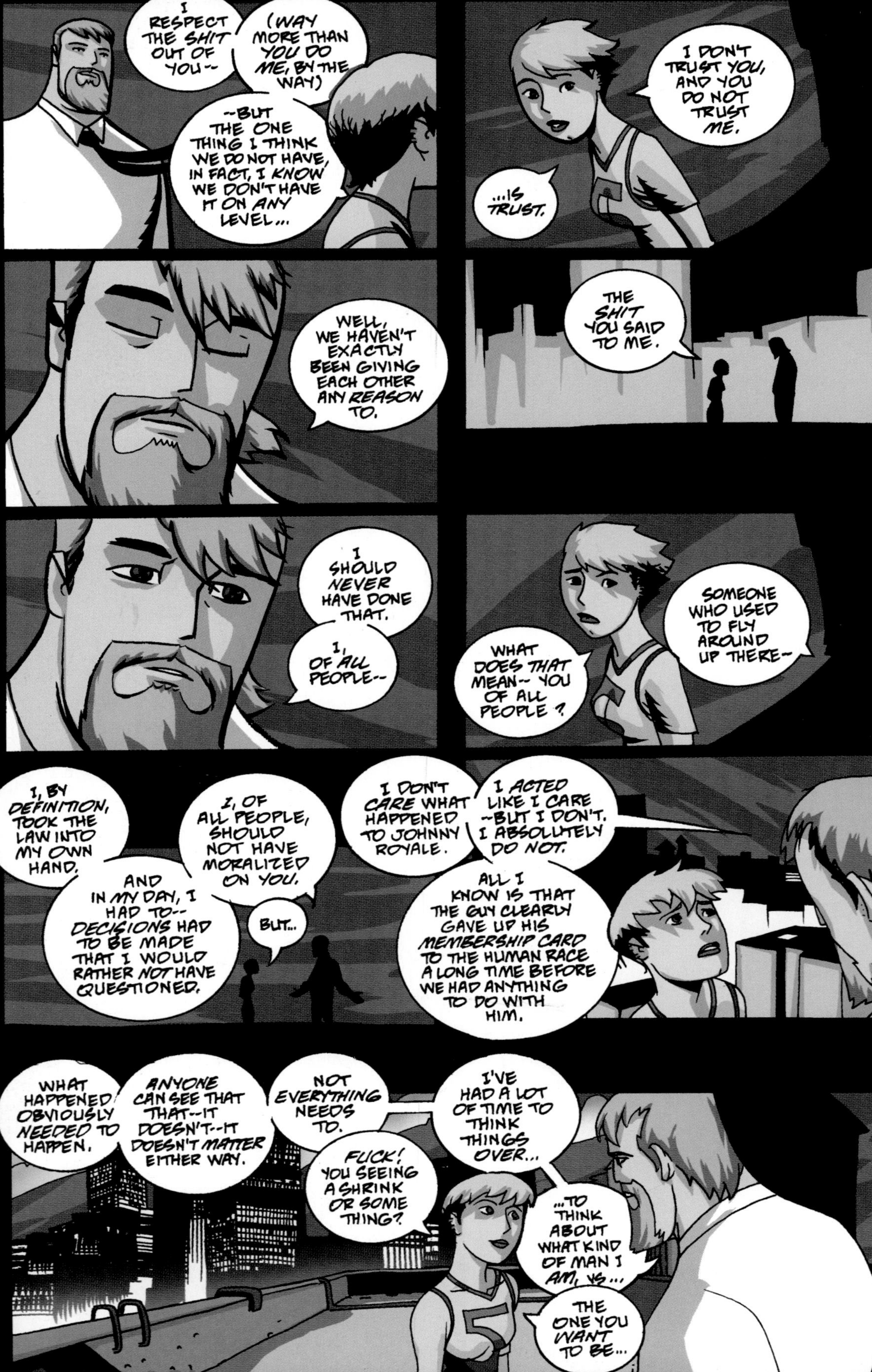
I RESPECT THE SHIT OUT OF YOU--
(WAY MORE THAN YOU DO ME, BY THE WAY)
--BUT THE ONE THING I THINK WE DO NOT HAVE, IN FACT, I KNOW WE DON'T HAVE IT ON ANY LEVEL...
...IS TRUST.
I DON'T TRUST YOU, AND YOU DO NOT TRUST ME.
WELL, WE HAVEN'T EXACTLY BEEN GIVING EACH OTHER ANY REASON TO.
THE SHIT YOU SAID TO ME.
I SHOULD NEVER HAVE DONE THAT.
I, OF ALL PEOPLE--
WHAT DOES THAT MEAN-- YOU OF ALL PEOPLE?
SOMEONE WHO USED TO FLY AROUND UP THERE--
I, BY DEFINITION, TOOK THE LAW INTO MY OWN HAND.
I, OF ALL PEOPLE, SHOULD NOT HAVE MORALIZED ON YOU.
AND IN MY DAY, I HAD TO-- DECISIONS HAD TO BE MADE THAT I WOULD RATHER NOT HAVE QUESTIONED.
BUT...
I DON'T CARE WHAT HAPPENED TO JOHNNY ROYALE.
I ACTED LIKE I CARE --BUT I DON'T. I ABSOLUTELY DO NOT.
ALL I KNOW IS THAT THE GUY CLEARLY GAVE UP HIS MEMBERSHIP CARD TO THE HUMAN RACE A LONG TIME BEFORE WE HAD ANYTHING TO DO WITH HIM.
WHAT HAPPENED OBVIOUSLY NEEDED TO HAPPEN.
ANYONE CAN SEE THAT THAT--IT DOESN'T--IT DOESN'T MATTER EITHER WAY.
NOT EVERYTHING NEEDS TO.
I'VE HAD A LOT OF TIME TO THINK THINGS OVER...
FUCK! YOU SEEING A SHRINK OR SOME THING?
...TO THINK ABOUT WHAT KIND OF MAN I AM, VS...
THE ONE YOU WANT TO BE...

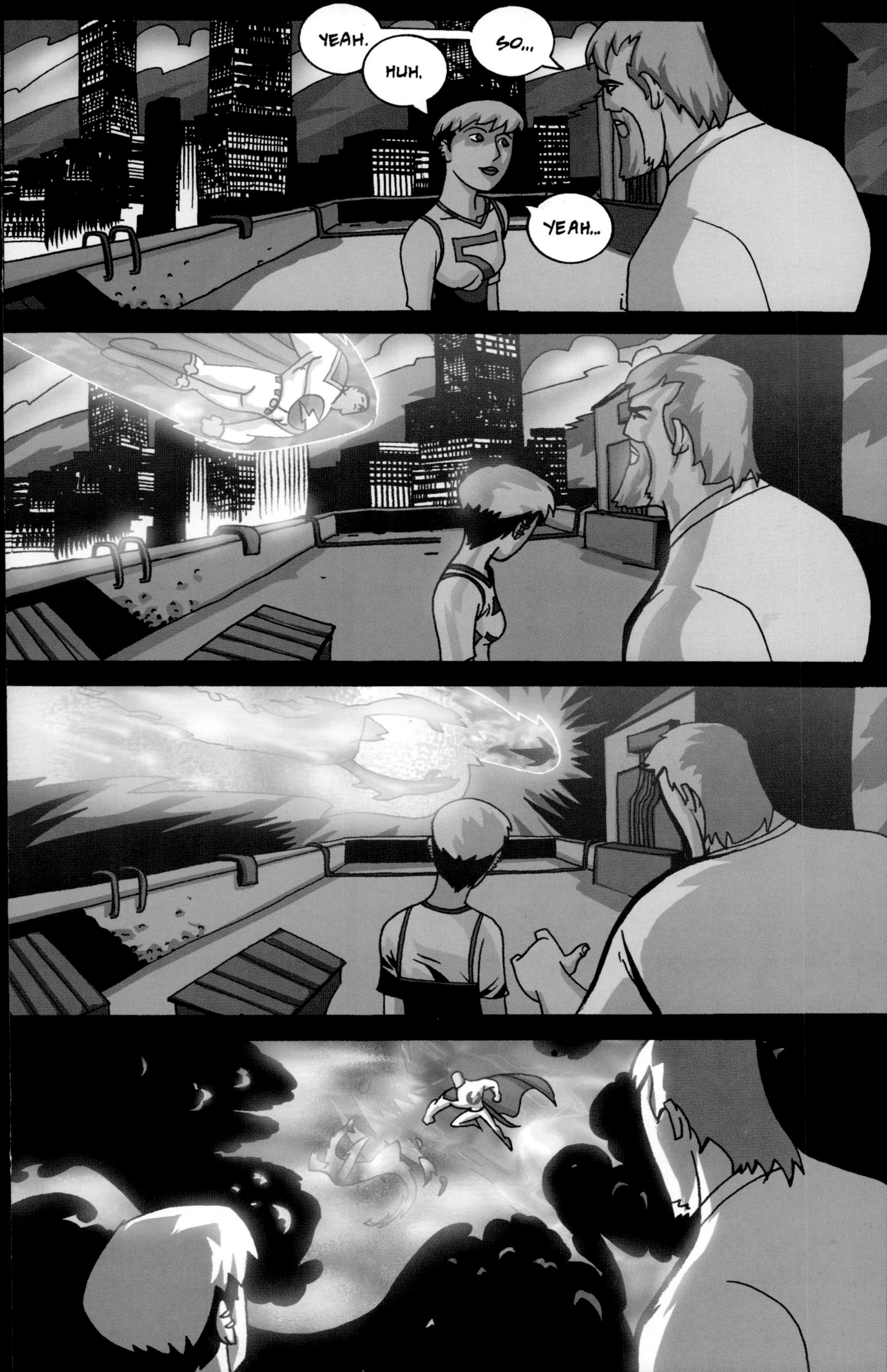
YEAH.
HUH.
SO...
YEAH...

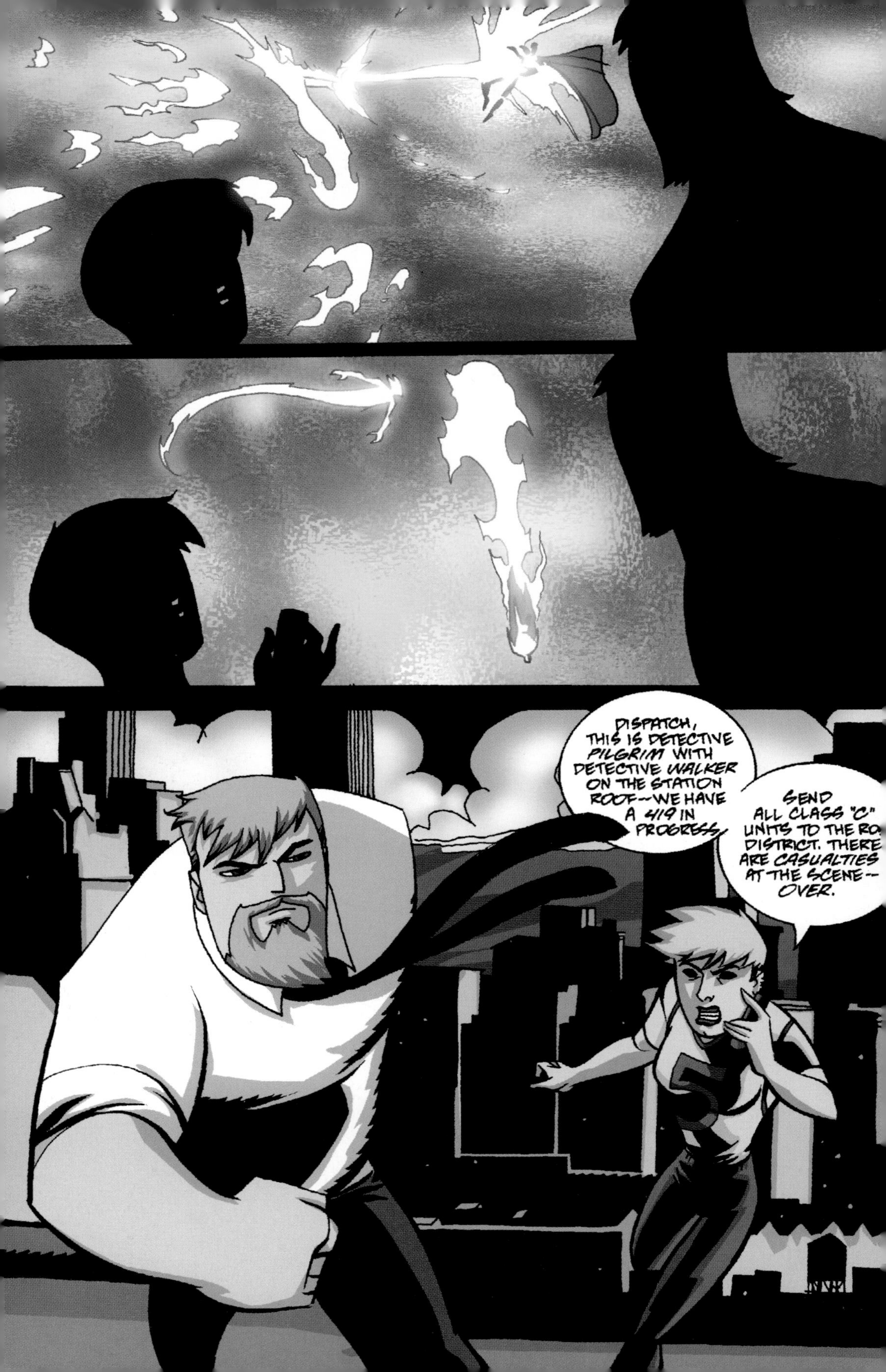
DISPATCH, THIS IS DETECTIVE PILGRIM WITH DETECTIVE WALKER ON THE STATION ROOF--WE HAVE A 419 IN PROGRESS.
SEND ALL CLASS "C" UNITS TO THE RO DISTRICT. THERE ARE CASUALTIES AT THE SCENE-- OVER.

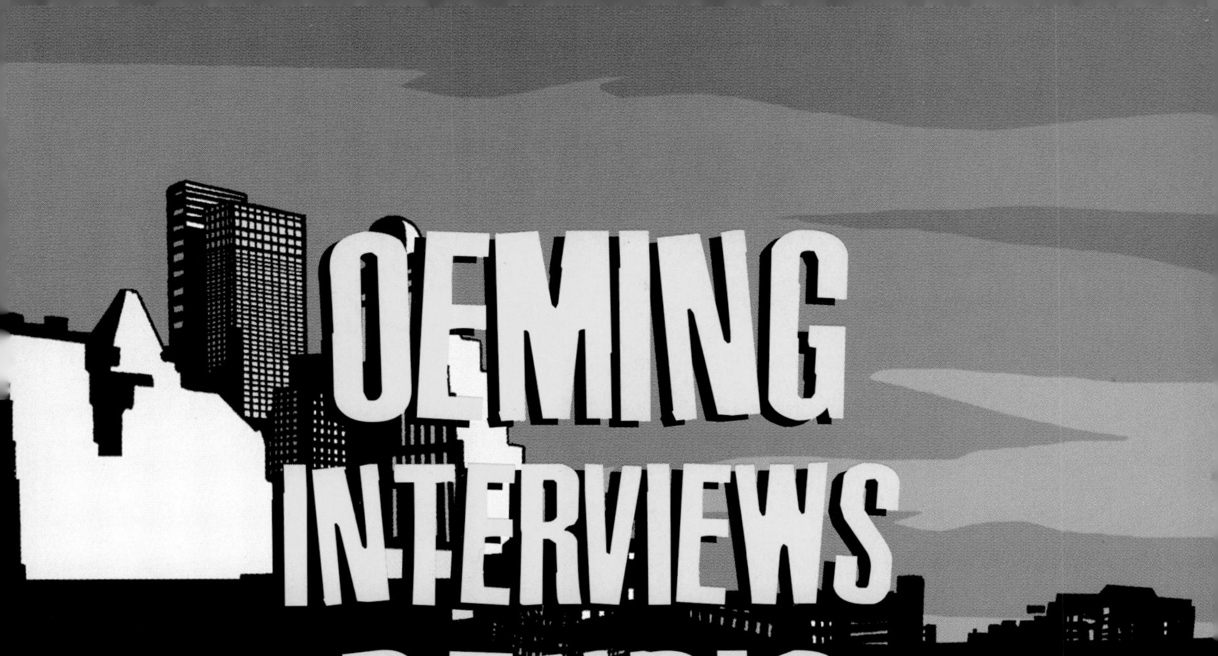

OEMING INTERVIEWS BENDIS AND VICE VERSA

So, this is something you don't see everyday. The creative team of the comic you just read raking each other over the coals a bit. We always thought our private talks were more interesting than the interviews we gave, so here, exclusively for you, is an unedited discussion between Mike and myself on everything that we could think of at the time we thought to do this. We may make this a regular feature in the collections.

This section also features rough page layouts by Mike Oeming

OEMING: Why writing? Why have you chosen writing over art? I know one comes more naturally to you than the other and you never had a commercial style, but clearly you could be drawing some of your own stories, if not on a monthly basis, as a special issue or so. I could clearly see you drawing an *Alias* issue.

BENDIS: Life is opportunities. I took the art gigs when they came, both in comics and outside of comics. And now it's the writing gigs that are coming. I just read a great quote: "A career is about what you say no to." That is so true. I think about what I have decided not to do and why and wipe my brow in relief, you know? I supported myself as a graphic artist for almost twelve years. I will draw again. I love to do it. Plus, I am so much more successful as a writer, it's almost sad.

OEMING: You started as an artist, doing work for local mags and papers, even doing caricatures—at what point did you want to start writing?

BENDIS: The first time I drew a caricature at someone's fucking nightmare *bar mitzvah*. That did pay well and it funded all my crime graphic novels, but it has to be the lowest form of artistic expression on the planet, I really hated it. And as I hated it more and more my caricatures got meaner and meaner.

What is the worst job you ever took for money? And don't say *Powers*, ass.

OEMING: It was last year. I did the cover to a children's book called *The Blue Avenger*. I thought it would be fun. Hey, this is a "real book" I'd be doing a cover to. It pays really well, too. But nothing on this earth is worse than a book editor. They know everything about words, but nothing about pictures. Example, they say they want a Zebra, so I give them a Zebra, but then they ask for no stripes. I say, then it will look like a horse...No, they say, they want a Zebra, just no stripes. So I do it...Then they say it doesn't look like a Zebra. This story had something to do with a donut. So I drew one in the background like they wanted. Well, I put sprinkles on it, because without sprinkles or something, it just looks like a tire. They say "make it glazed," so I do and it looks like a tire. I assure them with colors, it will look like it's glazed. Then they say it looks too literal, it should be a "cosmic donut." No shit. So I made it look like there was space swirling out of the fucking thing like it's giving birth to the universe. In the end, I don't think any of us were happy with it. This was worse than doing porn comics in the early '90s, because at least then I could get excited, jerk off, and get something out of it. But this was pure torture.

When did writing really click for you, meaning you went beyond writing stuff to facilitate your art to where the art was there to facilitate your writing?

BENDIS: It was never about writing only to facilitate my art. It was more about just overall storytelling. The only thing odd about the whole thing is how natural the expression of writing is for me and what a struggle

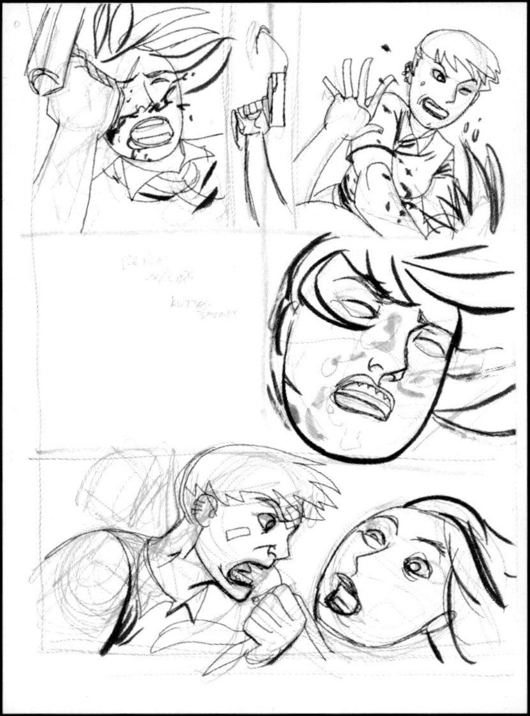

drawing is and was, and yet I wasn't even considering the idea of writing for a living, because that seemed just insane to me.

Why did you start drawing? Not when, why?

OEMING: I'd always drawn because of my mom. She would draw a lot. She had a drinking problem (well, actually drinking wasn't the problem, she did that fine, but the rest of her life went to shit) and I had to be raised by my Aunt and Uncle for about four to seven years. For the first five, she didn't live with us, she was trying to get sober, but still drinking. Anyway, she'd write me letters with drawings in them. I've always associated art with life, I guess, because of that. I remember once getting a letter from her with some happy clowns on it she drew. For the most part, I was patient, I knew what was wrong with her and it was just a waiting game until she got better. But when I got that letter, it set me off. Usually she drew flowers and butterflies, but this had happy clowns on it and I guess a happy clown was the last thing I felt like. I remember ripping it up. I was about five. The only thing worse than the happy clowns was ripping them apart. We kept drawing though, and it became a cheap pastime.

I stopped drawing shortly after mom came to live with us. I think I didn't "need" it anymore, but most importantly, I remember a teacher telling me a drawing I did wasn't very good and that I was much better than that. So I stopped. I didn't really draw for a long time after that. A few times, but not all the time like I had been. Then I moved from Jersey to Texas (mom and I did this once before when I was younger and she first got custody of me, but we came back to Jersey, in about he 6th grade and it was terrible for me. I didn't adjust at all. It was actually traumatic. I locked myself in my room, I learned to jerk off properly and read comics. Funny how those two go together so well. Anyway, I found comics at a flea market and fell in love with Spider-Man all over again. I started tracing and tracing. We moved back to Jersey, I went from tracing to copying o drawing. Then *X-Men Annual* #9 came out and it was all over for me. Art Adams made me want to be a comic book artist for sure, and I've been on that path ever since.

Before Robert McKee's *Story*, what was your major writing influence? Was it simply reading other writers that turned you on, or was there a specific school of thought that you worked on? Or was it mostly instinctual?

BENDIS: I was taken away by three writers: Richard Price, David Mamet, and Woody Allen. The three best dialogue writers in the history of any medium. Characters that talk to each other and not at each other. I studied their work, and it sent me on a quest for the work they loved and I started reading that, and then I started making my own decisions as a writer. People hate when I say this, but I am totally self-taught, never took a class.

You write, as well. What are your influences other than *Penthouse Forum*?

OEMING: Well, not to kiss your ass because I've already got the *Powers* gig, but at this point it's you. Not so much what or how you write, but the things we discuss through the making of *Powers* have become the new tools I carry with me in writing and storytelling. There are writers and books you've introduced me to and ways to study a story that have equipped me with new writing skills. So you can only blame yourself when I'm off writing and not drawing *Powers*!

Before you, I was into superficial writing. I wrote stories around cool things, not around story. That was one problem with *Ship of Fools*. I gave Bryan Glass *ideas* to write around, a bunch of disjointed weird shit he had to try and put together in a story, so in the end it had no focus. We plan on reissuing *Ship of Fools* slightly rewritten and some art moved around to open up the story and give it focus. At that point, my main writing influences were Mike Baron from *Nexus*, which I feel is the best overall series ever written, and Douglas Adams of *Hitchhiker's Guide*. I still love that stuff.

BENDIS: Also, not many people know how many things you can do and how varied your art and linework can be. What got you on the road you are on now?

OEMING: Shortly before *Powers*, I think I had finally started on a good "realistic style." I did a short *Kabuki* story like that. But then at the same time, that's when my career hit a dead end (like a lot of pros in the mid-90s crash) and I had to get a "real job." My son Ethan was born so I needed to bring in money on a regular basis. So, with the new job and baby came less time to work, so I needed to focus on a more simple, less time-consuming drawing style. It had really started about a year earlier when I was really trying to be Alex Toth, but then I found Bruce Timm and married the two in a way that worked and was less time consuming. Don't think you can just jump into a simple style, it's actually very difficult at first stripping the work down like that. It really makes your weaknesses shine through; it takes a long time to develop. So I eased into it. I tried working on *Batman Adventures*, but I still couldn't do the style. I think I got real comfortable with it just as I started *Hammer of the Gods*. Then *Powers* happened and by that time I was really into it. Look at the first trade of *Powers* and the work coming out now, you can still see a progression. While it's still there, I've gotten pretty far away from Timm and Toth, almost more into general animation, especially during the *Supergroup* and *Anarchy* story arcs, when I was using the mono dead lines. They look like animation cells.

Was there a genre you were into before crime stories?

BENDIS: Marvel superhero comics.

OEMING: At what point did those crime stories really take hold of you?

BENDIS: Yeah, this is still odd to me, because I didn't know that this is what I wanted as a writer until I started writing. Everything that came out of me were these poppy Jim Thompson graphic novels and I didn't even know who he was. No one was more surprised than me. It's the idea that in crime fiction you can examine a character by really throwing him into a corner and seeing what he will do.

OEMING: Do you think that interest in crime comics, the idea of someone being thrown into a corner emotionally, is a reflection of your own experiences? I know like many people, you didn't have a perfectly happy childhood. Do you think any residual anger from when you were younger is what attracted you to crime stories?

You really introduced me to crime stories and noir. Who introduced it to you, or did you discover it, consciously or subconsciously? I've always been into European Mythology, but it wasn't until recently that it became conscious. I can trace it back to my childhood. How far does a fascination with crime stories go back for you?

BENDIS: Hmm...I started my love of the genre in comic form. All those crime comics like Steranko's and all the Munoz novels, really got under my skin. Then, like my writer heroes, I backtracked to find Jim Thompson and Hammett. I read every Thompson novel in a three week period, like I was taking a course in it.

Then I saw the *Visions of Light* documentary and they started talking about the rules of film noir. I knew them but I had never heard them spoken out loud before and when I heard them I literally stood up in the theatre and yelled, "Halleluiah," I knew that this was for me.

OEMING: When a story comes to you, what part of it comes first--the overall idea or specifics of the story?

BENDIS: Could be anything, sometimes it's just an image, like a dead superhero lying in a playground, or a one liner that you think is so good you start constructing a story about it for the soul purpose of publishing that one line.

When you read the script, what do you do, just read it through and take it in, or start thinking as the artist immediately? What goes on in that head of yours? We have never discussed that.

OEMING: I think I'm lucky, because images come to my head immediately. I really mean immediately, sometimes before I finish the sentence I know what the panel is going to be. I rarely even do a second layout or change a panel when I first draw it, unless it doesn't fit the story and you ask me to, which is fine. But images come to me like an attack, to the point that it's distracting. I think that comes from my childhood. My Aunt and Uncle always had the radio on--if the TV wasn't on, the radio was, and when we slept, we slept with the radio on. It was always easy listening, that '70s and '80s singer-songwriter stuff. Crosby, Stills, and Nash, James Taylor, Billy Joel, Cat Stevens, Carly Simon, Simon and Garfunkel, Gary Numan, Harry Chapin, that sort of stuff. All those songs had stories. So I'm sleeping there, or trying to sleep and listening to these songs. Each of them told a loose story and with my eyes closed, I saw the stories or played them out in my head. I'd have to say that singer-songwriters may have been the single most important writing influence on me; artistically as well, because that's where the immediate imagery comes from.

To this day I hear a song and I can build a story around it. That's where *Hammer of the Gods* came from, Led Zeppelin's "The Immigrant Song." *"We come from the lands of ice and snow, from the midnight sun and hot springs flow, the Hammer of the Gods will drive our ships to new lands, to fight the horde, sing and cry, 'Valhalla, I am coming!'"*

Those words made me write what became *Hammer of the Gods*, although it has little to do with the words of the song...well, except the last line, that's almost

Do you think in terms of the themes, then the story builds around that, or do you have an idea you bring the themes to?

BENDIS: After I decide on the story, I start questioning what the purpose of it is. I really don't think enough people do this—ask themselves why they are writing what they are writing. It needs to say something other than just being cool. And sometimes I clearly state the purpose in the material and other times I don't. I just let it hang there. And sometimes the theme can derail the original story and take it in another direction. You have to be open to it. You've seen me do that, do a 180° on what I told you the story was going to be, because the characters or theme dictate it.

OEMING: That's awesome. I try to do that, too. I either have the meaning and build the story around that or have a cool story with no meaning and then find that meaning and go back and work it in. Like in *Powers*, it's a superhero universe seen through the eyes of police. The theme is how it is observed by the media and everyday man. What came first, was it the media

he eyes of cops?

BENDIS: At first it was the clichés of the superhero genre through the harder eyes of the cops. And then when we both decided to add the *VH-1 Behind the Music* twist to it, that every arc has some footing in a famous rock star story, and that's when it became magic to us. That's when I knew it was worth publishing, because now it was about a lot of things.

OEMING: How do you structure a story? I think now you mull it over in your head and then go straight to writing, but was there a time when you wrote step-by-step outlines and built it around that?

BENDIS: I think I learned how to do that, so now I am much more interested in fucking around with the three act structure. Like, with you I have shorthand, so I can

BENDIS: H
movie that
Ha!

Well, no. I
love a big a
another per
get slappe
write the ac
I like to lea
about it for

OEMING: V
in comics?
is the most

BENDIS: Ot
more into

...cally bums me out is I see a lot of comics that were failed movie pitches, or people writing comics to sell as properties. Now, we both have had the luck of selling movie properties, including *Powers*—but we never, ever, ever consciously created something for that purpose. Comics are a vital medium and form of expression and entertainment, not a stepping stone or a slum for your shit *Aliens* knock-offs. I really hate all the clutter that is thrown into *Previews* that is so clearly made to get Hollywood's attention.

OEMING: What is it specifically about the writers you admire? The work, not the person. Greg Rucka, for instance.

BENDIS: He is a real writer. He is the best technical writer I have ever met or talked to. And he isn't afraid to talk about the craft, like so many are. Many writers are afraid to talk about it because they think people will find out how full of shit they are.

OEMING: Mamet.

BENDIS: There's so much I couldn't even type it here. He is my guru. I have a huge book of interviews by him that I keep on my nightstand like the Bible, I go to it if I am lost. Seriously.

OEMING: Alan Moore.

BENDIS: He's the gold standard. He's like our DeNiro. He is so good so often that he is often taken for granted. I won two consecutive best writer Eisners, and I don't think I did anything as inventive as anything he did in one double-page spread of *Promethea*. It seems insane to me that his books aren't higher on the charts. But listen, he's a witch living in the blue dimension, so he's fine.

Okay, I got some for you. Mike Mignola.

OEMING: He's my Mamet. Honestly, when I am lost or uninspired, I flip through his work. The looseness, especially. He's not afraid of the line, he's not a slave to it, he rules it! I love tight artists, I really do, but the tight lines often suck the life out of their work. Mike's lines are so loose they can be sloppy and abstract and still work. Besides the lines, Mike's work exudes a mood I find almost hypnotic. He is mythology on the page, his work evokes the subconscious.

BENDIS: Alex Toth.

OEMING: Storytelling and black spotting. While he doesn't do storytelling like I do, I like a much more "in-between" feel to the panels, he cuts to the chase. He's the master of simplicity and yet his work is more complex than most. He's a genius and a master of the medium. His black spotting and composition is just something few, if any, can compare to. My favorite work of his is the late '60s into the early '80s. I still write him from time to time and he writes back.

BENDIS: Bruce Timm.

OEMING: He actually helped me understand Alex Toth's work better. From Timm, I learned a lot about form, keeping the exterior of a body simple, smooth lines on the outside that make the character flow, not interrupted by lines that break the form. Timm flows better than any artist I know of.

BENDIS: Adam Hughes.

OEMING: Adam taught me a lot. Hands on. I worked with him when we lived in the same town. We met just before he broke into comics. He introduced me to Steve Rude's work (Neil Vokes showed him Rude, Neil showed me Toth and Timm, Neil is another big influence on me) and taught me a lot about storytelling. There is a panel in a *Star Trek* novel he did where there are guys running off a ship in line. He drew them as if it were animation, each guy in the next pose a person would be in, as if running, left foot, right foot, and in-betweens. We talked a lot about art and artists. He tends to like more refined artists while I like them looser and sloppy. Adam is also a very close friend.

BENDIS: Steranko.

OEMING: I've never been into Steranko's work. If you see any there, it's the Jack Kirby influence probably, or the influences of others. I love Jim's work, but didn't discover it until recently.

BENDIS: David Mack. In fact, let's gossip about all the shit we know about David Mack.

OEMING: I happen to know that David is a great wrestler and can fart really loud. Thankfully, he never farted on me when we wrestled. His design sense, the lack of respect for the borders of a page, really influenced me. You can see that a lot in *Bulletproof Monk* and in the *Oni Press Color Special* issue with the *Powers* story we goofed around on. All done in love. He's also in need of Ritalin.

What is something you see in your favorite writers (not one I mentioned above) that you like the least?

BENDIS: Well, I think I get annoyed at how criticized they are by people who don't get it. I get very annoyed at how much shit Aaron Sorkin gets from critics when his work is so vastly superior to everything else on television, it's amazing to me.

You hate *The Watchmen*? Explain this travesty.

OEMING: I don't hate it, it just doesn't get me. I think it's because it's been so influential on other books that when I try reading it, all those lessons have been used in good and bad ways so the effect is watered down when I read the original. I've tried reading it three times, and not once does it interest me. Now don't get me wrong, I love Alan Moore. I even love his music. In fact, there are ways I like his music more than the...

writing. I love most of his work. *Parliament of Justice* s very influenced by *V For Vendetta*. I just don't "get" *Watchmen*. It's just a mental shortcoming on my part. 'd die to work with Moore.

BENDIS: For a life-long comic professional, you don't seem very into comics on a monthly basis. Do you read a lot of comics? What do you read, what's your favorite comic? Why are you so standoffish to the business on some levels?

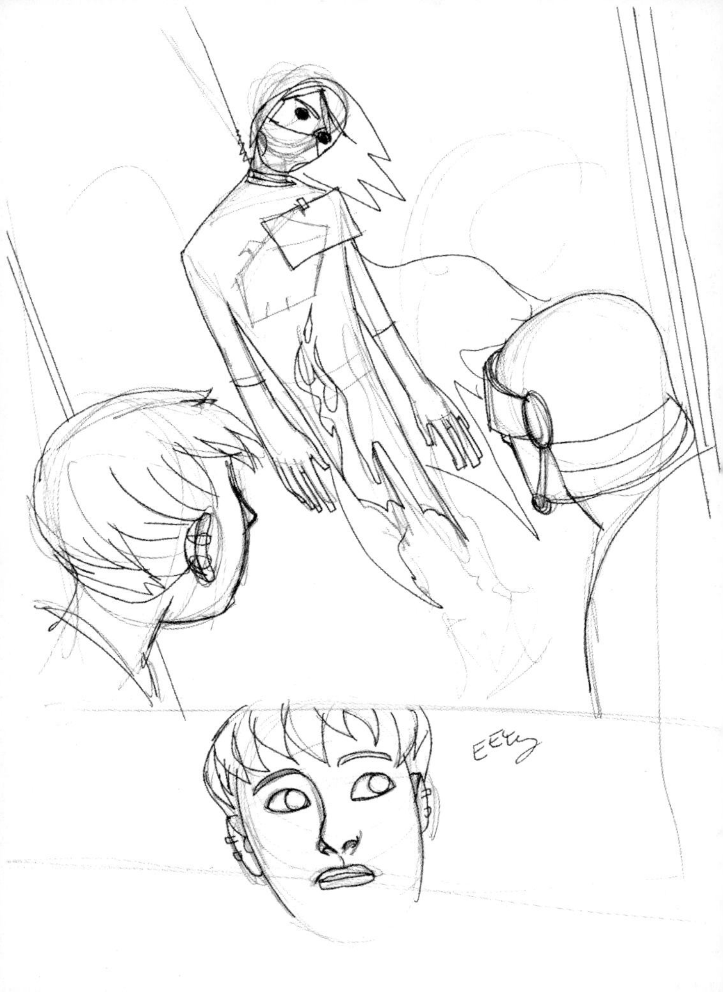

EE

DEMING: It's odd, but it's like this with a lot of comics people I know. The more you make comics, the less you read them. Nothing makes me more happy than writing or drawing comics, but reading them doesn't hold my interest. In fact, I rarely read the finished product of my own book. I think the last issue of *Powers* read when it was done is like issue #7. No shit. Same with *Hammer*. But with *Bastard*, I did read those when t was done to measure if we went too far in not explaining everything or *Parliament* because it was

Neil and I, and t
part I don't read
not reading the

I've been readi
love those. I've
than *Hellboy*, I c
away from the b
what new books
I feel that if it's r

in stories, I look
but it has to hav
there are ridicu
it's all true and

What's one of th
writing? Where
reading a book?

BENDIS: Well

my comfort zone, there are things I know I do well, and there are things I do not know if I do well, so I am trying to do them to experience it and see if it works. In *Powers*, particularly, I have attempted styles and genres I never thought I would try, specifically to see why.

What's the one thing about your art that you think you need to improve and why? And why haven't you tried it yet? And what are you waiting for?

OEMING: Hah, taking my time! I'd really love to have a project where I can slow down and think the shit out of each page and the story as a whole. Right now, it's largely instinct built from years of hands-on work, but I'd like to approach a project with no time restraints and really work it. I'd also like to work on my backgrounds more. I think taking my time would help, but I'm a speed freak.

In *Powers*, we have total freedom to do whatever we want or what the story wants us to do. At Marvel, you don't have that freedom. You have editors and bosses and characters that have to maintain a continuity. I've found that what you've done with *Daredevil* is amazing, you actually found room for character growth there, something rare and hard to do in a mainstream, established series. How much does that hold you back? Especially on *Ultimate Spider-Man*, I imagine there's much less you can do. Shouldn't Mary Jane be smoking pot and having sex with Peter?

BENDIS: Who says she doesn't? Well, I don't see the limitations at Marvel as limitations. I see them as opportunities to be creative. I read this interview with Ridley Scott recently and he said nothing makes him more inspired than a budget, he said every limitation put before him has created a situation where he forced himself to be more creative than he would have been otherwise. I have the same feeling. Also, it's the juxtaposition of creator-owned and work-for-hire that has made my work so fulfilling to me. Both experiences have pros and cons and I find they feed off each other, I think it has a lot to do with the way a lot of people have responded to my work.

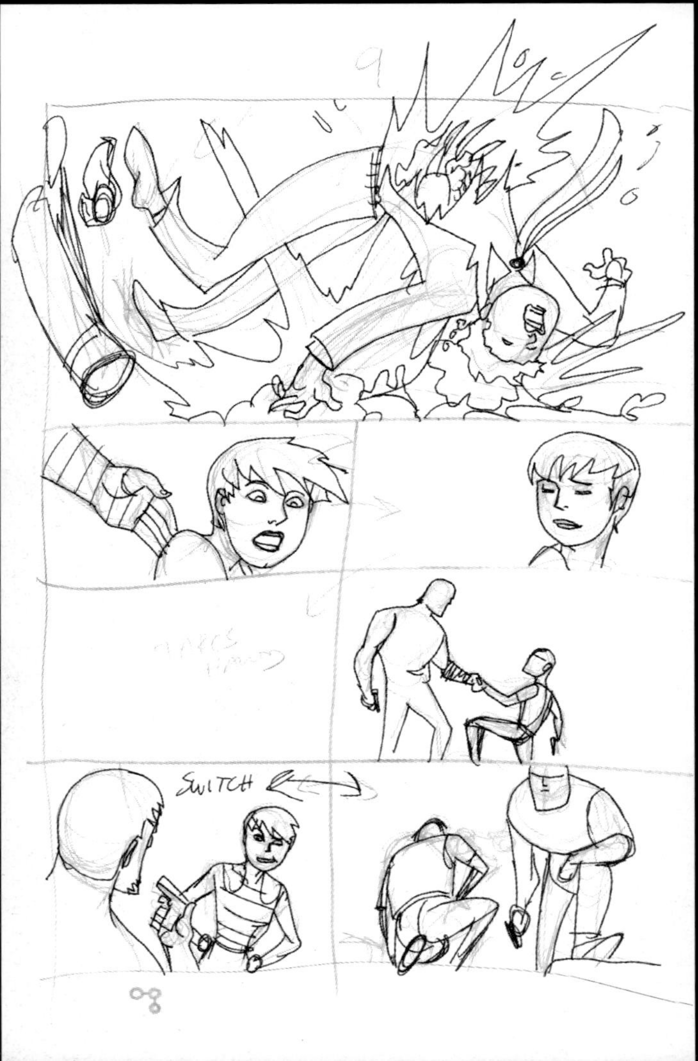
SWITCH

Also, Marvel is pretty damn trusting of me and I have been allowed to go out on the plank many a time. Anal anyone? And I will forever be the guy who used the F-word in a Marvel comic first. See, you have had some unfulfilling work-for-hire experiences, you need a fulfilling one, and I am going to make you do one so you can experience how awesome it could be.

OEMING: *Great*! I can't wait. Maybe that's the one I can take my time on. Obviously drawing an issue of a comic takes longer than writing an issue of a comic--or at least it should. *Powers* is my love but also a monthly gig, which can be hard at times, grinding work.

BENDIS: Boo-hoo, wahh-wahh.

OEMING: I do my "side projects" really to keep me sane. Even though you write several books at a time, how do you keep any of those gigs from becoming stale?

BENDIS: If they got stale, I would bail in two seconds, life is too short. And it's my name on the cover. Also, I stay ahead of schedule, so sometimes I don't write, let's say, *Powers* for months at a time, and then write it constantly for weeks. I write it when I am inspired to. That's the real key to everything. You have the attention span of a ferret full of Snickers bars, so it's harder for you to focus, but you're also a martial arts master, so it's odd. You are a conundrum wrapped in a package of contradiction.

DEMING: Thanks! How much longer do you see *Powers* going?

BENDIS: It's over. Bye, Mike.

DEMING: We know the ending, and we've talked it over. Not in terms of issues or years, but how many story lines do you see coming up? We've promised to never write or draw *Powers* beyond the amount of fresh ideas we have.

BENDIS: Exactly, we'll know when it's time to wrap it up. I think both of us were surprised at how challenging this year was creatively, we really pushed each other. I don't feel like we're even near the end.

DEMING: We've done less police procedurals, which are my favorite stories.

BENDIS: Me, too. They're fun to write. Why are you so into them?

DEMING: The pacing. I have trouble mixing noir and heroes. Sometimes you have Pete darken and thicken the lines because I have that problem. When I see cops walk into a room with a dead superhero, however, it's all mood and shadows. People are in danger in the *Powers* universe, you never know when Deena, Walker, the Captain, whomever might get killed. I like the dirtiness of the work.

They do unfortunately have repeating conventions to the story that people think are tired or predictable. Like there must be a murder in a murder investigation, there must be a body, it must be a hero, etc. How do we continue to do those in such a way that our less astute readers won't perceive it as repetitious? *Homicide* and *Law and Order* do it every week.

BENDIS: Also, at this point, there are tons of *Powers* knock-offs. I know I sound like Howard Stern, but man, I look through *Previews* and I get a nosebleed. It's flattering and I welcome it, but a lot of these publishers are sucking rejected *Powers*, so it's funny. But I think we have the freedom and the vision to stay ahead of the pack, so that's not that much of a concern. I think that we certainly shocked people with the last couple of stories, I think most people know for certain that even if the story starts with a body, they don't know how it's going to end. But yeah, it's my favorite part, too. We'll get back to it very soon.

But you just like drawing the talking heads.

DEMING: How much do you listen to your detractors? I know we get tons of mail saying how great we are, but it's always the few that tell us we suck that bug us, or even worse, the shrug off. At what point do we take

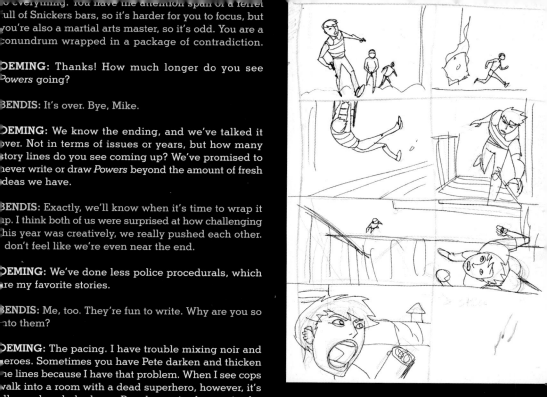

that into account? If we continually laugh it off, we can become one of the many burned out creators who only listen to the cheers who think they are still doing great work when it's actually crap.

BENDIS: That's a very good question. I don't know if I have an answer yet, because there's also the fact that it is absolutely impossible to make everyone happy. Every book I have ever been involved with has been someone's favorite and someone's least favorite, one person cried, the other person was bored, I don't know what the answer is. But a lot of times the critic tells you where he is coming from, which qualifies the critique. In the review he will say, "I wish *Powers* was more photo realistic." And we have to look at that and say, "Well, it's not, so what's your point?" That's like saying, "I wish *The Matrix* was funnier." They weren't trying to be funny, so why even analyze it like that? Or a critic will say, "I have been reading comics for fifty five years and Stan Lee could have told that story in six pages." Like somehow I don't know I am taking a different approach to the scenes than they did in the '60s, like somehow that idea totally eludes me. So, I don't know. Our approval rating is pretty high and people do vote with their wallets, so I guess that's really what you have to listen to. But even then, how much do you give people what they think they want versus what you need to say as a storyteller? See? No easy answer, I do not know. I think the best thing we both have done is not spend our time online arguing with work speak for itself. A lot of our peers bury themselves with online arguments when they should be working on the book. What it does do for me is it makes me work harder, because I know there's no bullshit that will fly, the people speak out. You know? But I know that sometimes my critics annoy you a lot, more than they do me. Also, people don't even get when they are reacting exactly how we want them to, like with a tease or a cliffhanger, some people get so fucking angry about a cliffhanger and they don't even see how much fun they are having. I'm like, "See, you care. It's fun."

I know in your porn chatrooms, you get a lot of criticism for your flowery metaphors, how do you deal with it?

OEMING: I deal with it in a big, pink bunny suit...Anyway, often in *Powers* I'm running against deadlines and can take shortcuts, such as not doing a full background or keeping the camera too close too often to avoid drawing more. Aside from that, what do you think I have to work on the most in my work?

BENDIS: I think you need to be more photo realistic. My only concern with you has always been style consistency, you have so many things you can do and so many tools at your disposal that you often forget the power of a consistent line through a story arc. We talk about that a lot. But this is a problem of you being too talented and eating too much sugar more than anything else.

OEMING: That's true, I especially think you see that in this compilation. As of *Foreverman*, however, I've decided to stay with the brush. I think I got the pen out of my *Powers* system. What about yourself? what is your biggest weakness? I don't mean the stuff you stay away from writing, like fantasy or group books, but in the work that you do, what is your weakest ability?

BENDIS: Clearly I have trouble with the format of a comic. I have trouble keeping to my page count and have for years. I either go over my page count or take a scene that could be a nice four pager and I cram it into two pages because I have no wiggle room. It bothers me. Also, I can't spell almost to the point of retardation, and like when I won all those nice awards this summer, I felt like a fake or something. Why don't I know the difference between "their" and "they're"? I mean, I know the difference, but I don't do it.

OEMING: If I had to name one weakness in your work, I'd have to say it was your inability to self-edit. I'm sure you see how much you actually cut out, but sometimes I look at the amount of words on a page and it goes beyond a wordy page to an impossibly wordy page. Sometimes I can't understand why there are so many words on a page. Sometimes there's as many words as there is art. Why can't you look at a page and say, "I have to cut this way down"? I'm not complaining, hey, it's less for me to fucking draw! But on a scale of 1-10, sometimes you're on a 12 or 13 when it comes to

a page with too much dialogue.

BENDIS: See, that was a very wordy response, Mr. Blah Blah Blah! I agree in theory, and often I think you are surprised by what I yank off the page at the last minute.

OEMING: Wait a minute, you "yank off" on the page? No, that doesn't surprise me...anyway, I know comics are limited in space, but instead of cramming lots of words into one place, why not change the pacing of the story so you end an issue on a different climax in order to pan out those dialogue scenes to make them fit without overcrowding the page? Just move the events down and find new climaxes if there's not enough room that issue?

BENDIS: See, I know I just gave you a bitch of a script this week and you are reeling, but, honestly, I fall in love with a particular cliffhanger, or a decide that this amount of story is worth the $2.95 we have to charge. I hate that comics are so expensive, so I try to cram a lot in. I feel very beholden to people to give them a good read.

But if I didn't write all those balloons, you'd have to draw backgrounds, so why are you pulling at this string?

OEMING: Hey, you said we had to ask the hard questions! Other than asking mean ones, like why you eat so much candy, I'm asking professional ones like this.

A major shift has happened in comics, where the art was more important than the story, to the point we had no stories. Erik Larsen even announced that writers were no longer needed! Now the shift has gone, thankfully, to the writers, but do you think in mainstream comics that's gone too far? Sometimes people just want to see shit blow up and men fight men. By sometimes I mean once an issue.

BENDIS: And, honestly, ninety percent of comics still do that. Only a few are allowed the arrogance/luxury to do whatever they want storywise. It just, to my shock above all others, there is a big audience for story driven-comics and most can wait for the fight scene, they don't need it.

OEMING: I know you're big into politics, but I never see it in your work, why is that? And please, don't change, I hate that whole world and those who drag it into their writing.

BENDIS: Oh, my politics, or I should say my feelings about politics, are all over my books. When you say politics, people think that means I'm like Susan Sarandon and I'm protesting and shit. No, I am aware and obsessed with the murky water that is our political process and how our government works. And more importantly how it affects us on a day-to-day basis, and *that* is all over my work. All my characters are oppressed by the man, as they are by your puritanical view of women.

OEMING: We love people talking about *Powers*, about the character stuff. At what point should we spell things out for people? Maybe long after we're done? People keep asking me if Deena killed Johnny Stomps, and I just ask them what they think. They also ask me why if Walker suspects she did it, why he doesn't really do anything about it.

BENDIS: As far as I can tell, most people get it, and then there's all the fun everyone has talking about it online. I say we let them have the fun. Why are you trying to spoil their fun, Mike? Fun-spoiling Nazi!

OEMING: I love when you write a character as an asshole and then we learn they are more valiant than most of the characters in that same world. *Powers* characters have a real depth. Do you find that in real

me very often?

BENDIS: Yes and no am talking to has sor don't. I guess that is what we want in life

OEMING: While it's will ever want to wr story? You have bee books, which you s write a really intellige much needed in that would bring out new

BENDIS: Well, techn comics. I mean, they

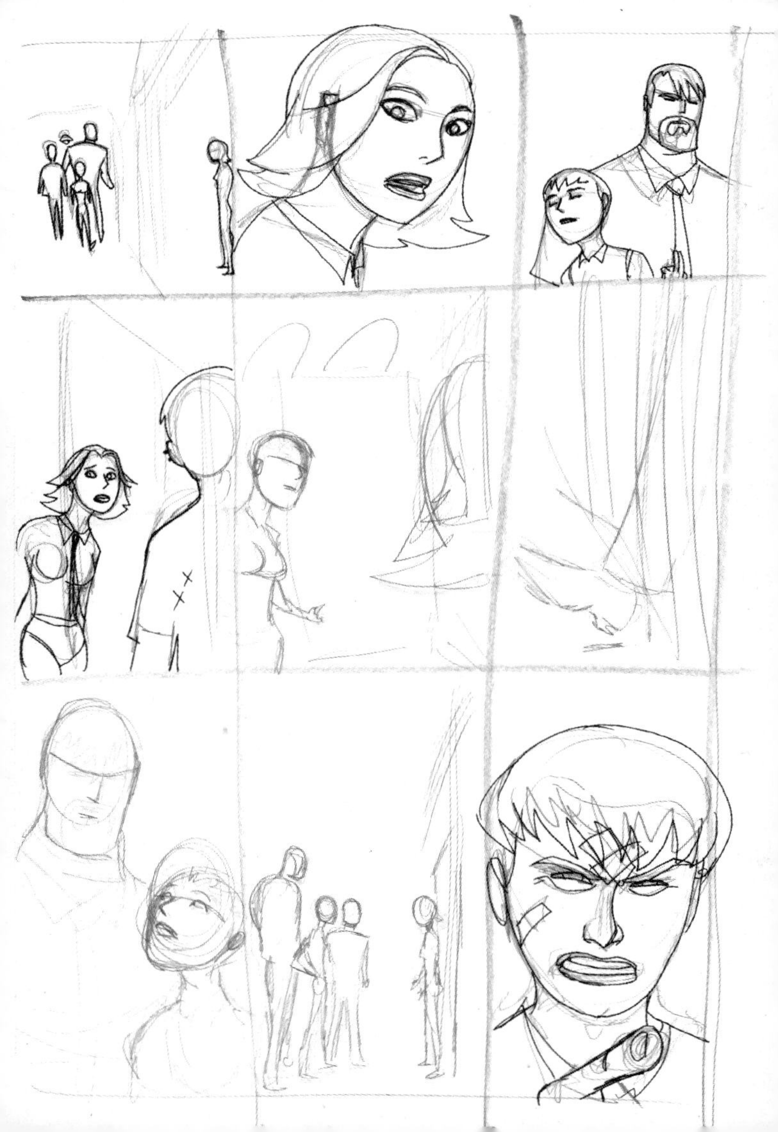

everyone else wanted.

Also, *Daredevil: Ninja* was a textbook example of the artist and writer having no ability to communicate with each other. Marvel offered me a parachute and I didn't take it, I should have taken it. I felt I could save it, but I couldn't. There's good stuff in there, but it could have

you seem to think you're the grunt artist of *Judge Dredd*. So, my question is, do you ever think you'll take a second and step outside yourself and look around and go, "Oh, hey, ok, I made it"? I'm not saying be an asshole rock star fuckhead, because I hate that, too, but many times I wish you knew your place in the biz.

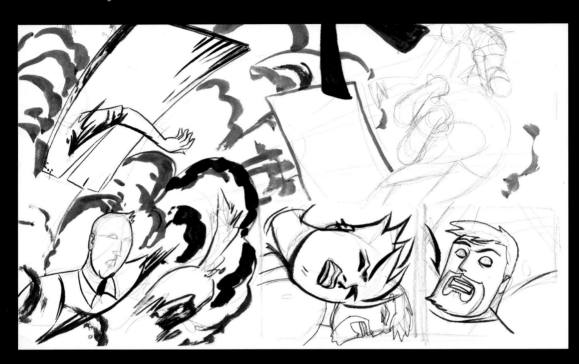

been great. Thank God for Alex Maleev.

OEMING: Yeah, that was a good example of communication breakdown. Another great Zeppelin song...

BENDIS: You got a pretty sordid comics past, Mr. *Edward Penis-hands*, how about you?

OEMING: Actually I don't have any problems with those early porn books, they were goofy. But everything up till *Powers*, with the exception of *Bulletproof Monk*, parts of *Ship of Fools* and *Foot Soldiers*, hurts my eyes to look at. I wish I had just gotten a real job and let my art grow out of the public eye!

What are the top five questions you hate being asked the most in interviews? We get a lot of repeat questions to the point it seems like the interviewer has put no thought into it.

BENDIS: Well, listen, being asked a question over and over is better than not being asked anything by anyone. Speaking of which, I both admire and am annoyed by how much you don't know you're a big deal in comics. You are one of the best artists in comics, you have won awards, all of your projects are successful, you have sold all kinds of stuff, yet

OEMING: I know I've "made it," but honestly, you can take the boy out of the ghetto, but not the ghetto out of the boy. I come from a really mentally beat-down background and will always carry something about me that says I haven't done enough. Remember I said I love the journey, not the destination? I think the bad part of that is I always feel like I'm on the journey and once I reach the destination, I'm dissatisfied and want to move on. I'm amazed I have just enough common sense to not self-destruct. Maybe because I've seen enough of that in those I love. *Powers* keeps changing and evolving so it always feels like a journey. Thanks for the confidence, I've always been grateful to you for that. That's why you're the only one allowed to call me a Nazi.

BENDIS: What do you want from *Powers* next year creatively?

OEMING: I'd like to see Walker and Deena become more personable to each other, eventhough I like their standoffish relationship. They really are opposite sides of the same coin at this point. I like how they react to each other, it's unpredictable. Deena is unpredictable. After *Foreverman*, I really look forward to getting back to those two. I love how you write them. A gunfight would be cool, too, one where someone shoots a gas tank and it explodes at the end. :)

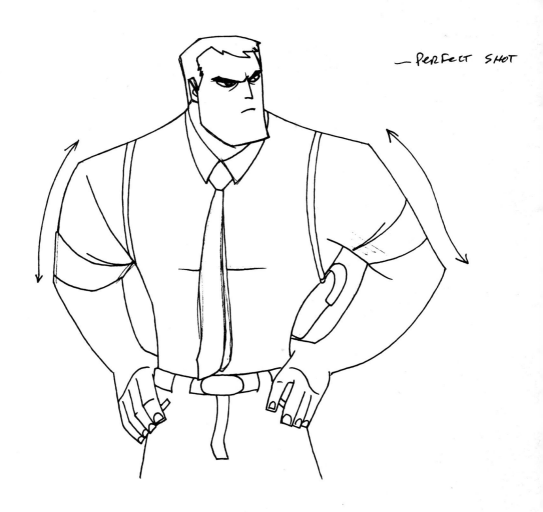

— PERFECT SHOT

WALKER FRONT | AVAN 12-31-01

WALKER STATUE DESIGNS

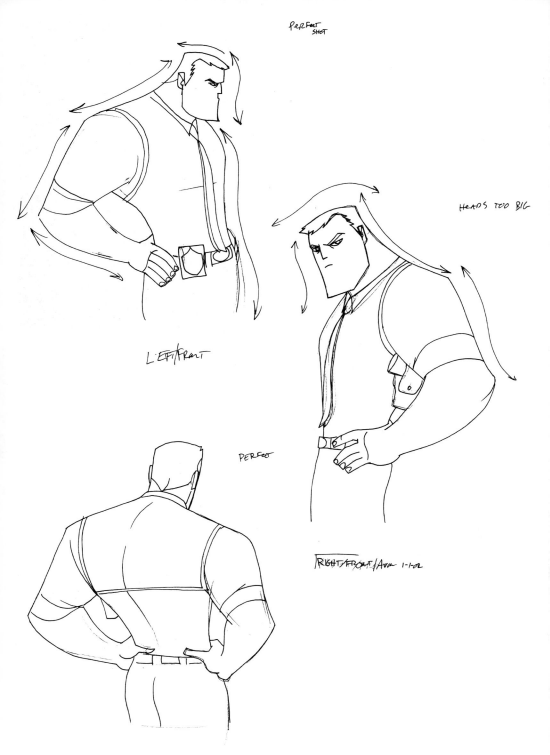

PERFECT
SHOT

HEADS TOO BIG

LEFT/FRONT

PERFECT

RIGHT/FRONT/Ava 1-1-02

BACK/LEFT

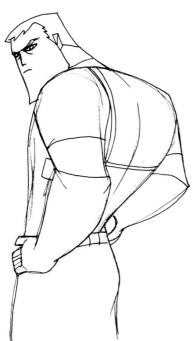

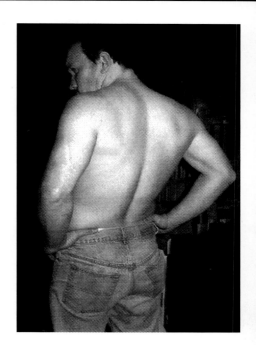

RIGHT / BACK

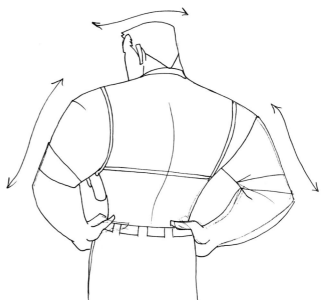

BACK / AVM 1-1-02

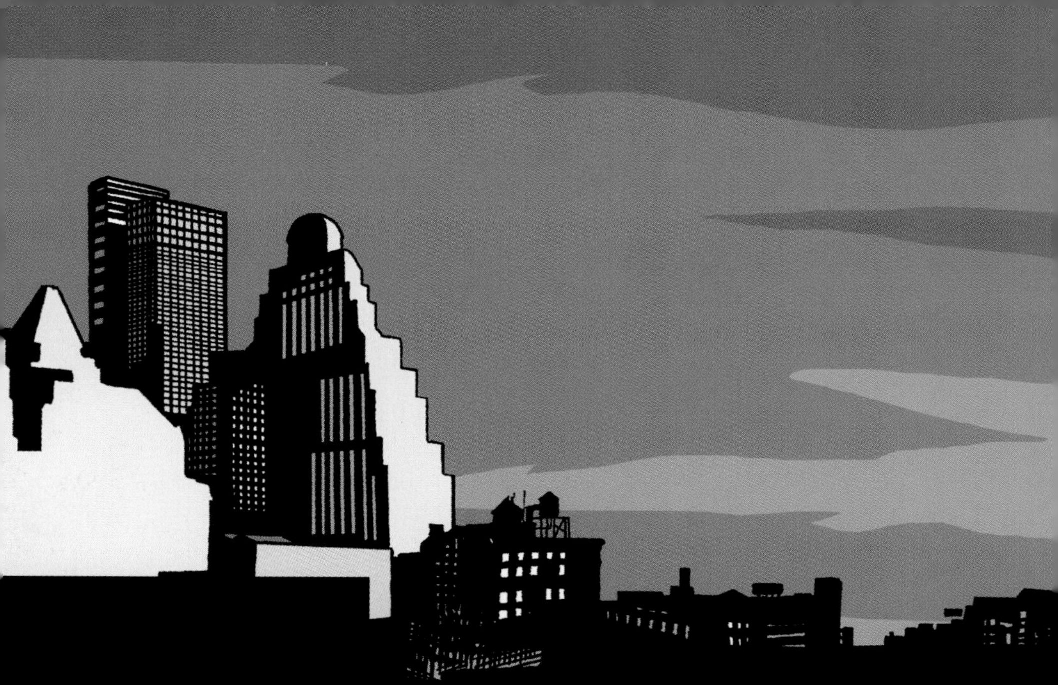

POWERS

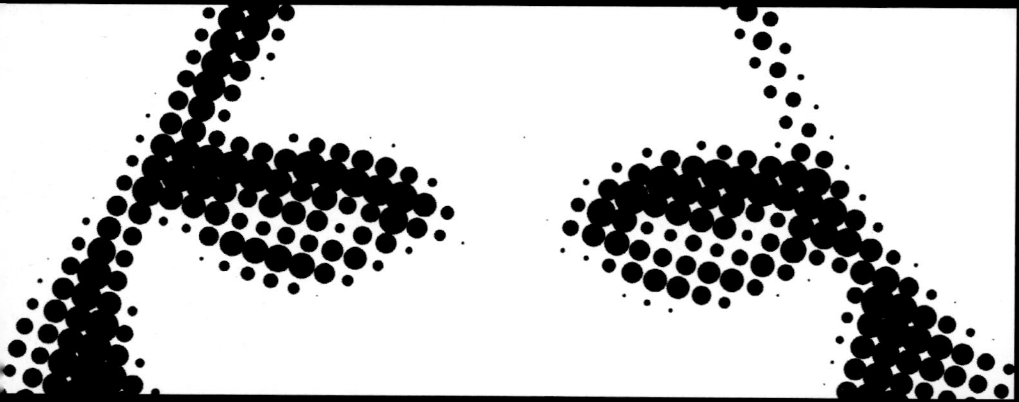

COVER GALLERY

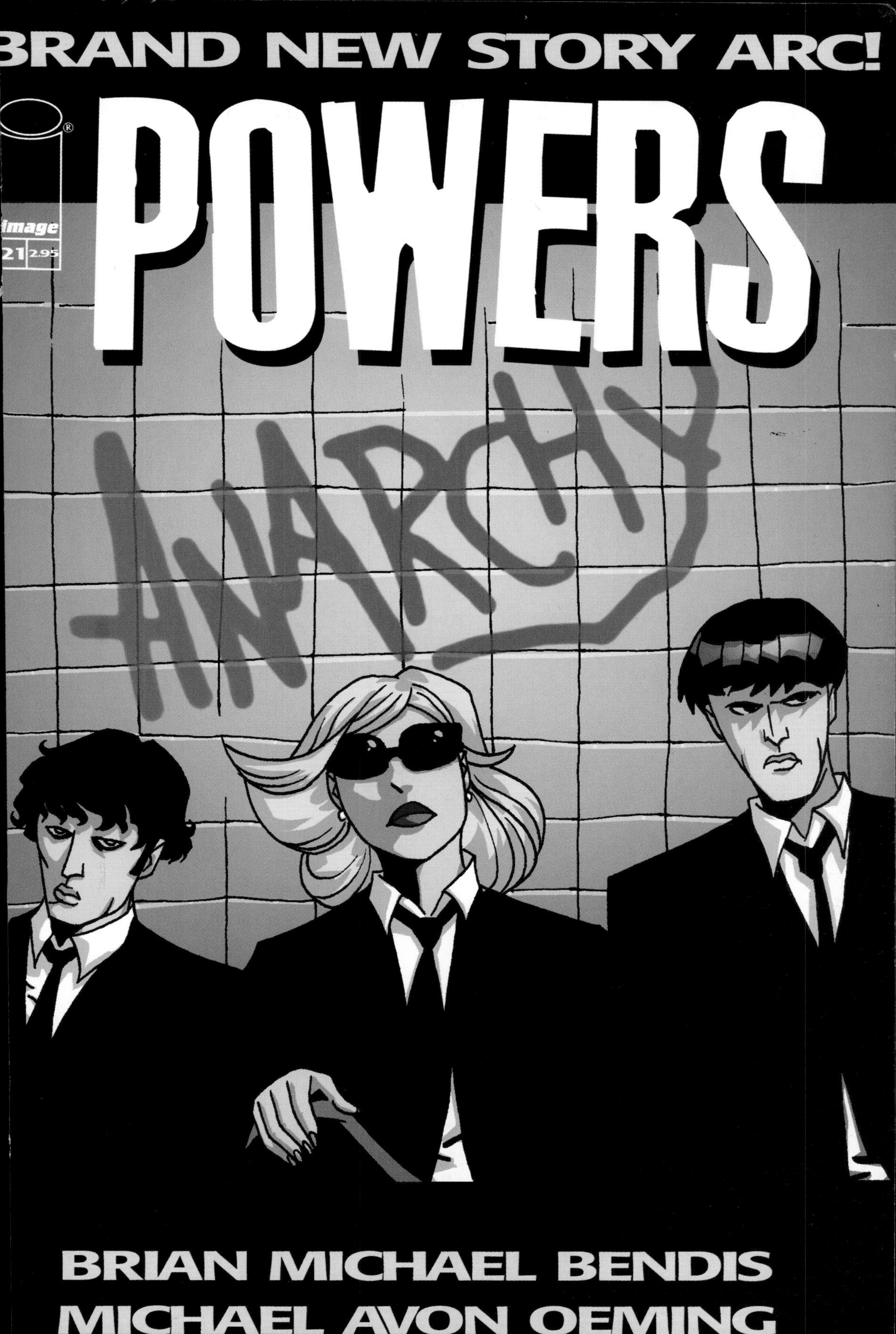
BRAND NEW STORY ARC!
POWERS
image
21 2.95
ANARCHY
BRIAN MICHAEL BENDIS
MICHAEL AVON OEMING

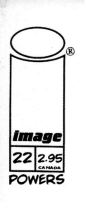

image
22 2.95 CANADA
POWERS

POWERS

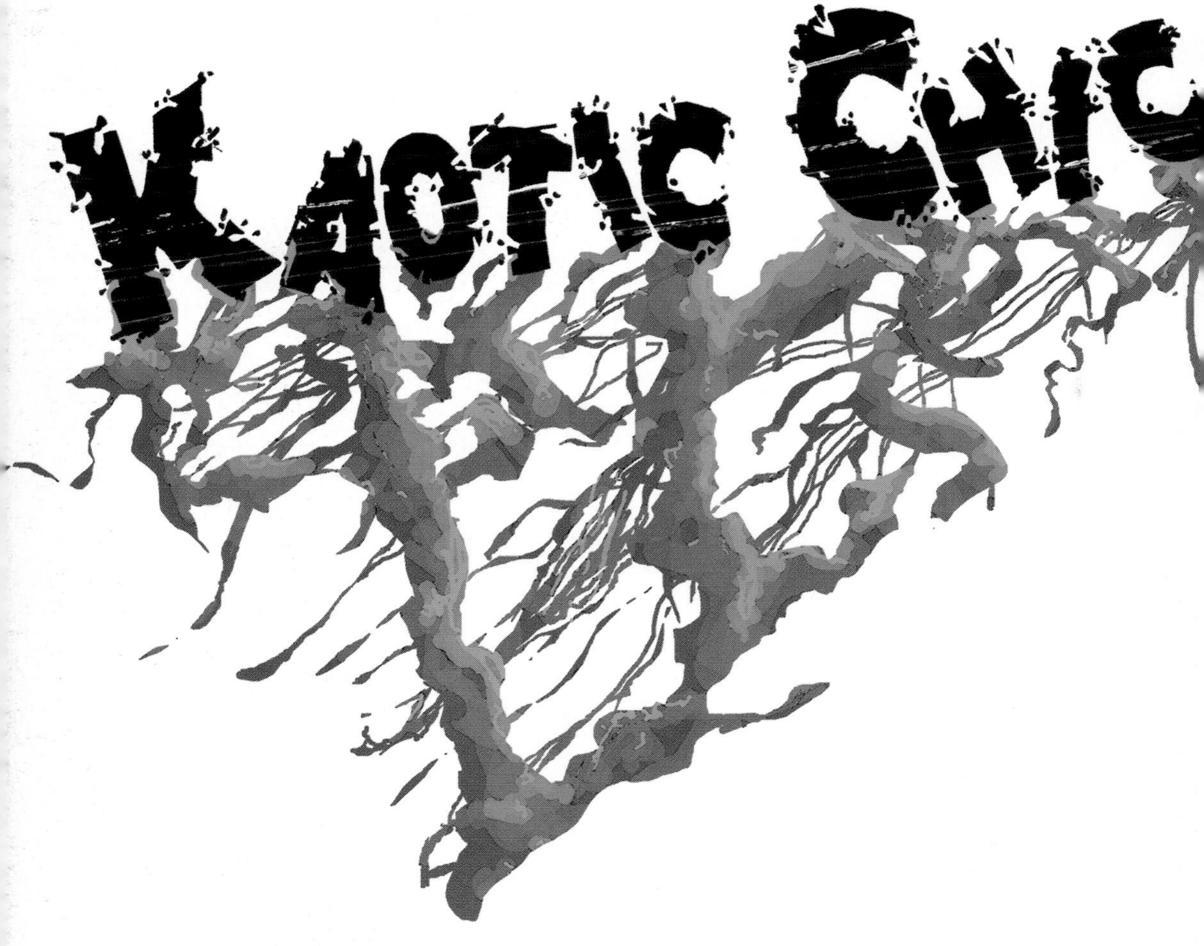
KAOTIC

"POWERS IS A WORK DESERVING OF THE RARELY JUSTIFIABLE TITLE... MASTERPIECE!"- GRADE: A!
-COMIC BUYER'S GUIDE

BRIAN MICHAEL BENDIS
MICHAEL AVON OEMING

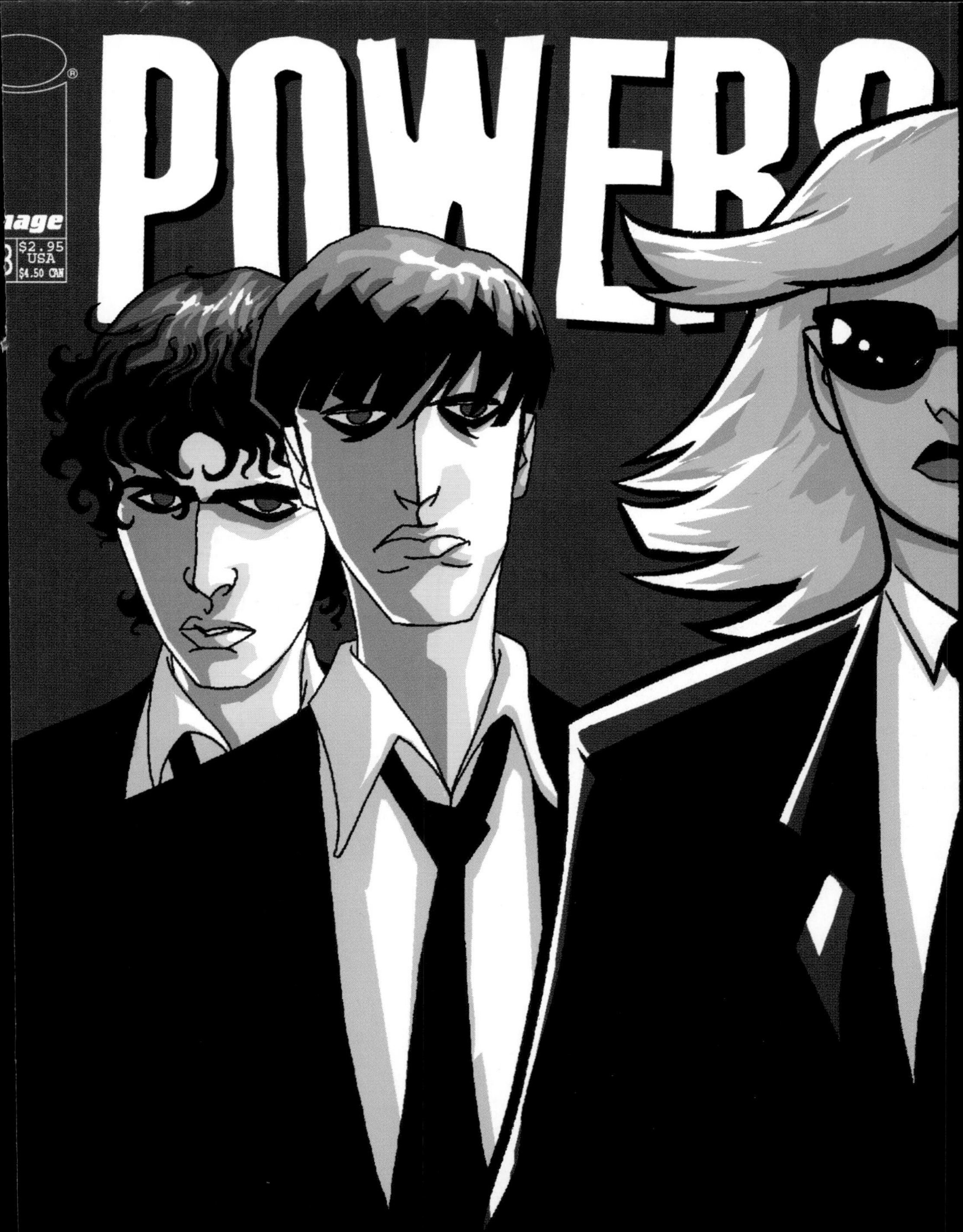
POWERS
$2.95 USA
$4.50 CAN

"One of the bes collaborations in comics today!"
-Ain't-it'cool-news

BRIAN MICHAEL BENDIS
MICHAEL AVON OEMING

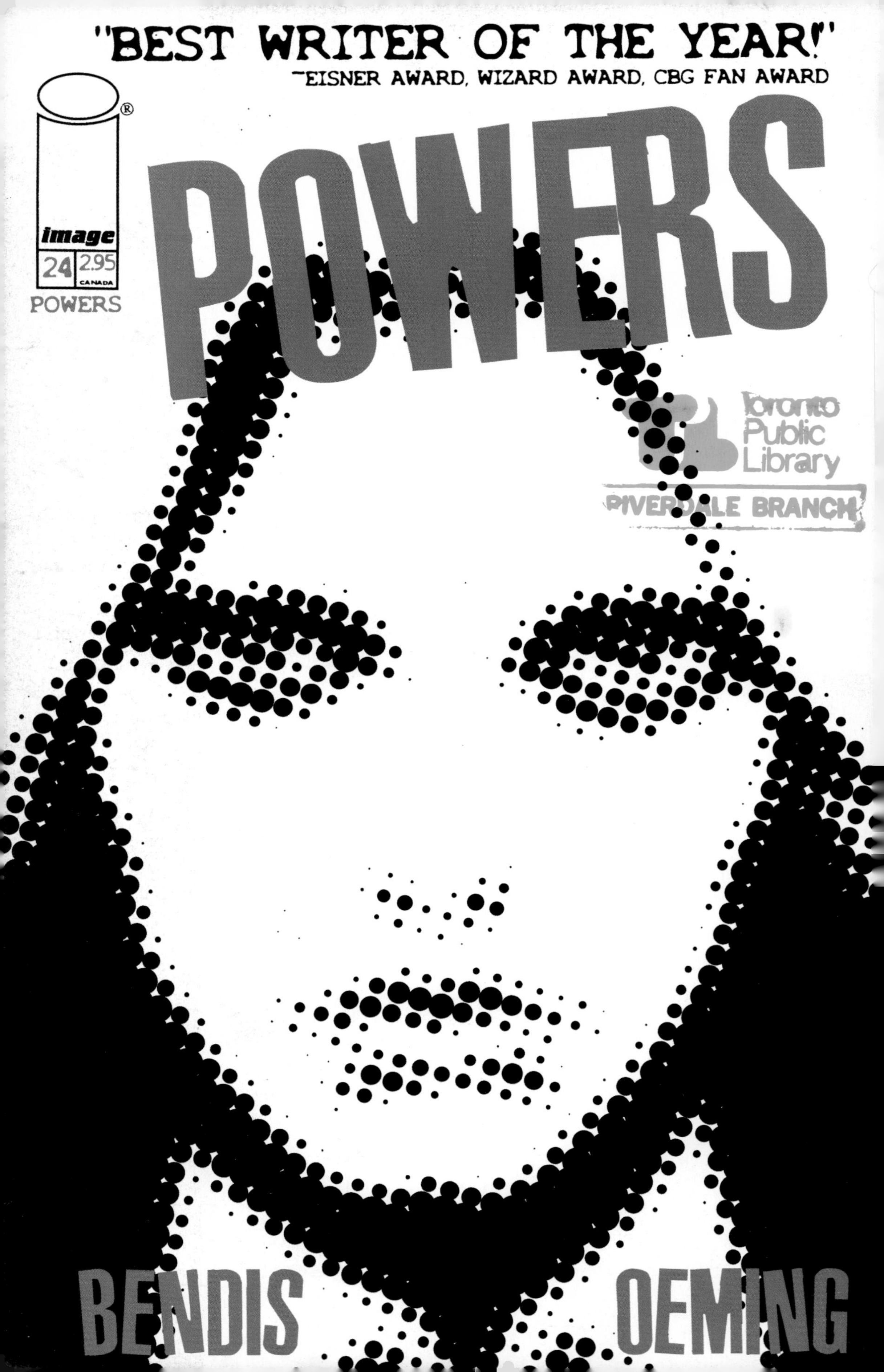
"BEST WRITER OF THE YEAR!"
—EISNER AWARD, WIZARD AWARD, CBG FAN AWARD
image
24 2.95 CANADA
POWERS
POWERS
BENDIS
OEMING

MORE GREAT TITLES FROM IMAGE

image®
COMICS

BACKLIST

GET THE REST OF THE STORY

POWERS
Who Killed Retro Girl?
BRIAN MICHAEL BENDIS
MICHAEL AVON OEMING

POWERS
ROLEPLAY
AVON
BRIAN MICHAEL BENDIS
MICHAEL AVON OEMING

Exposed
COSTUMED CONSPIRACIES TAKE FLIGHT
POWERS
EXTRA!!
BRIAN MICHAEL BENDIS
MICHAEL AVON OEMING
VICTIMS?
OR SMUT RACKETEERS?
OLYMPIA CAUGHT RED HANDED WITH THIS RED HEAD!!
SECRET ORIGINS NOT SO SECRET ANYMORE!
SUPERHERO HUSBAND LEFT HER 13 TIMES
IS THIS SUPER COP A SUPER HERO?
THE SHARK: THE DISGRACE

POWERS
SUPERGROUP
BRIAN MICHAEL BENDIS
MICHAEL AVON OEMING

POWERS

BY
BRIAN
MICHAEL
BENDIS

AND
MICHAEL
AVON
OEMING

BROWSE
OUR BACKLIST
ONLINE!

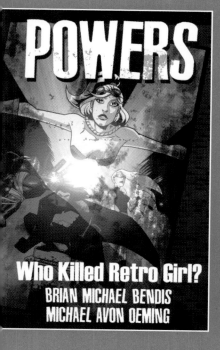

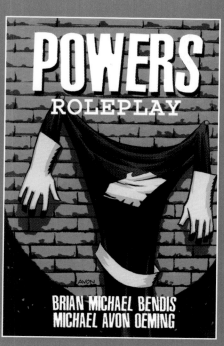

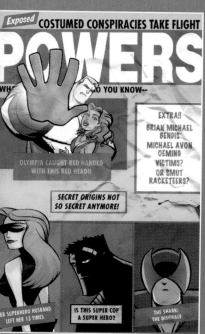

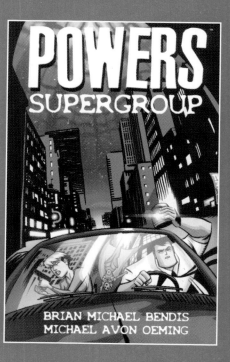

MORE GREAT TITLES FROM IMAGE

A DISTANT SOIL VOL I
THE GATHERING
ISBN: 1-887259-51-2
STAR07382

AGE OF BRONZE VOL I
A THOUSAND SHIPS
ISBN: 1-58240-2000
STAR13458

ARIA VOL I
THE MAGIC OF ARIA
ISBN: 1-58240-139-X
STAR11559

AVIGON
ISBN: 1-58240-182-9
STAR11946

BLUNTMAN AND CHRONIC
1-58240-208-6
STAR13070

BULLETPROOF MONK
ISBN: 1-58240-244-2
STAR16331

CHASING DOGMA
ISBN: 1-58240-206-X
STAR13071

CLERKS
THE COMIC BOOKS
ISBN: 1-58240-209-4
STAR13071

DARKNESS VOL I
COMING OF AGE
ISBN: 1-58240-032-6
STAR08526

DAWN VOL II
RETURN OF THE GODDESS
ISBN: 1-58240-242-6
STAR15771

DELICATE CREATURES
ISBN: 1-58240-225-6
STAR14906

E.V.E. PROTOMECHA VOL I
SINS OF THE DAUGHTER
ISBN: 1-58240-214-0
STAR13075

FATHOM VOL I
ISBN: 1-58240-210-8
STAR15804

G.I. JOE VOL I
REINSTATED
ISBN: 1-58240-252-3
STAR16642

GOLDFISH
THE DEFINITIVE COLLECTION
ISBN: 1-58240-195-0
STAR13576

JINX
THE DEFINITIVE COLLECTION
ISBN: 1-58240-179-9
STAR13039

KABUKI VOL I
CIRCLE OF BLOOD
ISBN: 1-88727-9-806
STAR12480

KIN VOL I
DESCENT OF MAN
ISBN: 1-58240-224-8
STAR15032

LAZARUS CHURCHYARD
THE FINAL CUT
ISBN: 1-58240-180-2
STAR12720

LEAVE IT TO CHANCE VOL I
SHAMAN'S RAIN
ISBN: 1-58240-253-1
STAR16641

LIBERTY MEADOWS VOL I
EDEN
ISBN: 1-58240-260-4
STAR16143

MAGDALENA VOL I
BLOOD DIVINE
ISBN: 1-58240-215-9
STAR15519

MAGE:
THE HERO DEFINED VOL I
ISBN: 1-58240-012-1
STAR08160

NOWHERESVILLE
ISBN: 1-58240-241-8
STAR15904

OBERGEIST VOL I
THE DIRECTOR'S CUT
ISBN: 1-58240-243-4
STAR15853

POWERS VOL I
WHO KILLED RETRO GIRL?
ISBN: 1-58240-223-X
STAR12482

RISING STARS VOL I
BORN IN FIRE
ISBN: 1-58240-172-1
STAR12207

SAVAGE DRAGON VOL I
BAPTISM OF FIRE
ISBN: 1-58240-165-9
STAR13080

TELLOS VOL I
RELUCTANT HEROES
ISBN: 1-58240-186-1
STAR12831

TOMB RAIDER VOL I
SAGA OF THE MEDUSA MAS
ISBN: 1-58240-164-0
STAR03000

TORSO
THE DEFINITIVE COLLECTIO
ISBN: 1-58240-174-8
STAR12688

VIOLENT MESSIAHS VOL I
THE BOOK OF JOB
ISBN: 1-58240-236-1
STAR160053

WITCHBLADE VOL I
ORIGINS
ISBN: 1-887279-65-2
STAR07991

ZORRO
THE COMPLETE ALEX TOTH
ISBN: 1-58240-090-3
STAR14527